IMAGES
of America

BOW

On the cover: **GET A HANDLE ON IT.** Bow's vintage road crew awaits the call to tend and repair our well- or not-so-well traveled roads. It is hard to believe that with water, a few rakes, and strong backs and arms, roads were maintained in a mannerly fashion. From left to right are (first row) unidentified, Harry Drew, Bill Nordine, Fred White, Carroll Flanders, and Nils Nordine; (second row) Perley Clough, Martin Christensen, and Frank Clough is on the back of the machine. The location of this photograph is the junction of Logging Hill Road and Grandview Road. The home was owned by the Colby family and is currently the home of Harvey Moody. (Courtesy of the Bow Herritage Commission.)

IMAGES
of America

BOW

Bow Heritage Commission

ARCADIA
PUBLISHING

ISBN 978-0-7385-4944-6

Published by Arcadia Publishing
Charleston, South Carolina

Printed in the United States of America

Library of Congress Catalog Card Number: 2006932973

For all general information contact Arcadia Publishing at:
Telephone 843-853-2070
Fax 843-853-0044
E-mail sales@arcadiapublishing.com
For customer service and orders:
Toll-Free 1-888-313-2665

Visit us on the Internet at www.arcadiapublishing.com

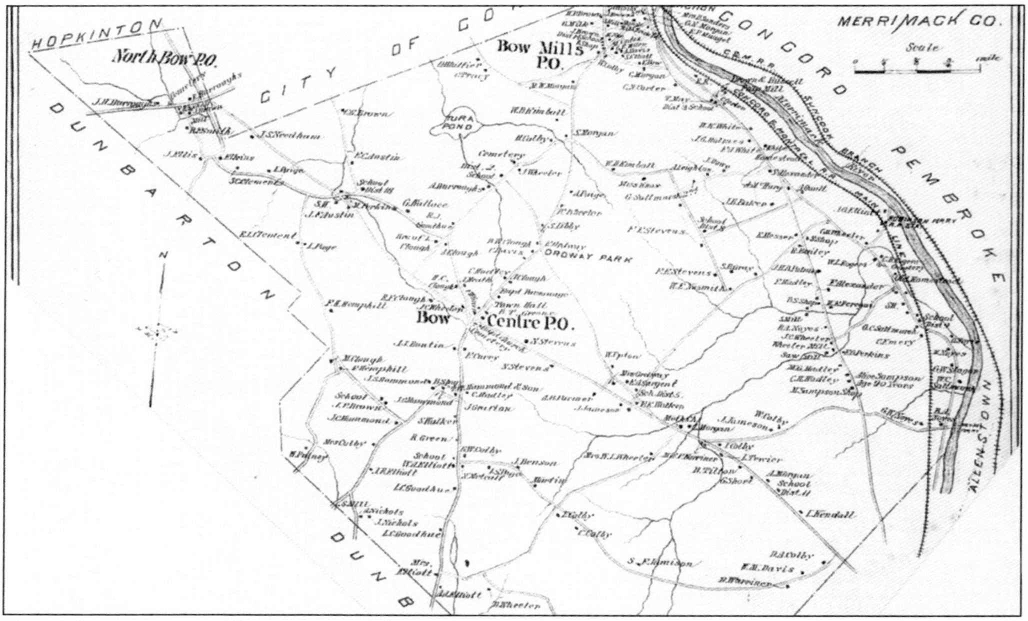

BOW MAP OF 1892. This 1892 map shows Bow surrounded by Allenstown, Dunbarton, Hooksett, Hopkinton, and Concord. In response to Gov. Benning Wentworth and his allies on May 27, 1727, Bow's proprietors were granted land along the Merrimack River. At the time, the charter required that families settle into 75 houses within three years. Furthermore a meetinghouse had to be built within four years. Still unsure of the danger caused by Native Americans, there were provisions for interruptions in settlement. The proprietors were mostly close friends of Wentworth and were also designated for land grants. These proprietors were not farmers, but were wealthy merchants, politicians, and landowners from Portsmouth and Stratham. These men received 500 acres of land.

CONTENTS

ACKNOWLEDGMENTS

The Bow Heritage Commission would like to give many thanks to all the people and organizations who have contributed to the content of this book. Years of historical data and photographs brought together by previous Bow Heritage Commission volunteers and citizens of Bow contributed to the final structure and content herein contained. Of special note are Jane Lindquist, Carol Gouin, Bob Morgan, and Betty Hanson who compiled several photograph albums of images that have proved invaluable in our work on this book. This pictorial history of Bow is the product of the efforts of many participants, through both their knowledge and donation of images. If by circumstance, error, or omission we have failed to mention any persons in this acknowledgment, we ask your forgiveness and understanding.

The list of people who have contributed include: H. Dana and Barbara Abbott, Alexander family granddaughters, the Allbee family, Eric Anderson, the Horace Bailey family, Glen Berger, Norma Blanchard, Bow Board of Selectmen, Bow Ladies Service Club, David Bundy, Charlotte Buxton, Vicky Cantara, Rae Clough Carson, Chum Cleverly, Alice Ordway Cate, Arthur Cheney, Peter Cheney, the *Concord Monitor*, the Ted Downs family, Myrton Fellows, Mary Foote, Mark Goodwin, Carol Gouin, Paul Hammond, Betty Hanson, the Muriel Howard family, Nancy Knapp, the Earl Lamora family, Eva and David Lindquist, Barbara Macauley, Dane Malcolm, Brent Michiels, Bob Morgan, Rita Morgan, the Paul Nadeau family, New Hampshire Historical Society, the Adin Noyes family, Cilla Ordway, Dennis Ordway, the James Ordway family, Gert Bowen Page, James Pitts, Susan Colby Saltmarsh, Mildred Tappan Sanborn, the Hilda Sargent family, Dick Shaw, Dorothy White Shaw, Dick Stevens, Jane Langley Strablizky, Sara Swenson, Richard and Katrina Swett, Mildred Blake Thompson, the Bruce Vandyke family, the Dick Welch family, the Lillian Welch family, Bryan Westover, Jessie Wheeler, and the Frank Woodbury family.

Heritage Commission Members
Jacquelyn Jennings, Nancy Knapp, Gary Nylen,
Roger Ordway, Janet Shaw, Beth Titus, Susan Wheeler,
and selectman representative Eric Anderson

INTRODUCTION

Bow is typical of most southern New Hampshire towns, dealing with explosive growth while trying to retain a rural character. Noted for its excellent schools and a focus on education, conversely, the town has hundreds of acres of conservation land. The forests and swampy areas on this land make it a prime location for moose, deer, turkey, and bear. Bow was once the home to mostly farmers, noted for products from Jersey cream to strawberries. The construction of the Public Service Plant and the routing of Interstates 93 and 89 through town in the mid-20th century was a turning point for the town, making it desirable for development because of low taxes and easy commutes. New residents extol the virtues of Bow's rural character, while old timers yearn for the simplicity of the days depicted in this book.

The town of Bow already has a written history, *100 Acres More or Less*, by David Bundy, which was published in 1975. Bundy's book covers land and border disputes; people, religions, and politics; a changing economy; and the progress of the town. This retrospective is to complement that history by sharing photographic reflections of people and times, past and present. It is planned to be a way of identifying places that should be enjoyed, appreciated, and preserved for the future. These reflections will highlight some of these places and events as well as the people that built a "town known for its livability."

Meeting houses, churches, civic buildings, mills, and other structures will be depicted along with events that have taken place within these buildings. Early in Bow's history, social clubs, farm associations, and children's clubs were formed to promote community spirit. Many continue to this day, with new groups formed as population needs changed. The early sawmills, brickyards, and farms have given way to modern industry and a power plant. Photographs of some of the early district schools will be shown as well as those of the new schools. This will be contrasted with the growing importance of education and local control of the schools, which resulted in the construction of the town's own high school.

Locations lost because of time and the construction of interstate highways will be highlighted. There will be photographs of various sites which are currently recognized by historic markers. Cemeteries provide an important personal link to the past and photographs of some of these sites will be included.

Bow was the home of two congressmen, three ambassadors, and the founder of a worldwide religion. The town's rich history was shaped by its location on the river. Expansion of railroad lines and the introduction of the Interstate Highway System contributed to, and continue to mold the future. This retrospective will trace the development of the town in photographs, from Native American campsites along the Merrimack River, to farms whose land was rich with soil from river runoff, to the current suburban mecca that is Bow today.

Housing needs in town have changed with Bow being proactive in passing regulations to control growth. The town has also been aggressive in preserving open space, purchasing hundreds of acres of land, and building an extensive trail system. These initiatives have worked to balance a much desired rural environment with neighborhood development and business opportunities. A large segment of the population devotes much volunteer time and resources to maintain this balance.

What does the future hold? The 2004 Master Plan is "Bow's vision for the 1st quarter of the 21st Century and beyond," Some of the subjects covered include land use, conservation and preservation, its water resources, economic development, transportation and access, community support services, and infrastructure and schools. Implementation is now the driving force necessary to shape and maintain the town of Bow's livability.

One

MEETING AND GREETING

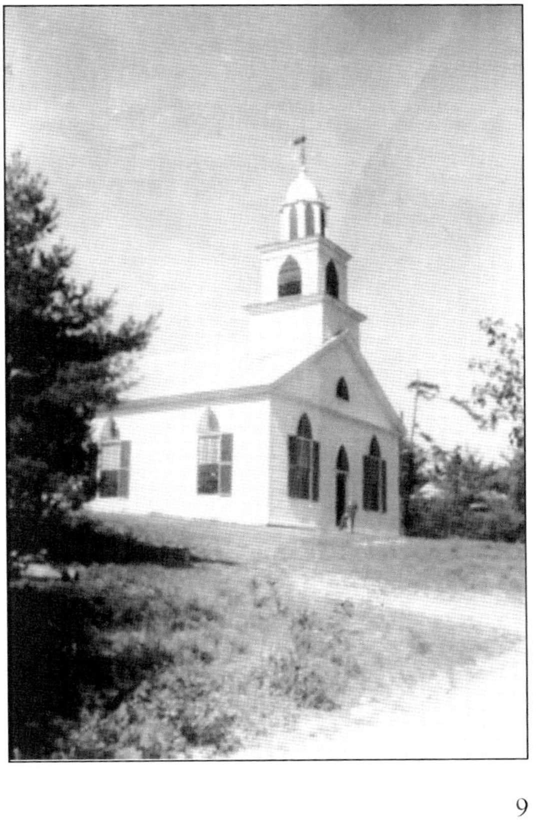

GATHER TOGETHER. Early gatherings were based upon long established traditions. People of all nationalities and faiths were brought together by common goals and ideals. The need for government rules, regulations, and civil order brought people to town meetings. Churches played a prominent role in social and religious activities. The Bow Community Baptist Church, as shown, was built in 1832 under the ministry of Rev. William Boswell. The congregation originally met at the White Rock Hill Road Meeting House or at members' homes. When the meetinghouse was relocated, parishioners voted to build their own church on Branch Londonderry Turnpike East, appropriating $1,600 for construction. Boswell was succeeded by Rev. Henry Archibald, who became the leader of the town's antislavery group. Recently the church was renamed the Crossroads Community Church.

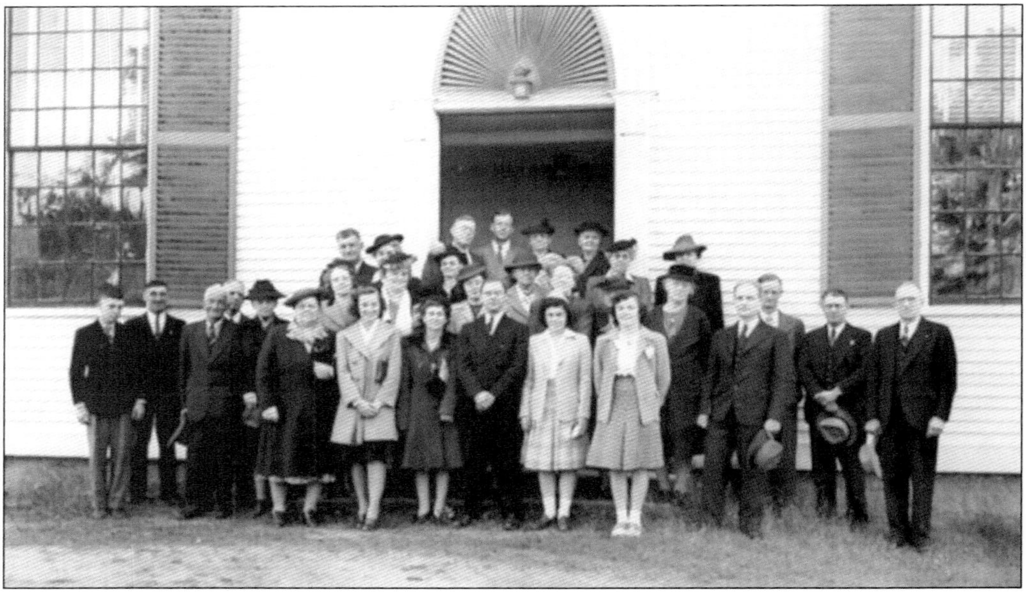

Bow Baptists. Parishioners are shown in this 1945 photograph. Identified here are Paul Hammond, Ai Hammond, Richard Putney, Carroll Flanders, Maude Putney, Annie C. Foote, Grace Mack, Elsie Houghton, Rev. Glenn Rogers, Priscilla Houghton, Maureen Prussia, Alfred Jenks, Ruth Chamberlin, Edith Knauf, Mabel Hammond, Catherine Rogers, Phoebe Focht, Ethel Mack, Robert Focht, Arthur Knauf, Horace and Bea Mitten, Ralph Houghton, Raymond Chamberlin, Cora Flanders, and Bertha Flanders.

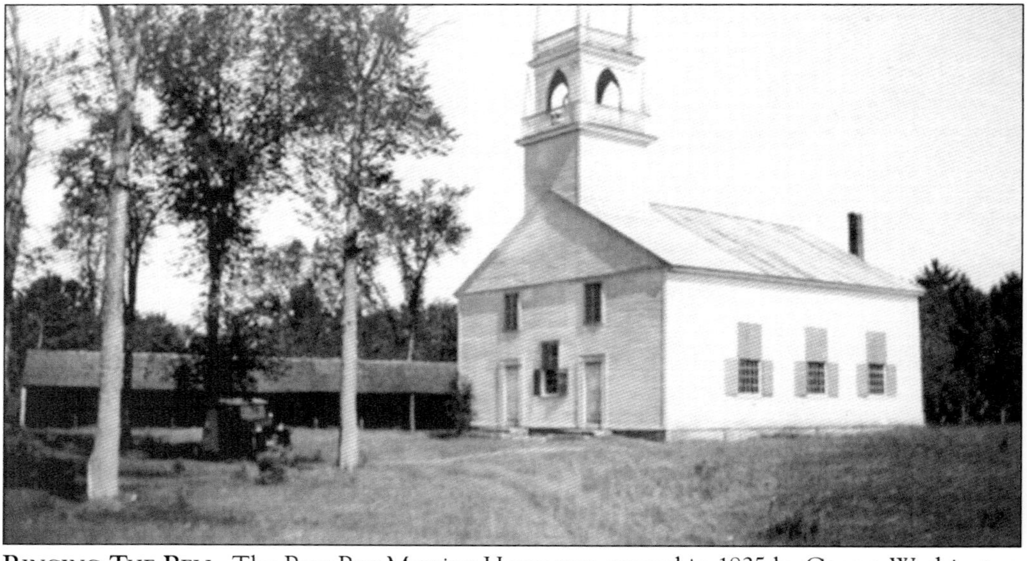

Ringing The Bell. The Bow Bog Meeting House was erected in 1835 by George Washington Wheeler. It was once the hub of community life. Abandoned in 1951, the building was saved and restored by the Bow Bog Meeting House Society, which in turn donated it to the town in 1985. The meetinghouse is available for use by community groups. It is on the town's historic buildings list and map.

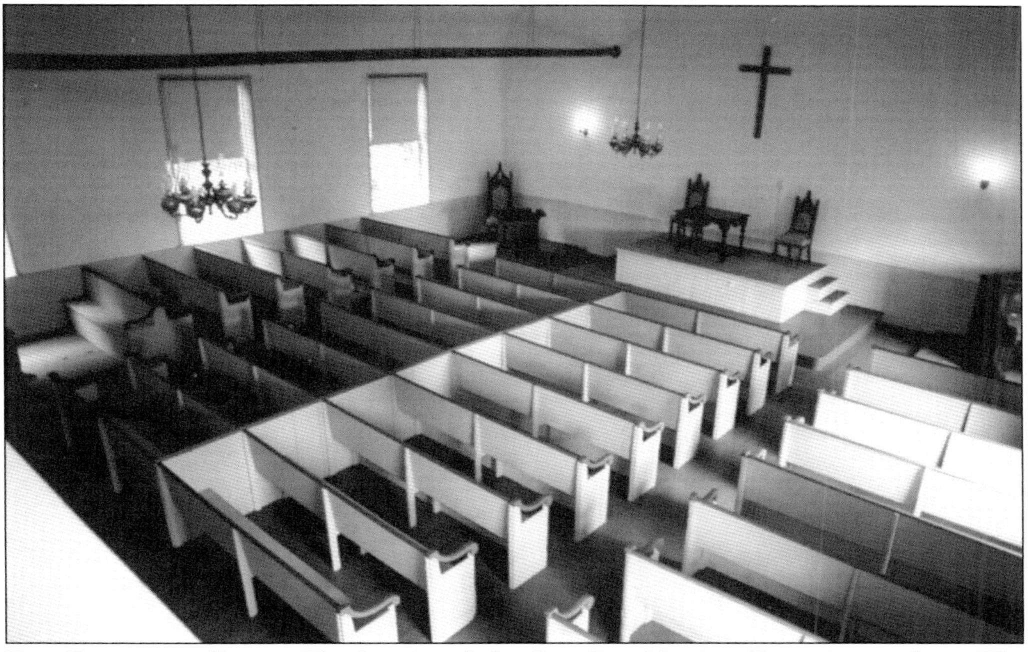

The Gathering Place. The interior of the Bow Bog Meeting House is seen here. The photograph is taken from the balcony and shows the altar section and the rows of pews. The building is an authentically restored Methodist church meetinghouse.

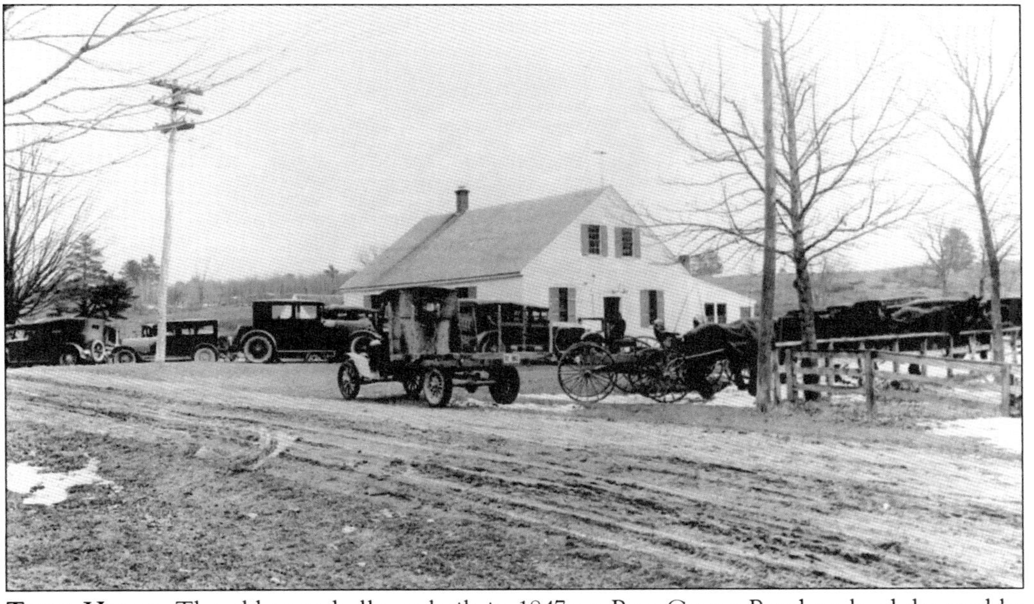

Town House. The old town hall was built in 1847 on Bow Center Road on land donated by Col. James Green. The photograph shows the old town hall on town meeting day in 1923. The use of the building for annual town meetings was discontinued in 1957, upon the completion of the Bow Community Building. Extensive repairs and updates have been made in recent years by the town, Bow Community Men's Club, and other interested citizens. As a result, the hall is used by many organizations for meetings and gatherings.

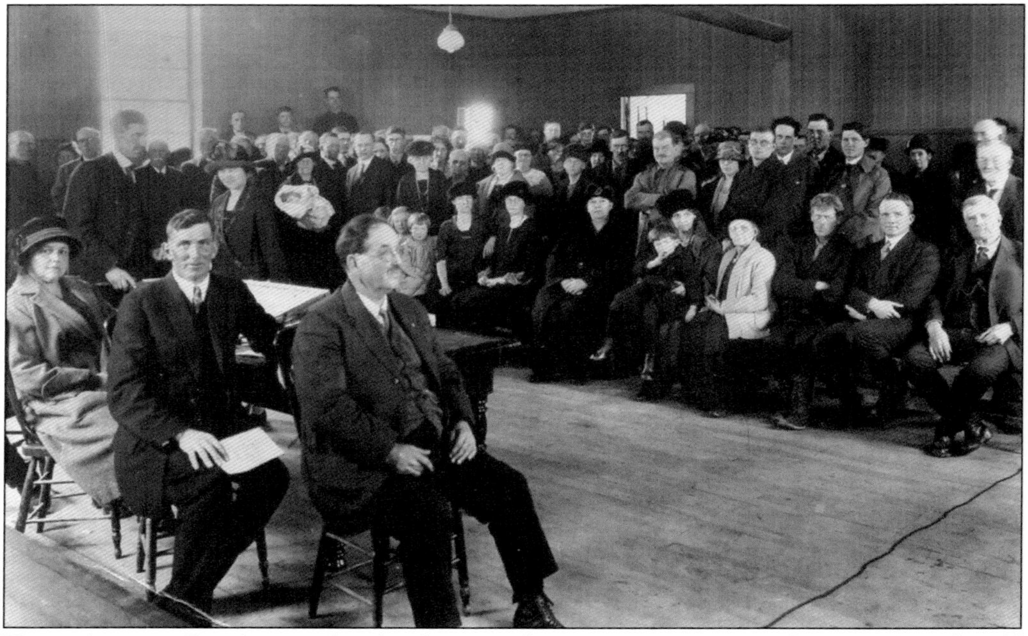

TOWN AFFAIRS. Residents gather for the annual town meeting on March 11, 1925, at the old town hall. Town moderator Charles Goodrich is standing in the foreground on the left. Seated at the table are, from left to right, Annie C. Foote, town clerk for over 30 years; and selectmen Fred Shedd and Arthur Case.

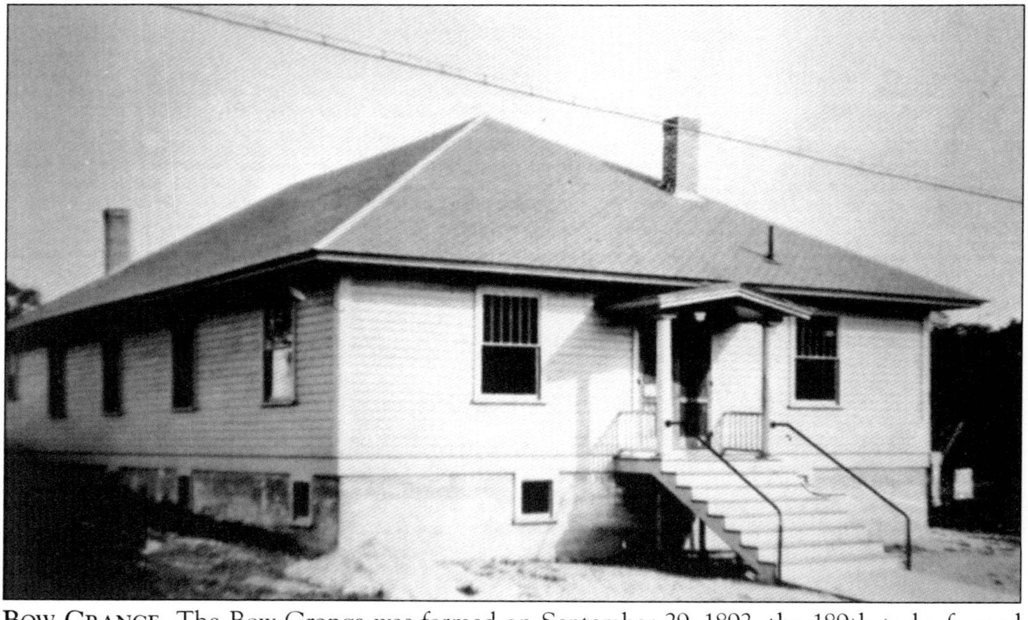

BOW GRANGE. The Bow Grange was formed on September 29, 1892, the 189th to be formed in the state. There were 39 charter members at the time of the National Grange Convention held in Concord in 1892. The Grange hall in this photograph was built in the 1920s on South Street, at the current site of Bow Mobil. In addition to Grange events meetings, shows, school graduations, and other entertainment gatherings were also held at the hall.

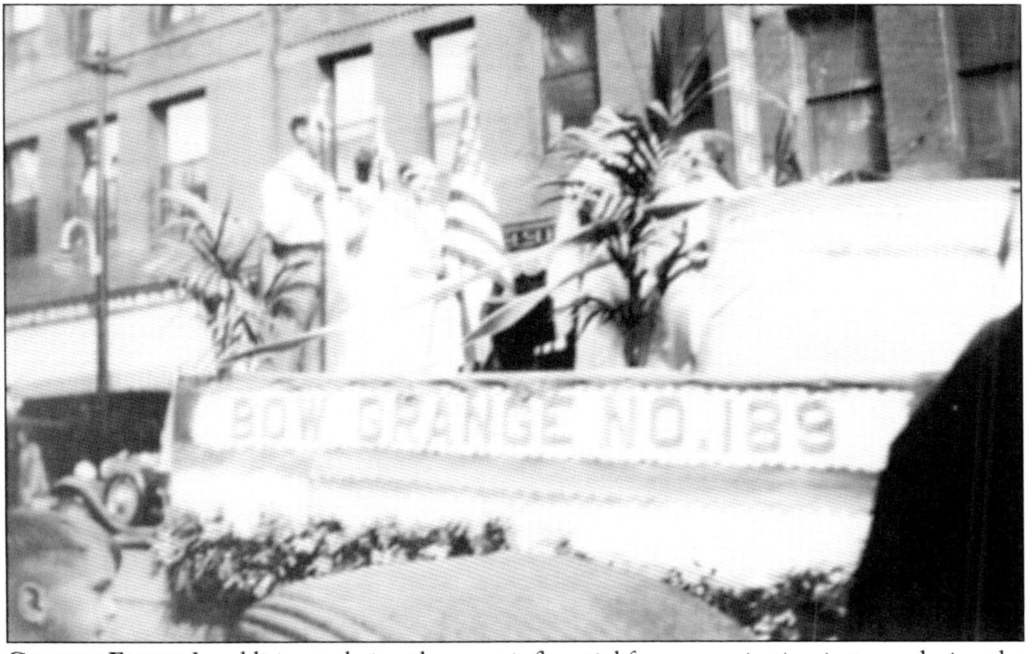

GRANGE FLOAT. In addition to being the most influential farm organization in town during the early 1900s, the Grange was the major social activity. Meetings often included exhibitions of agricultural products and handiwork, recitations, plays, and dances. Here the Bow Grange float passes in review in the 1938 Concord centennial parade.

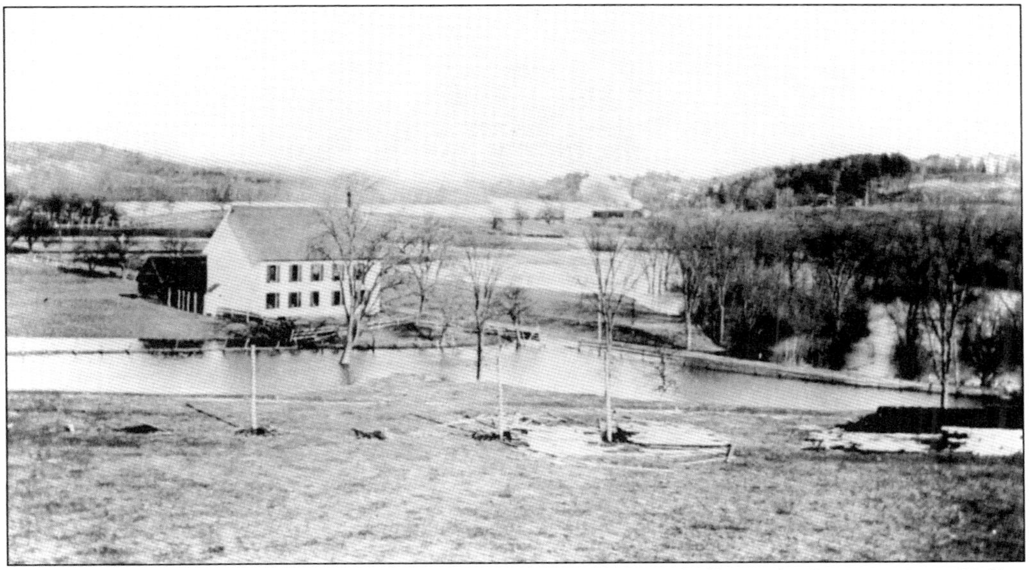

UNDER WATER. The Women's Christian Temperance Union hall was built in 1892 on Valley Road. The hall was deeded to the Bow Mills United Methodist Church in 1909 and used by the congregation until 1956. There were also many social activities held here. As seen in this photograph, the hall weathered many floods of the Merrimack River. The hall was demolished after 1954 to make way for Interstate 93.

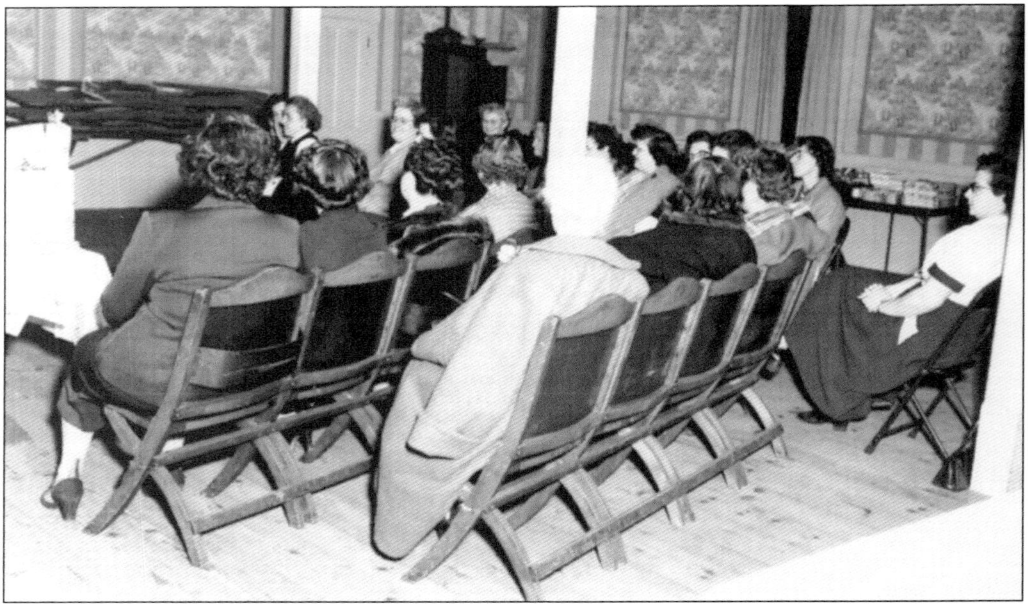

LADIES AID SOCIETY. The Methodist Ladies Aid Society was formed in 1905 and was renamed the Women's Society of Christian Service in 1940. This group raised enough money to pay for the operation of the church by holding public suppers. They also volunteered in community service projects, such as working in hospitals and assisting fire victims. Members of the group are shown at a meeting at the Women's Christian Temperance Union hall in the 1940s.

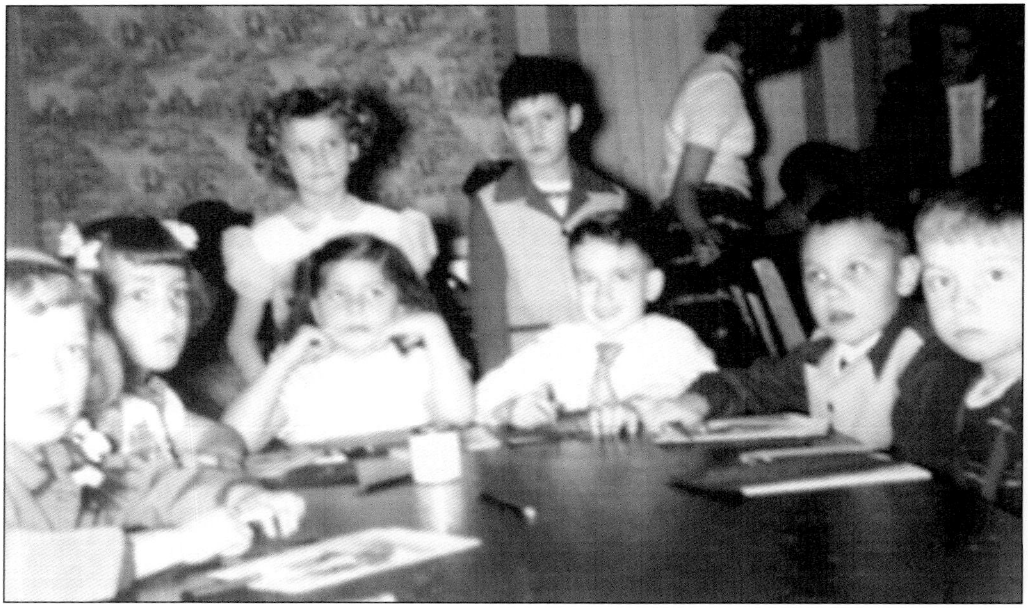

SUNDAY SCHOOL. Children in this photograph are attending a United Methodist Sunday school class at the Women's Christian Temperance Union hall in the mid-1950s. They are, from left to right, (seated) Barbara Foote, Linda Alexander, Bonnie Lewis, Thurston Hogdon, Werner Lehto, and Parker Morgan; (standing) Sandra Sargent and Jimmy P. The two people in the background are unidentified.

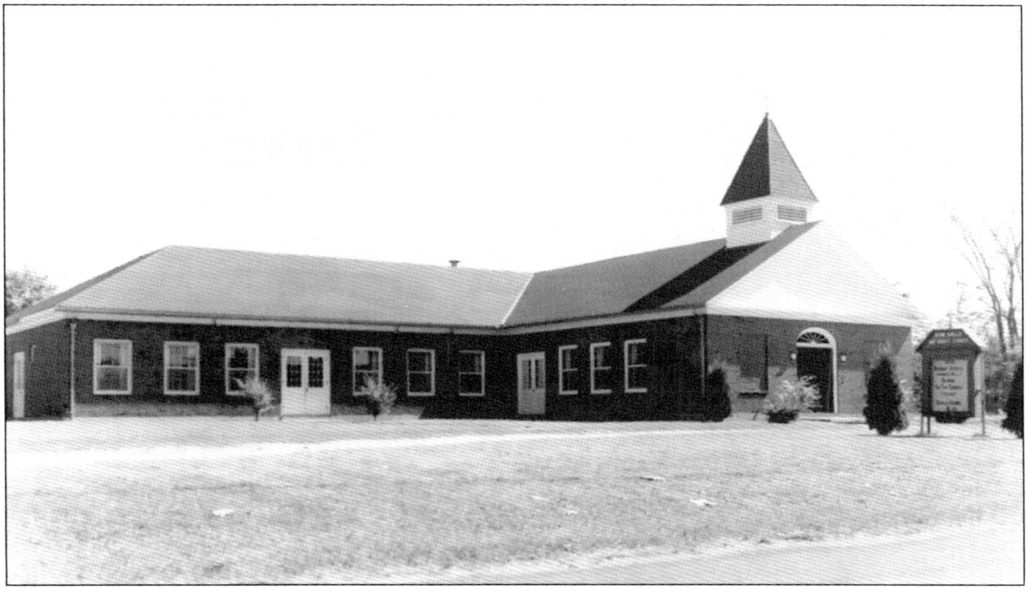

Bow Mills United Methodist Church. Plans to expand the Women's Christian Temprance Union hall/Methodist church at Bow Mills were scrapped when it was announced that the interstate highway would be located on the site. The new Methodist church was built on land at 505 South Street using mostly volunteer labor. The building as shown here was completed in 1956, with a wing added on the left portion in 1997 and a remodeling project undertaken in 2006.

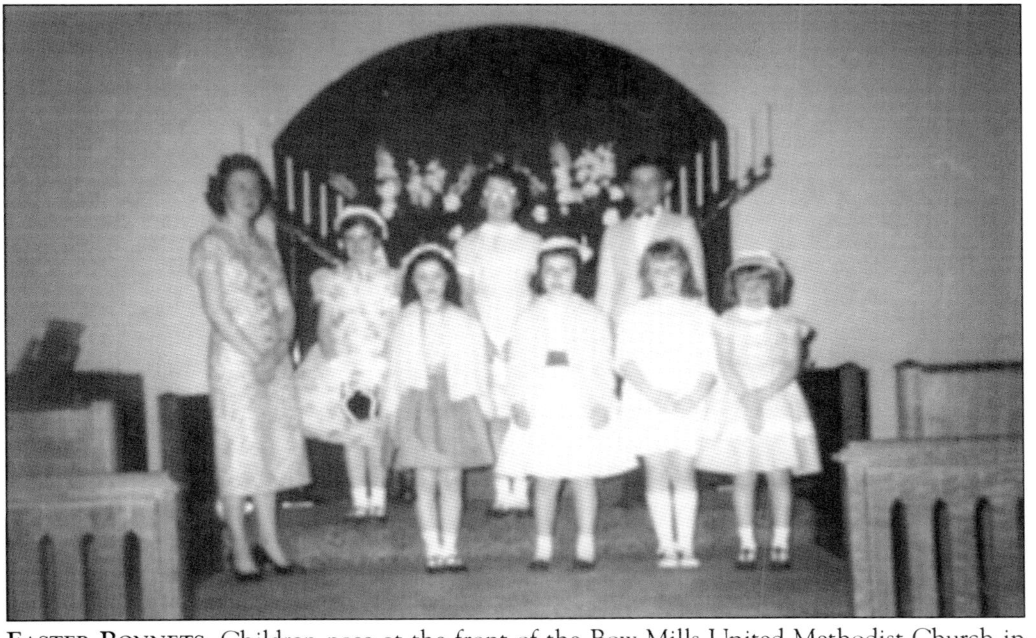

Easter Bonnets. Children pose at the front of the Bow Mills United Methodist Church in their Easter finery in 1962. From left to right are (first row) Anne Foote, Karen Blanchard, Roberta Warriner, and Anita French; (second row) teacher Jackie Lee, Linda Hogdon, Kay French, and Wayne Blanchard. The raised portion where they are standing and the partitions were removed in the renovation project in 2006.

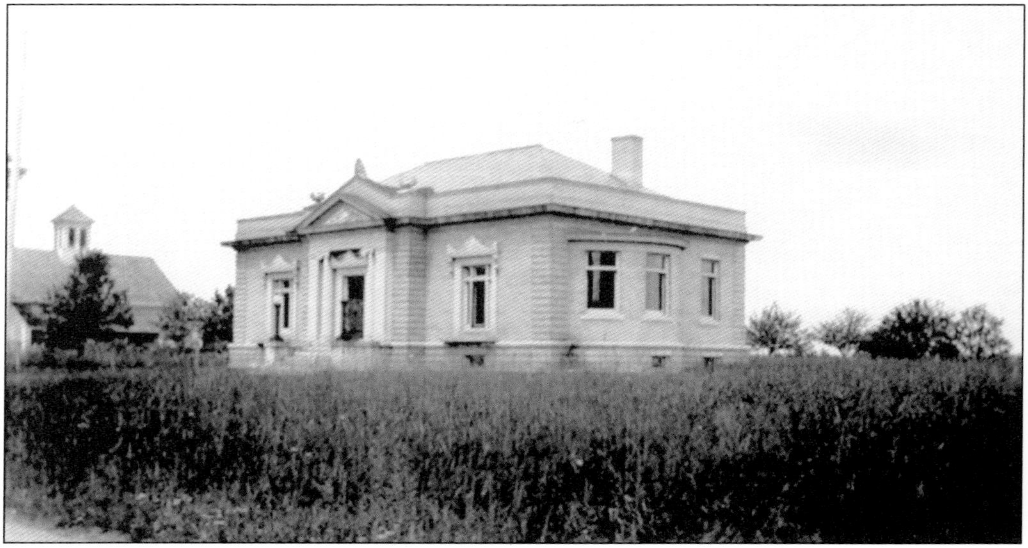

BAKER FREE LIBRARY. The Baker Free Library was built in 1914, using land and funds donated by Congressman Henry Baker in 1912. Baker also donated his personal library of books which are part of the collection today. This photograph, taken in 1919, shows a portion of the Baker homestead in the background.

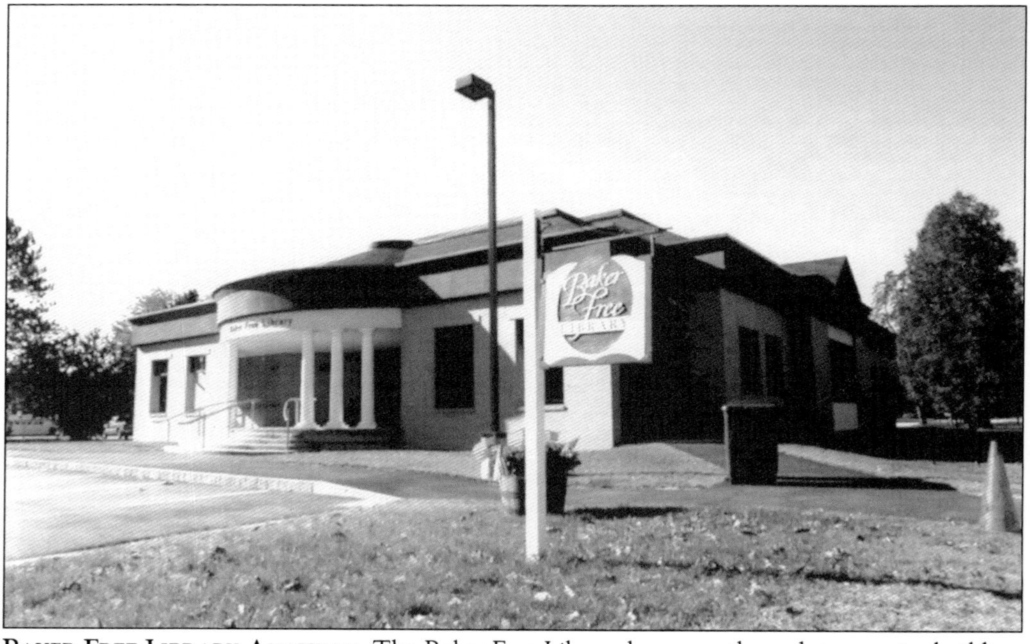

BAKER FREE LIBRARY ADDITION. The Baker Free Library has gone through two major building projects, one in 1967 and the other in 2002. The original portion of the library has been preserved and the new building has retained much of the original character. The main entrance has been relocated to the rear of the addition. The expanded space allows for improved programming. The library is also used as a meeting place by the community.

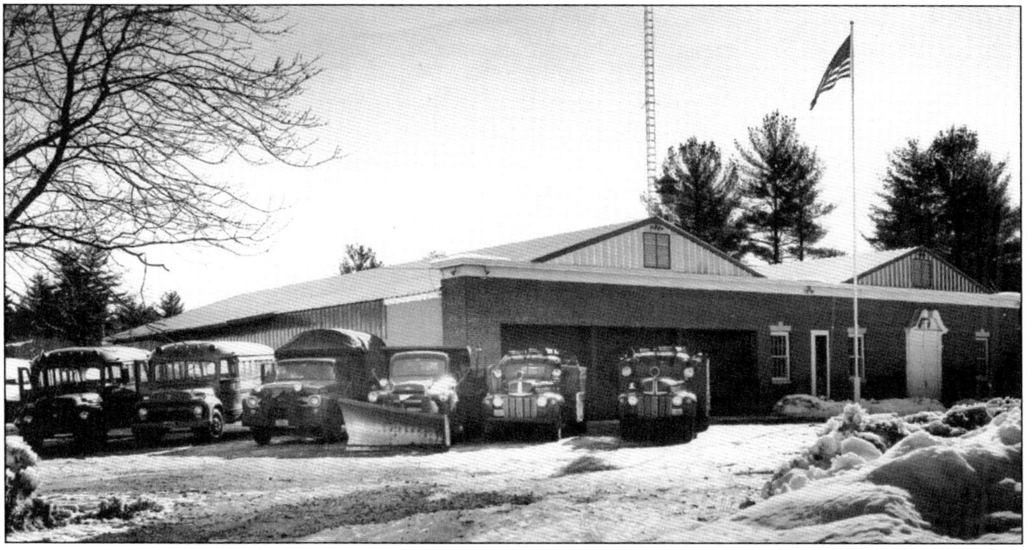

Bow Community Building. When the interstate highway was built, the fire station at Bow Mills was relocated to a site on the corner of Knox and Bow Center Roads. In November 1956, construction of the building was begun to not only house the fire department, but also the highway garage, the school bus depot, and the town hall/auditorium. Construction was completed within the year and an open house was held on October 5, 1957.

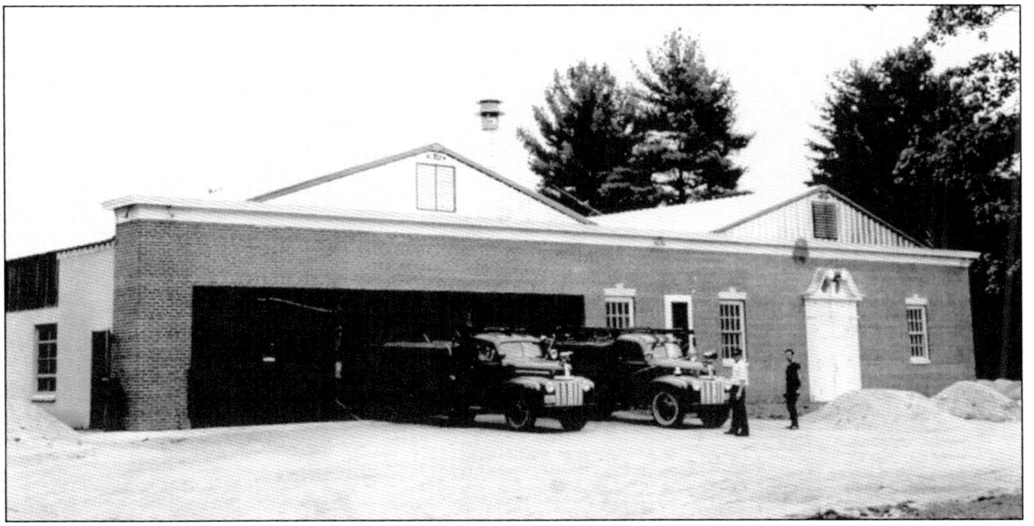

Bow Community Building Today. For many years the annual town meetings were staged here. Today the building is Bow's polling place, with town and school meetings being held at the high school. As its name implies, the Bow Community Building is also the site of many organizations' meetings and events. Presently the building is still home to the fire department and the recreation department. The highway department and school bus depot were both moved to Robinson Road.

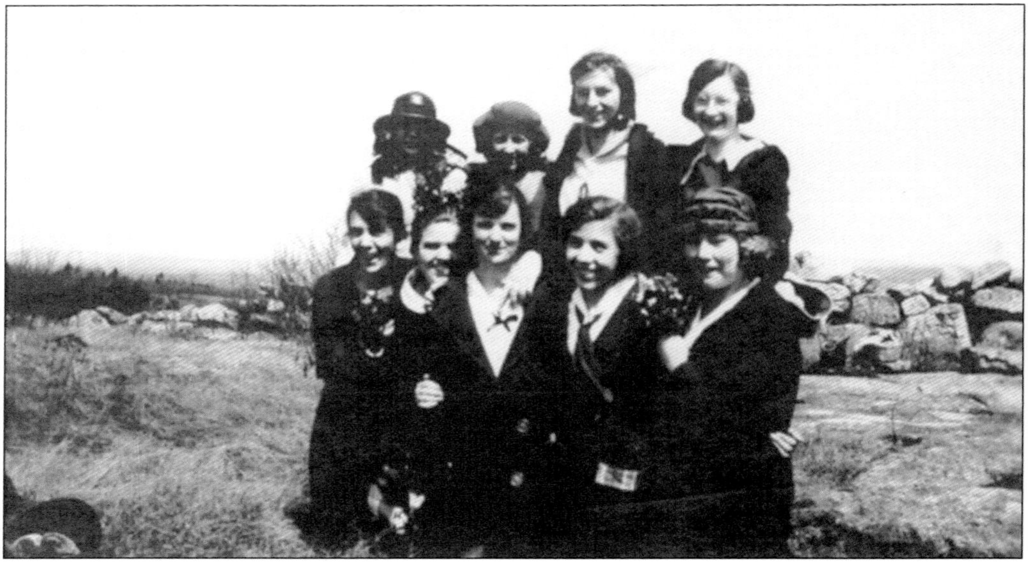

The Girls Sport Club. The club was formed in the second decade of the 20th century for women to engage in sporting activities. This was also a social group. They presented a comedy/drama at the WCTU Hall, with dancing after the play and homemade candy and ice cream for refreshments. Pictured from left to right are (first row) Helen Hartford, Hilda (Morgan) Sargent, Hazel Hartford, Hattie Alquist, and unidentified; (second row) Rachel Hartford, Madeline Palmer, Gladys Crawford, and Ruth Wheeler.

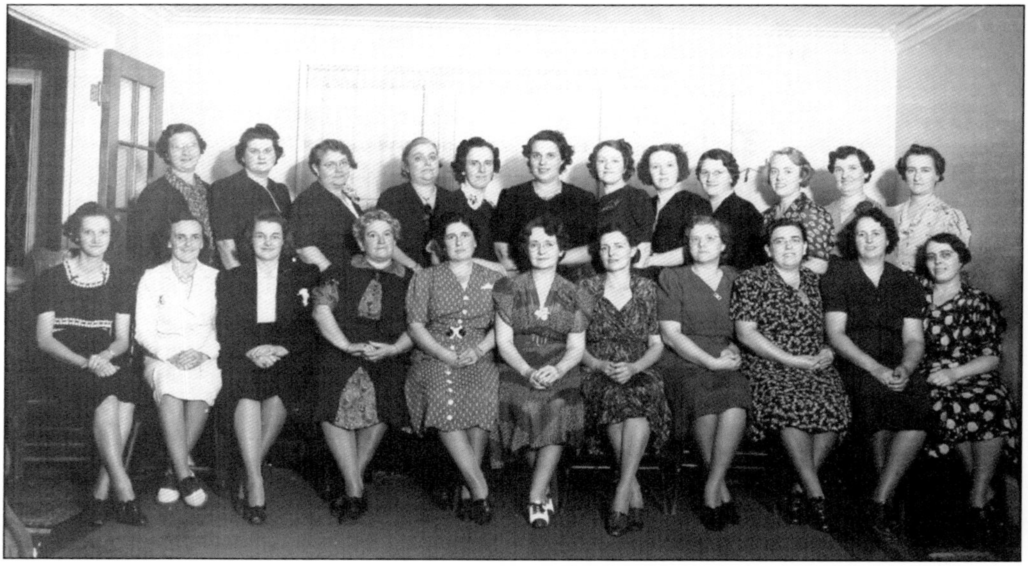

Tokalot Club. In 1921, the Girls Sport Club evolved into the Tokalot Club, a social group that supported many community projects. Members in this 1938 photograph are, from left to right, (first row) Beatrice Robinson, Margaret Allbee, Hazel Ordway, Edith Hammond, Doris Benson, Ann Clough, Lottie Morgan, Mary Hammond, Hilda Sargent, Cora Cook Pattee, and Helen Furbush; (second row) Laura Sargent, Ellie Nicoll, May Nordine, Ava Ordway, Lillian Hanson Ordway, Beatrice Tracy, Anna Ordway, Ethel Morgan, Freida Howland, Emma Cilley, Lena Bowker, and Gertude Lyford Peaslee. The club continued into the 1970s.

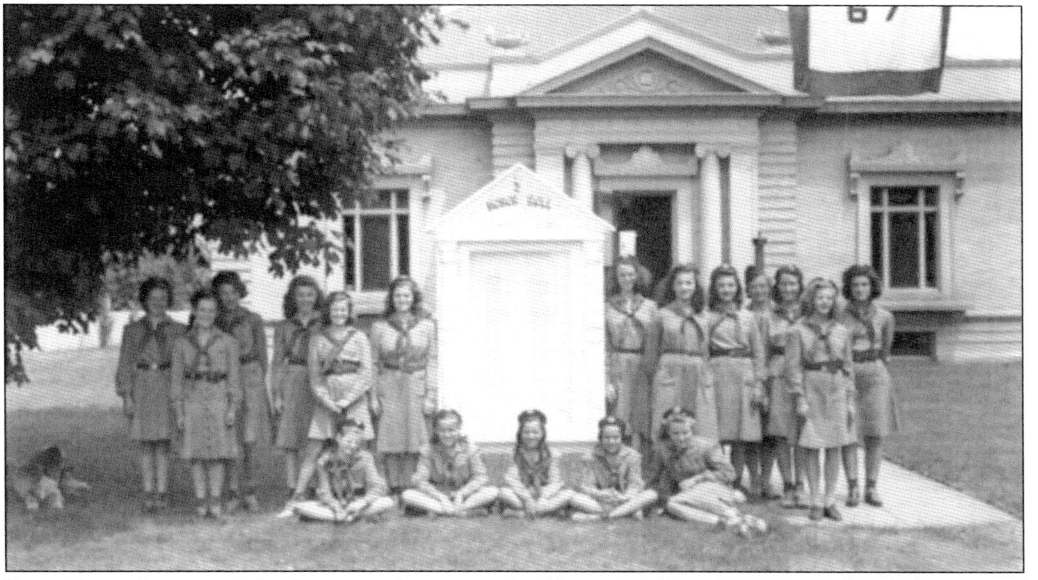

Bow Girl Scouts. Members are shown at the library on July 2, 1945, at the dedication of the service flag and honor roll for the 67 Bow veterans of World War II. From left to right are (first row) Norma Kilmister, Lyle Sargent, Helen Colby, Mary Howe, and Carol Allbee; (second row) Alice Hanson, Gert Bowen, Orissa Lee, Carolyn Butler, Theo Hutchins, Pauline Bowen, Joan Howe, Ardyth Coulter, Grace Heath, Leader Ervina Sherbourne, Thelma Whittier, Esther Bullock, and Elsie Avery.

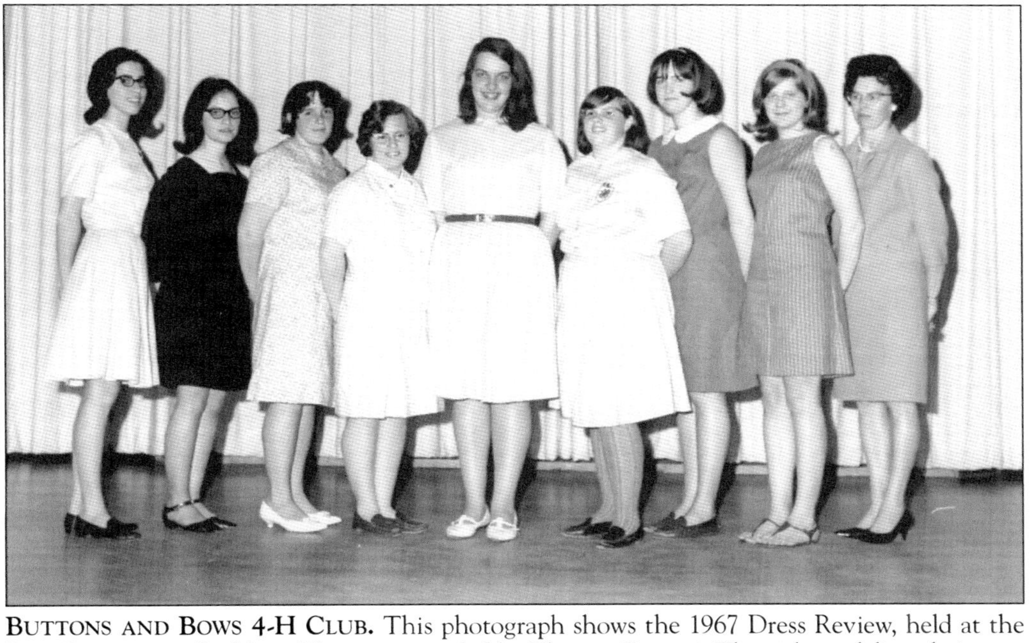

Buttons and Bows 4-H Club. This photograph shows the 1967 Dress Review, held at the Bow Community Building. The group was led by Theresa Capozzi. The girls modeling their own creations were, from left to right, Terry Capozzi, Anne Foote, Mary Lindquist, Marcia Goodwin, Sarah Morrill, Susan Goodwin, unidentified, Julie Thalin, and Theresa Capozzi. Other leaders not pictured were Shirley Barker and Grace Nesbitt.

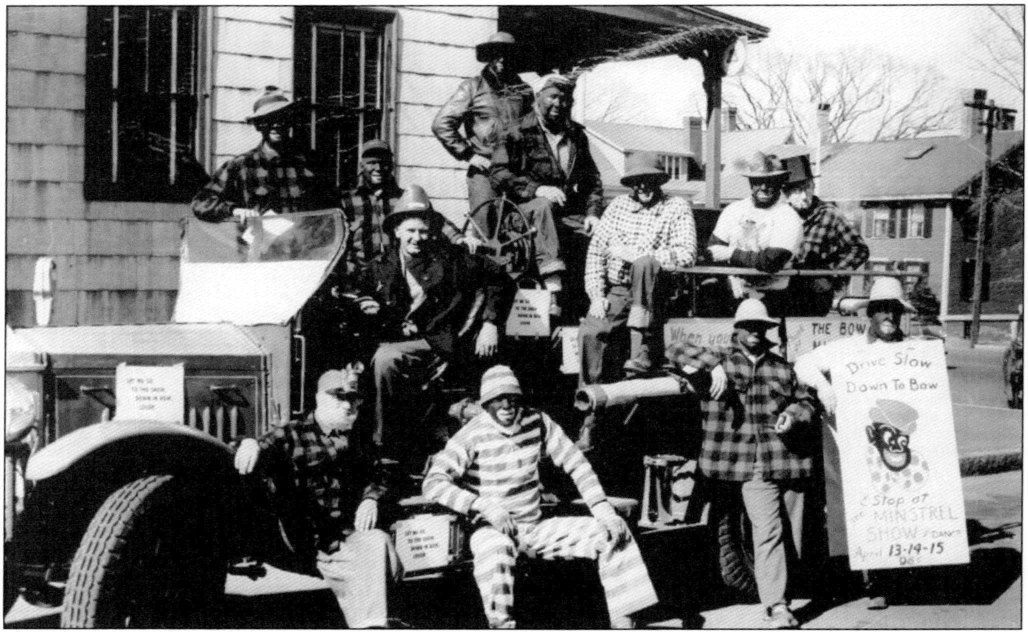

BOW MINSTRELS. The Bow Community Men's Club, which was formed in 1948, held annual minstrel shows in the early 1950s and 1960s. Identified here are Art Stickney, H. Chip Bailey, Dick Hanson, A. Wheeler Sargent, Dan Earnshaw, M. Farmer, Bow Chadwick, George Hancox, Art Chadwick, Stretch Wheeler, and Bob Day.

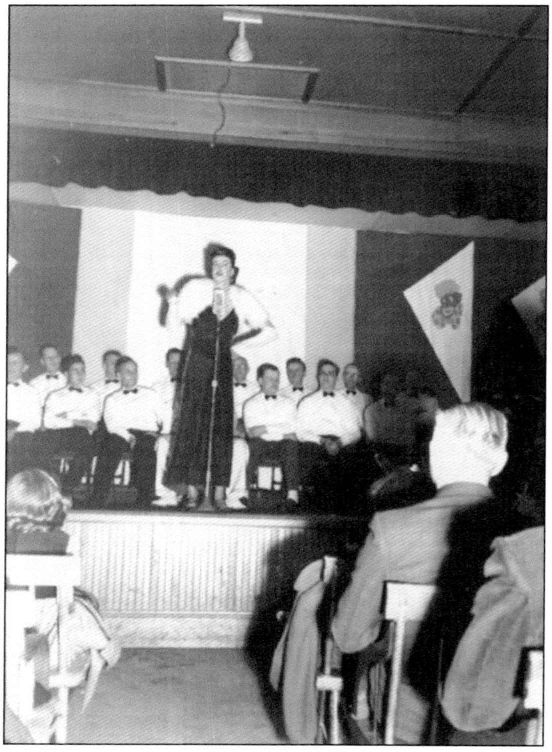

FASHION SHOW. Franklin Gregory performs as a female impersonator during 1952 Bow Community Men's Club minstrel show held at the Bow Grange hall. The shows were the main fund-raisers for the club, which purchased playground equipment, awarded scholarships, sponsored baseball teams, and supported many community projects. Some of the members of the chorus who can be identified are Richard Hanson and Paul Lindquist.

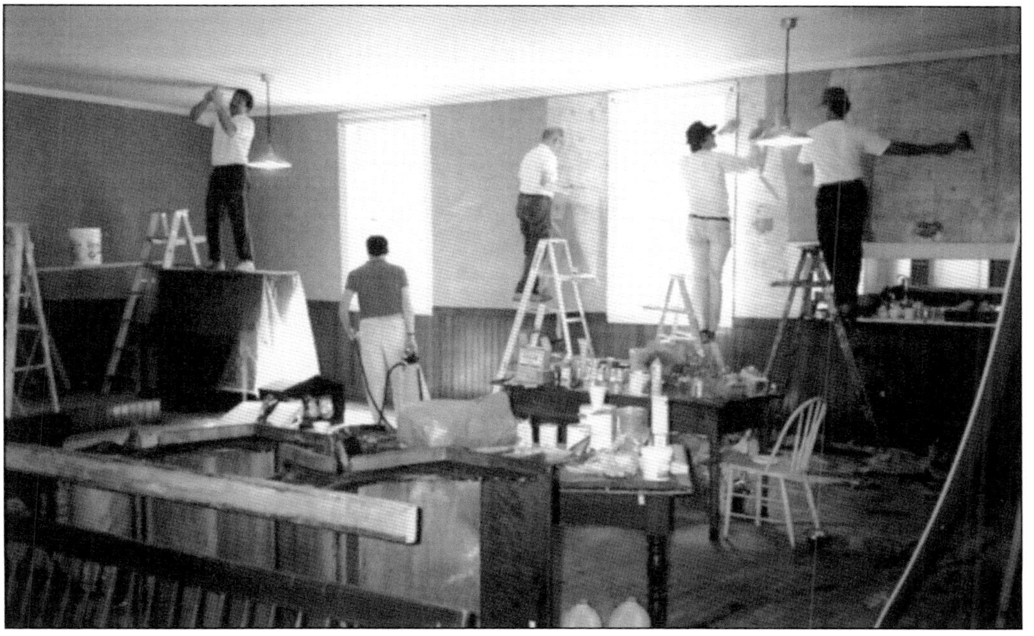

HELPING HANDS. The Bow Rotary was established in 1970. Members donate their time and money to help local, state, and international causes, programs, scholarships, and community projects. Shown here in the 1992 renovation of the old town hall are, from left to right, members Robert Dawkins, standing on the piano; Milt Shirlock; John Iffland; Chris Parkinson; and Jerry Carrier.

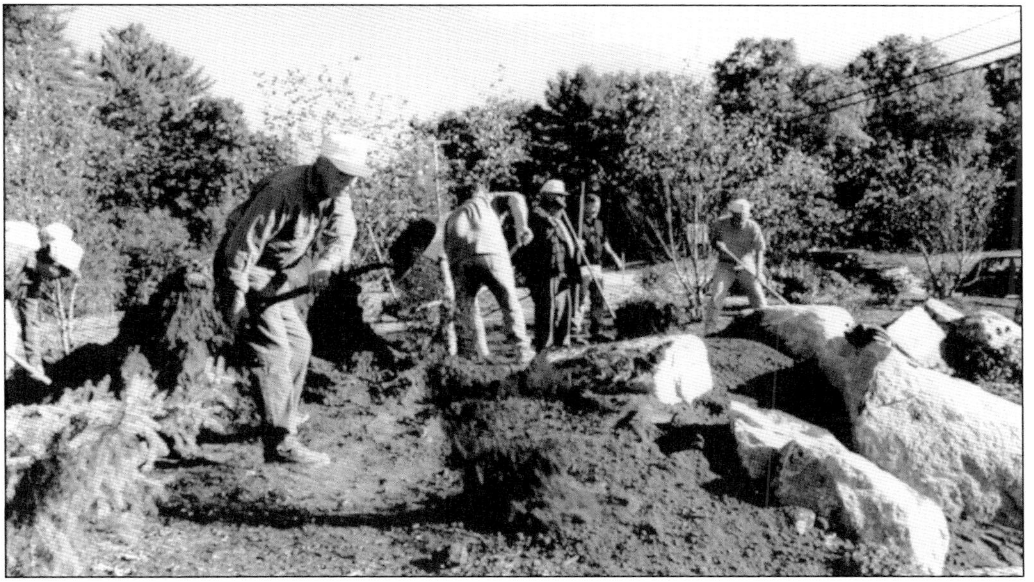

ROCK GARDENING. A major undertaking of the Bow Rotary Club was to develop the land at the corner of Logging Hill and White Rock Hill Roads as a Visual Park. With earth moving, rock siting, grass seeding, and the planting of trees, shrubs, and bulbs, the park took shape in 1998 and 1999. Perennial and annual planting and maintenance have been coordinated with the Bow Garden Club. Rotary club members are, from left to right, Harold Keyes; Ray Helgemoe, with spade; Chris Parkinson; John Lyford; Mark Lefebvre; and Ken Moulton.

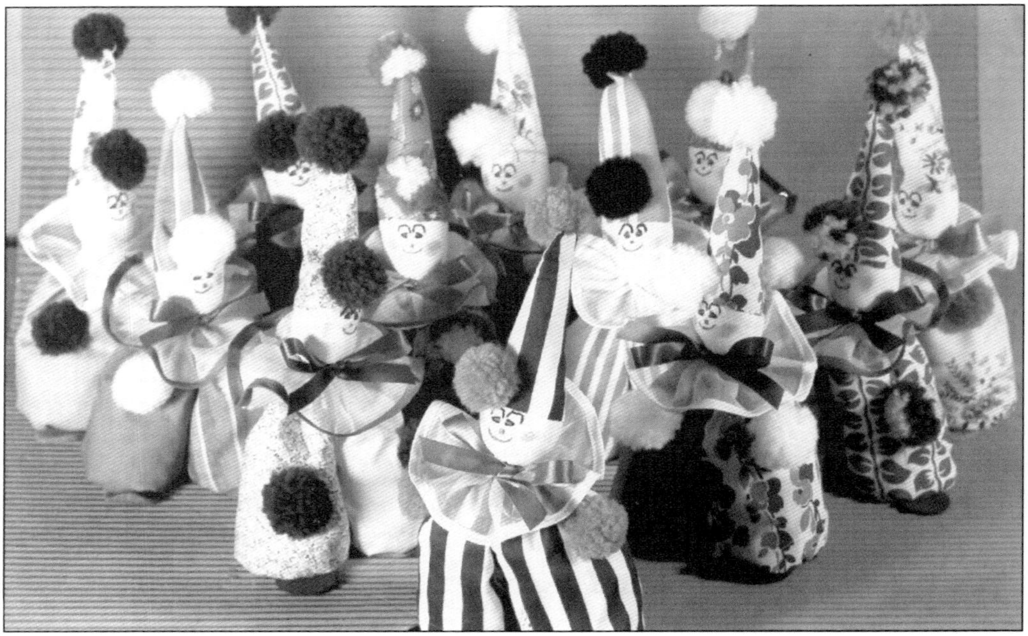

CLOWNING AROUND. The Ladies Aid Society of the Bow Community Baptist Church put together these clown dolls to sell at fund-raising events. The dolls' popularity gained in leaps and bounds, so much so that the ladies patented them. The dolls were made in the 1950s and 1960s.

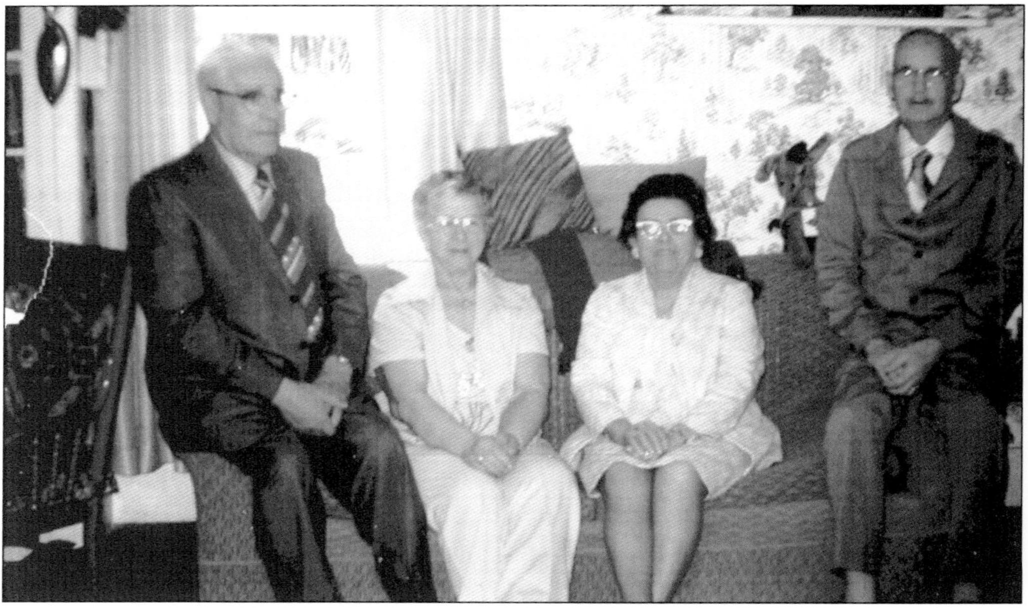

BOW YOUNG AT HEART CLUB. The Bow Young At Heart Club was started by recreation director Bob Wheeler as a social club for senior citizens of Bow. The group was chartered on April 27, 1976, with Evelyn Upton elected president and Helen Finch the secretary and treasurer. There were 29 charter members. With over 80 members, they meet at the Bow Community Building. This photograph shows the co-founders, from left to right, Arthur and Laura Sargent, and Hilda and Phillip Sargent.

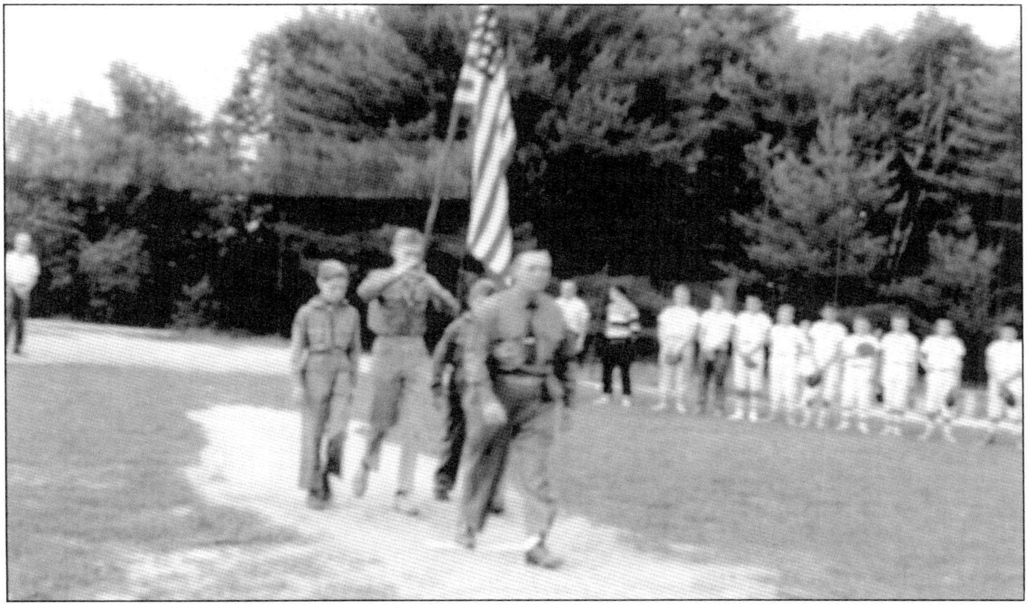

SARGENT'S PARK. Sargent's Park is located in back of the Municipal Building (formerly Bow Mills School). In the late 1950s, Arthur Sargent donated land to be used for a playground and baseball field. This picture shows George Barry, scoutmaster, and members of Troop 75 presenting the colors in June 1961 at the dedication. The playground was modernized in 2000 and the ball field is still used for T-ball, little league, and softball games.

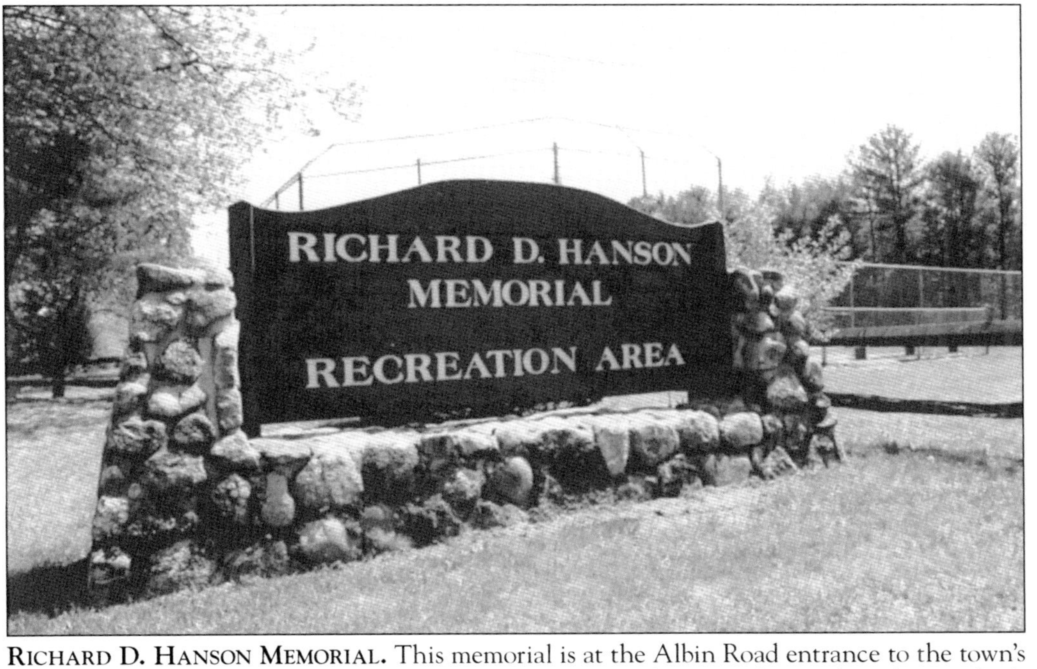

RICHARD D. HANSON MEMORIAL. This memorial is at the Albin Road entrance to the town's recreation area. The park includes four fields—Gergler, Goodwin, Gordon, and Gosling—which are used by the recreation department and the Bow Athletic Club for soccer, lacrosse, baseball, and softball games.

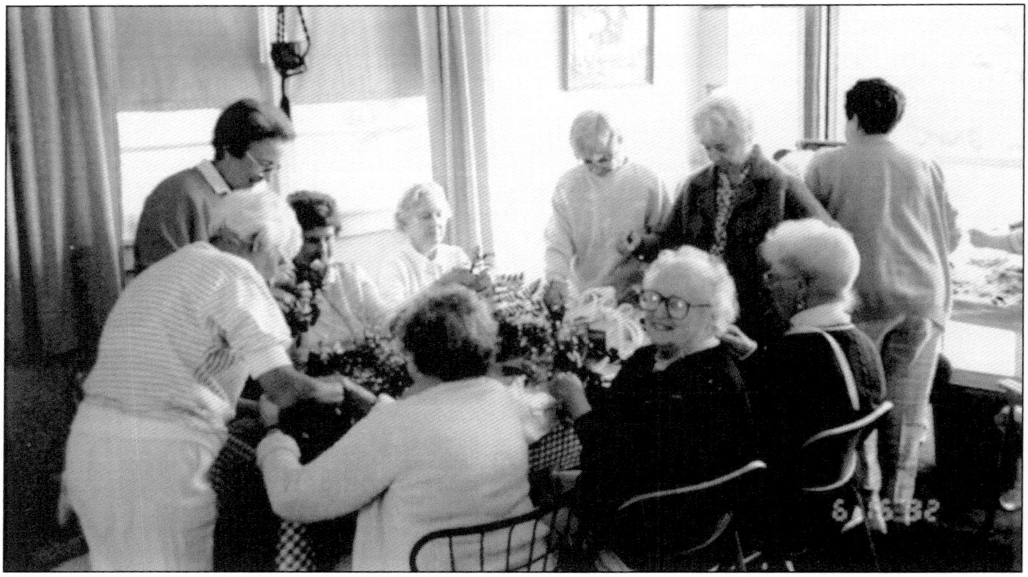

Bow Garden Club. The Bow Garden Club was organized in 1964 by Tempie Dahlgren. The objective of the club is to encourage interest in horticulture, protection and conservation of natural resources, and to assist in the beautification of the community. Here club founder Dahlgren guides members in making floral arrangements. Members shown are, from left to right around the table, Eunice Pinto, Clarise Bouchard, Hazel Ruggels, Tempie Dahlgren, Helen Smith, Erna Hamilton, Nat Macdonald, Jodie Mueller, Dot Wheeler, and Nellie Aldrich.

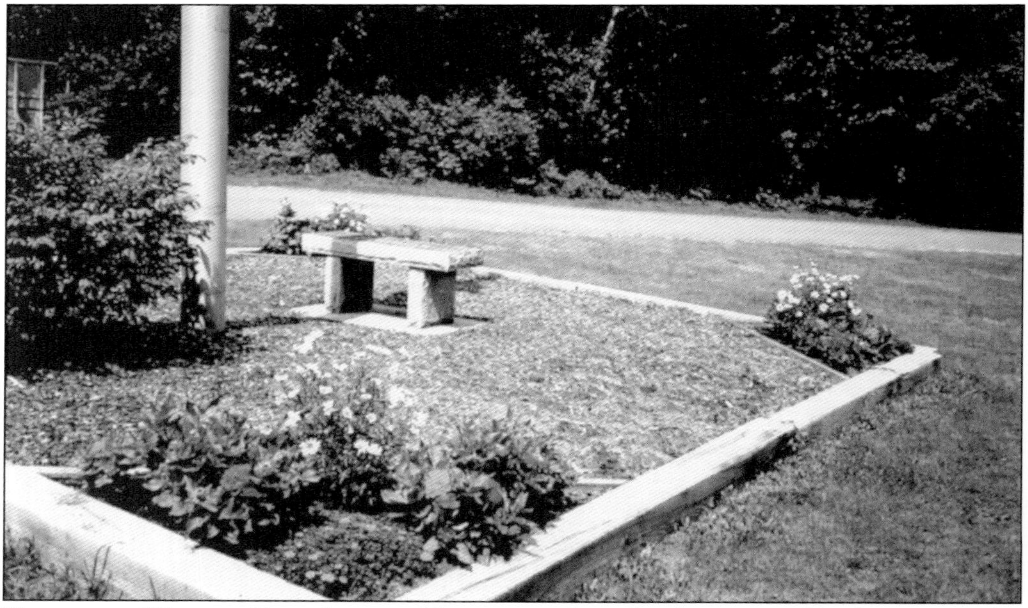

Volunteer Way and Flag Square. This square, planted and maintained by the Bow Garden Club, is sited at Hanson Park off Albin Road. A memorial bench donated by the Bow Rotary Club, Robert C. Gosling, and Public Service Company of New Hampshire is the focal point of Volunteer Way. In addition to providing a permanent memorial, the site is used for recognition ceremonies of individual volunteers.

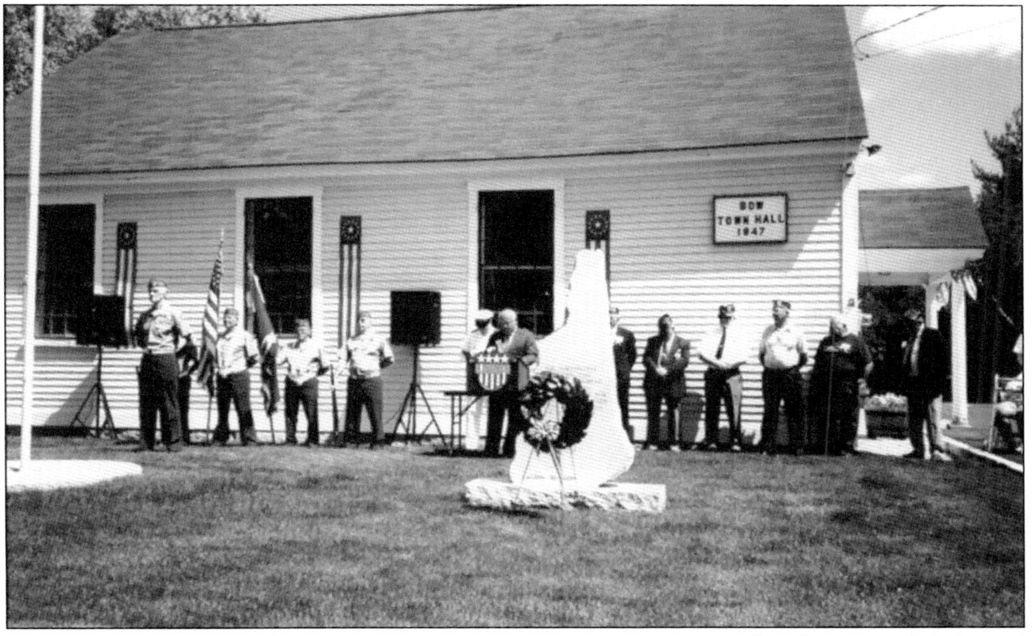

VETERANS MEMORIAL. A monument to town war veterans was erected at the site and dedicated on May 30, 2000. It reads "The Townspeople Dedicate This Veterans' Monument To The Brave Men And Women Of Bow Who Served With Honor In The Armed Forces Of Our Country." The old town hall is on the historic buildings list and map.

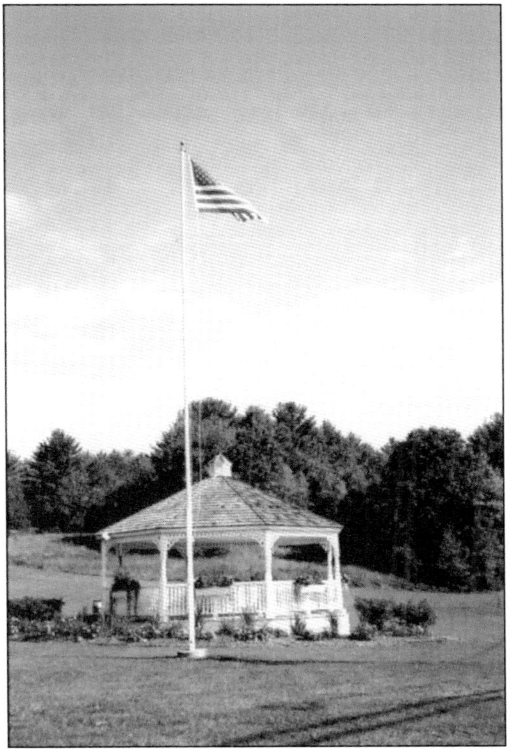

OPEN FOR FUN. The gazebo has provided an outdoor venue for summer concerts, weddings, Sunday sermons, and school and club activities. A summer concert in progress is shown in this July 2004 photograph. Flower boxes are maintained by Alice Jorda, a member of the Bow Garden Club. In 2006, the club created a memorial garden at the bandstand to honor Tempie Dahlgren, founder of the Bow Garden Club and past president of local, state, and national garden clubs.

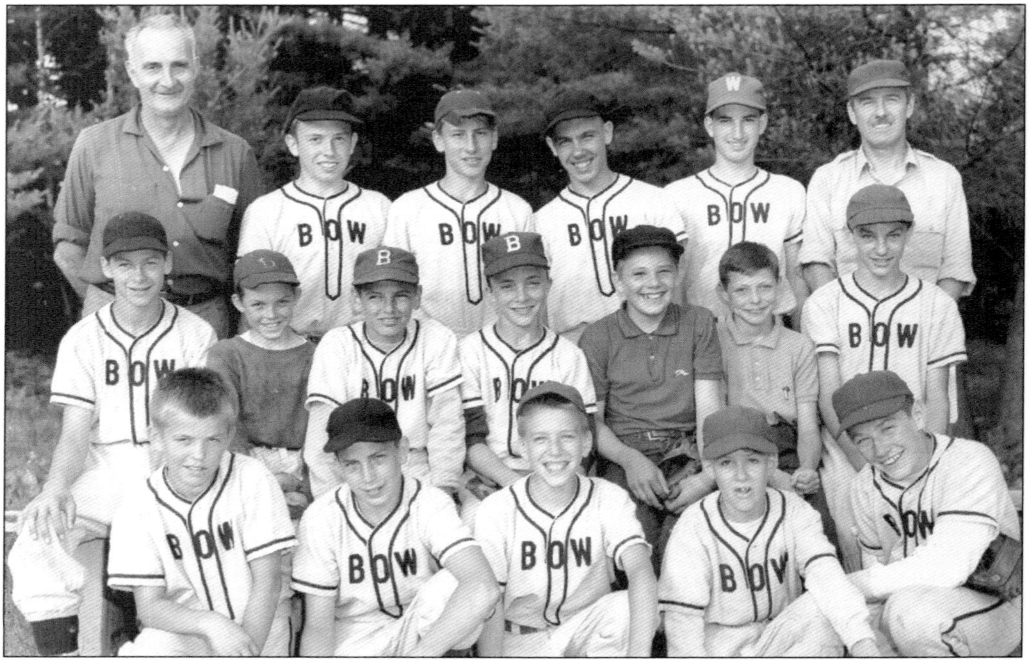

TOWN TEAMS. Before the Bow Athletic Club was incorporated in 1974, teams such as this 1961 baseball team were sponsored by the Bow Community Men's Club and the Bow Rotary Club. From left to right are (first row) Bruce Young, David Lindquist, Bill Maynard, Walter Chadwick, Bob Hill; (second row) Leonard Duckworth, Skip Ladd, Walter Herrick, Jerry Foote, Howard Wagner, Dana Abbott, and Ronald Sargent; (third row) Stretch Wheeler, Parker Morgan, John McPhail, Werner Lehto, Thurston Hodgdon, and Everett Duckworth.

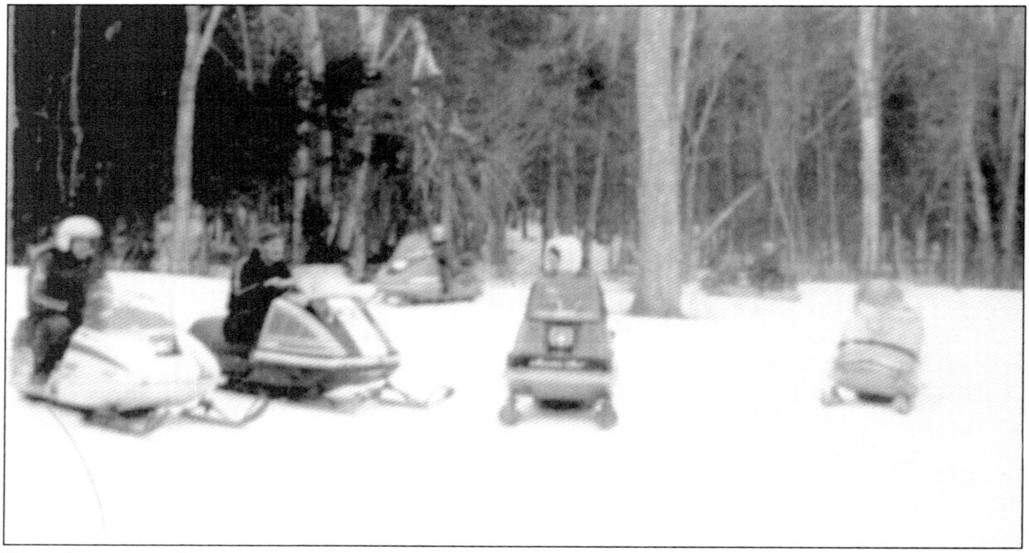

BOW PIONEERS SNOWMOBILE CLUB. The club was established in 1972 and has been a trailblazer for snowmobiling. They take the responsibility for grooming, putting up signs, and maintaining the snowmobile trail system. Not only has other areas of the state copied their formation, but they have networked and linked Bow's trails with theirs.

Two

CUTTING AND TILLING

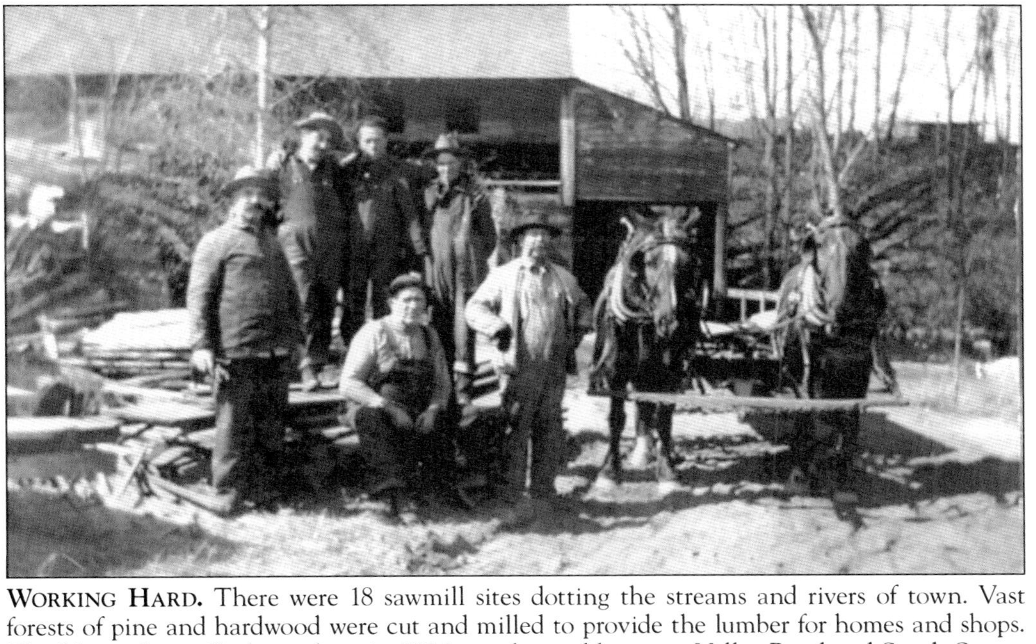

WORKING HARD. There were 18 sawmill sites dotting the streams and rivers of town. Vast forests of pine and hardwood were cut and milled to provide the lumber for homes and shops. The Upton Sawmill, shown here in 1926, was located between Valley Road and South Street. The mill workers, from left to right, are (first row) Mark Upton, Sanford Sidelinger, and George Drew Sr.; (second row) Lee Morgan, Fred Drew, and Harry Flanders. Flanders was a lifetime logger who remembers looking into the valleys from atop Wood Hill in the early morning and seeing the steam from 8 to 10 sawmills. Many of the later mills were portable mills, powered by wood fired steam boilers and capable of being moved between woodlots.

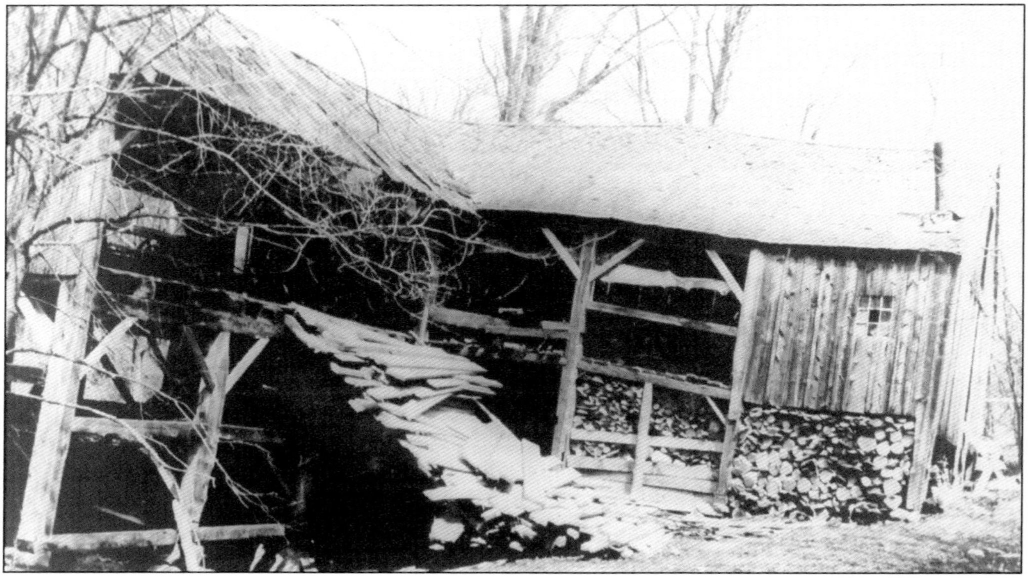

UP AND DOWN. The Up and Down Sawmill was located at the lower end of Putney Meadow Pond. The saw was a single long blade that moved vertically, hence the name. The original owner was Seth Ordway, followed by three generations of the Nichols family, and then a few generations of the Colby family (it was also known as the Colby-Nichols mill). The building was mostly destroyed by the hurricane of 1938. The remaining parts were salvaged and the mill restored at Old Sturbridge Village, as part of their historic tourist attraction.

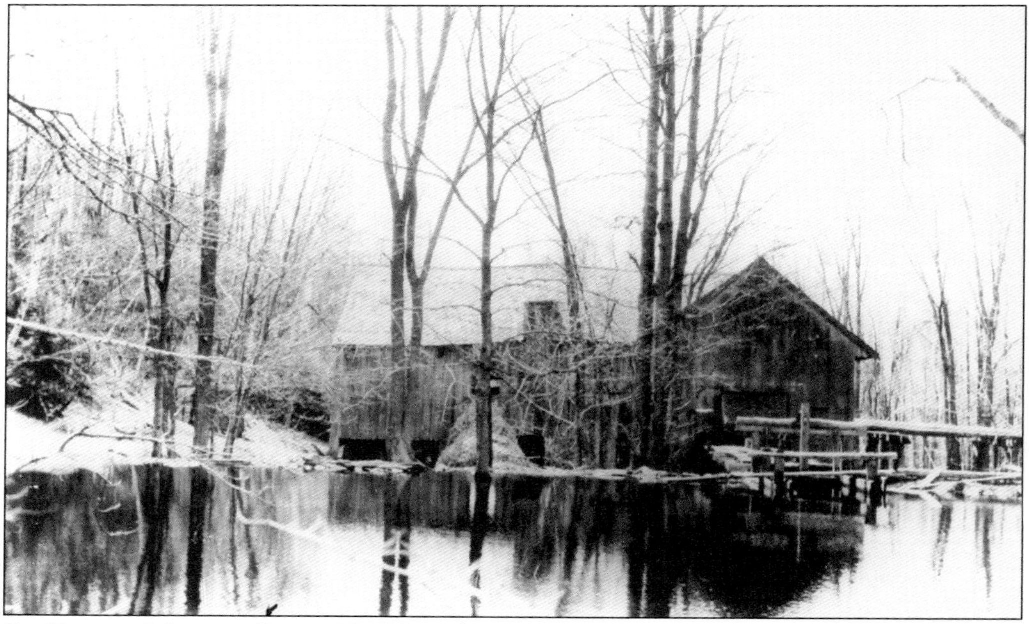

ON PUTNEY MEADOW POND. The Up and Down Sawmill was idle during the summer months when the meadowland was used for farming. From November to April, the dam was built up and the field flooded to form the holding pond. The dam and pond remained until the late 1990s, when the dam was dismantled and the pond drained.

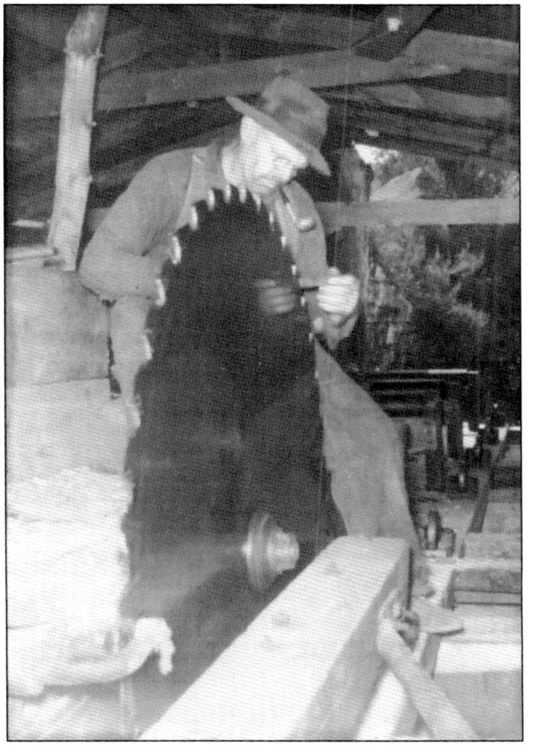

ROUND AND ROUND. The Scott Wheeler Mill was located close to Brick Yard Brook in south Bow. The circular saw, as shown, evolved from previous technology and was far more efficient than the up-and-down saw. This blade was cleaned and sharpened frequently by Sam Eliott, one of the logging crew.

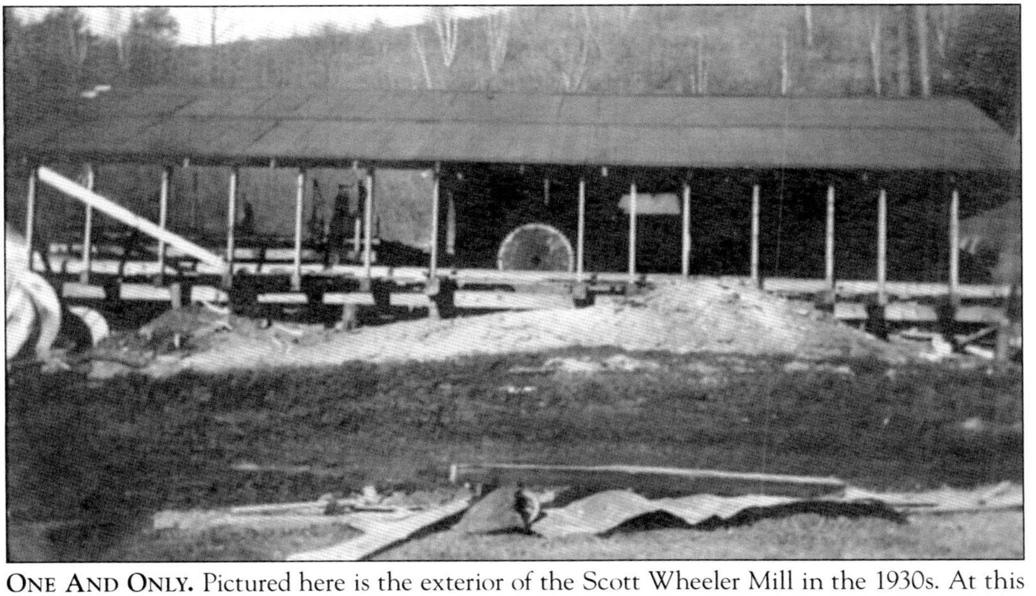

ONE AND ONLY. Pictured here is the exterior of the Scott Wheeler Mill in the 1930s. At this time, Warren Davis, who lived on Ordway Lane in south Bow, was the biggest lumber dealer in town. He would often bring lumber to this mill to be sawed, as it was the only permanent sawmill in the area.

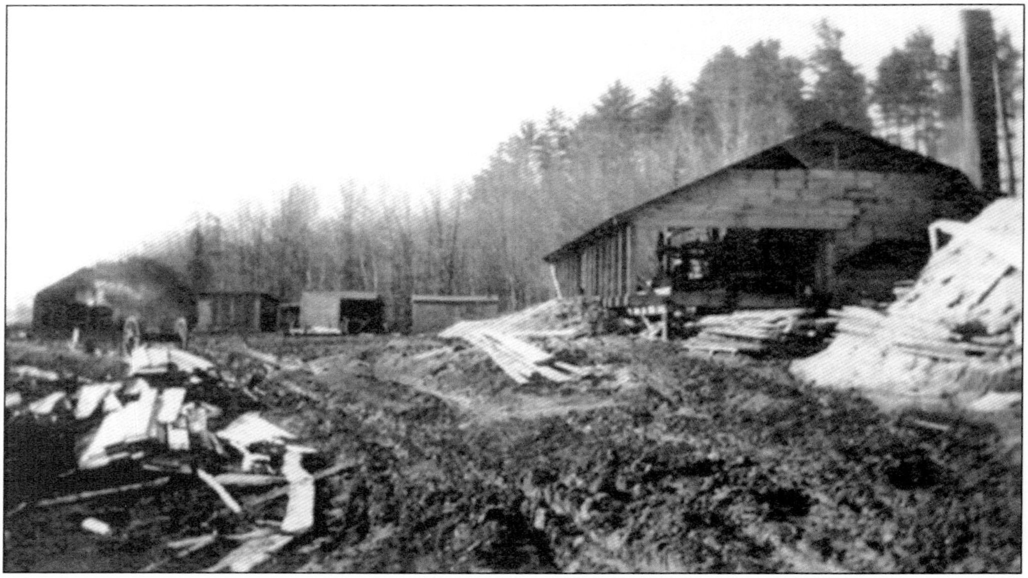

Lumber Yard. This photograph is a wider view of the entire operation of the Scott Wheeler lumber yard. On the left, the steam from a portable sawmill can be seen. Also visible is the smokestack of the furnace that powered the stationary mill. They were certainly busy, as evidenced by the huge pile of sawdust on the right side of the main building.

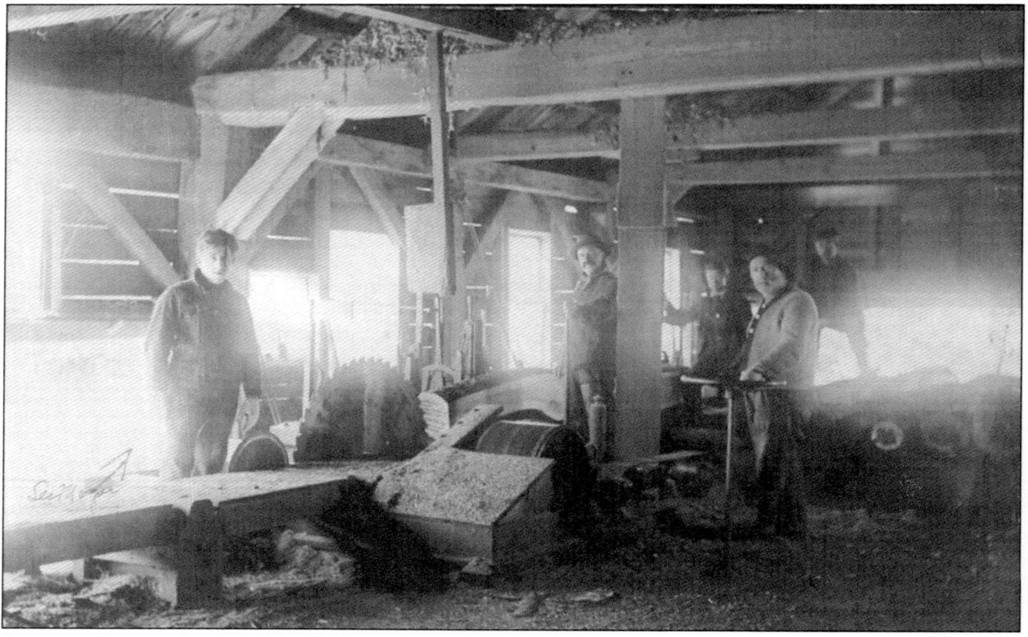

Seesaw. Pictured inside Mark Upton's sawmill at Bow Mills are, from left to right, Lee Morgan, Mark Upton, Nat Foote, George Drew Sr., and Fred Drew. Well before the enactment of safety standards, the mills were dangerous places. Fred Drew was killed in a tragic accident at the mill. A wooden wheel under the mill was connected to the saw by a belt and pulley. The belt had slipped and he was trying to replace it when his shirt was caught on the wheel and he was turned around and around and crushed to death.

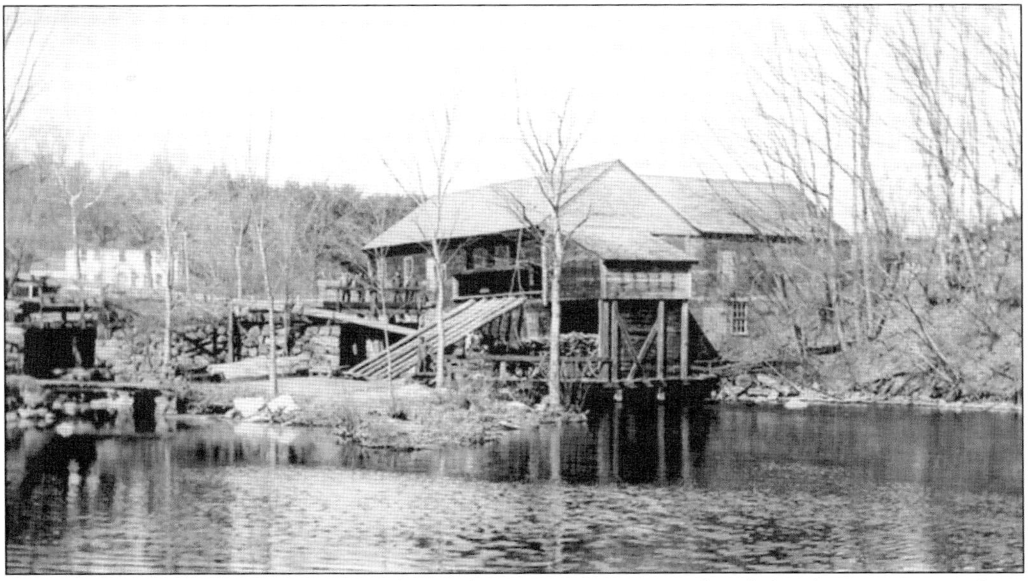

TURKEY RIVER. The mill sites on the Turkey River were considered the finest in town. Saw, shingle, and gristmills were operated here from 1748 to 1940. The mills passed through many hands, ultimately being owned by Mark Upton. This photograph shows the main sawmill and the middle dam located off of Valley Road. The Allquist home can be seen in the background with South Street passing in front of the home. The mill and home no longer exist and the site is now the Interstate 89 interchange.

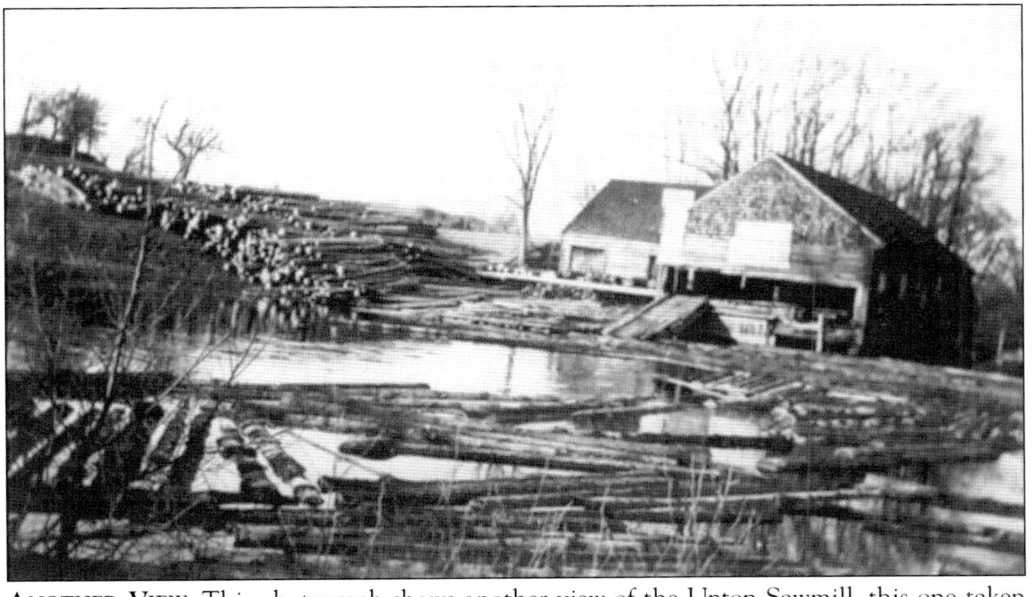

ANOTHER VIEW. This photograph shows another view of the Upton Sawmill, this one taken from the mill yard around 1925. Here the size of the holding pond formed by the mill dam can be seen. The logs were easier to handle and could be quickly moved to the mill when they were floated on the water.

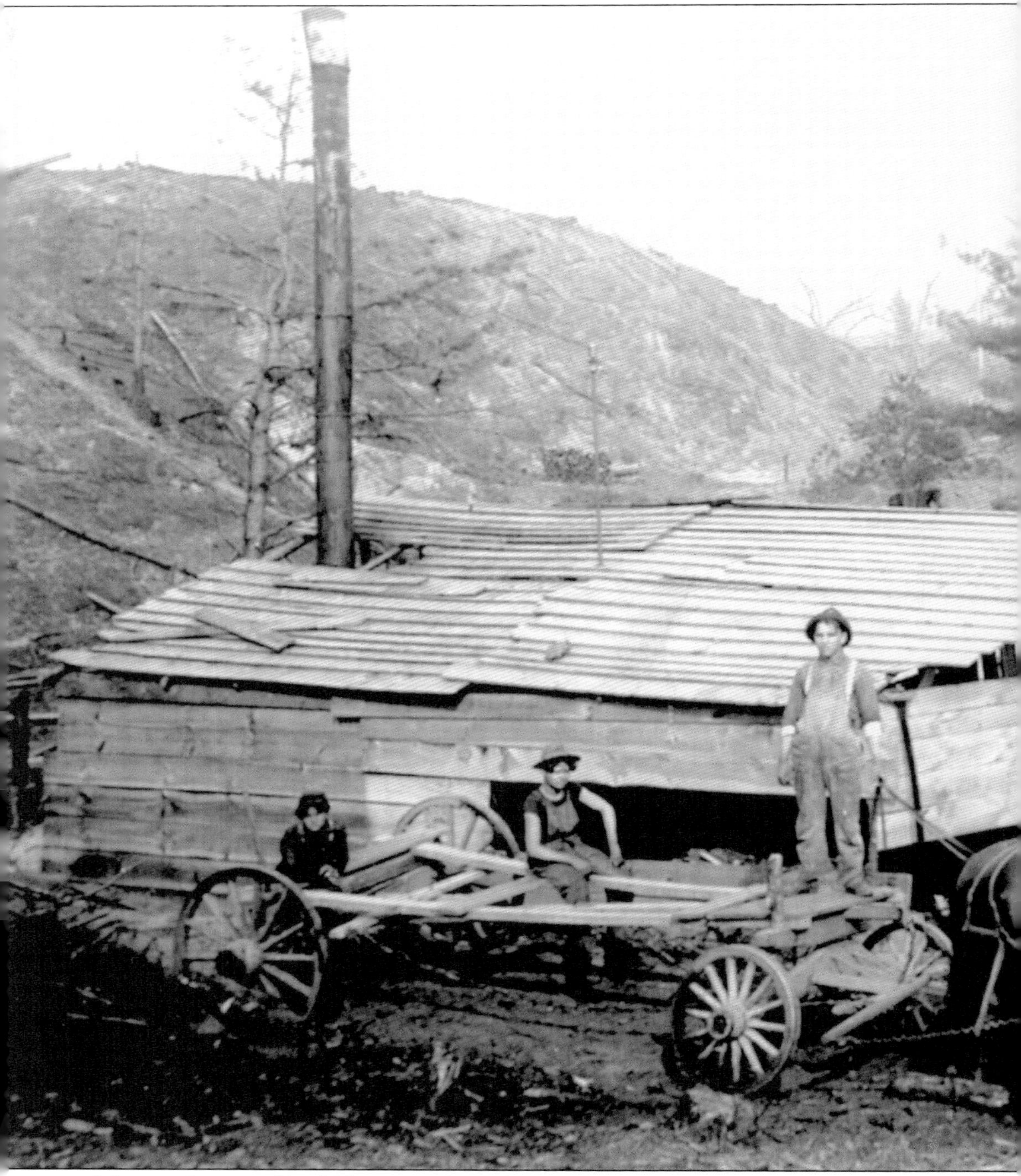

MILLING AROUND. Frank Noyes, grandson of Benjamin Noyes who was one of the original settlers of Bow, was heavily involved in the lumbering business. This picture, taken around 1901, depicts his stationary mill located off Route 3-A near Dunklee Road. Prior to this, Frank also owned several other mills, including one off Route 3-A at Moore's Brook (across from the current Bow Auto Parts) called the Merrymeeting Mill, that was first owned by Benjamin. He also owned

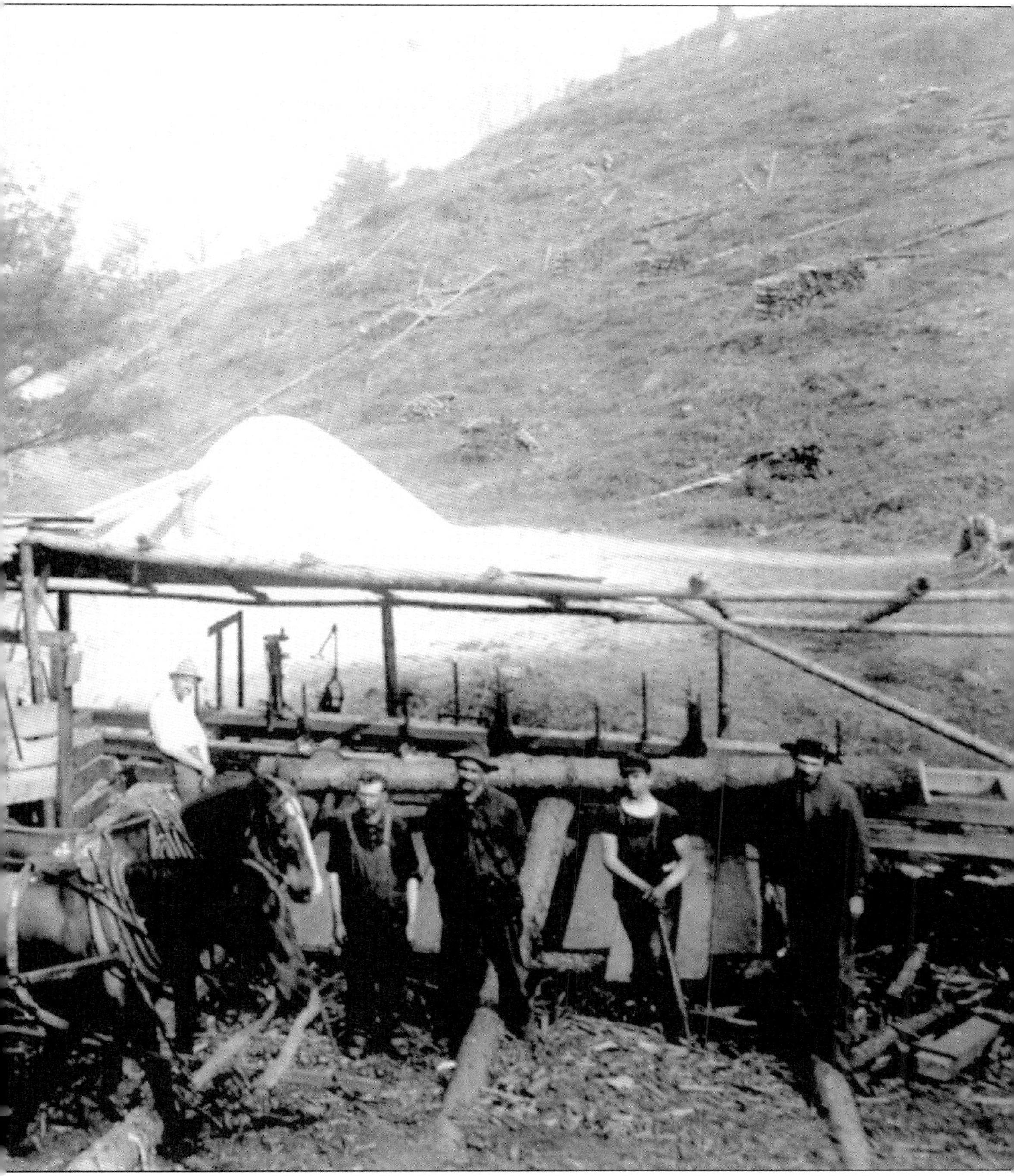

several portable mills on various woodlots around town. Frank was a highly regarded lumberman, who could, as quoted from *100 Acres More or Less*, "saw faster than anyone in the business." Lumbering was a big business around 1900, with railroads providing both ease of transport and a market in fuel for the locomotives. The lack of trees anywhere in the background and the huge pile of sawdust are testament to the scope of the operation at this site.

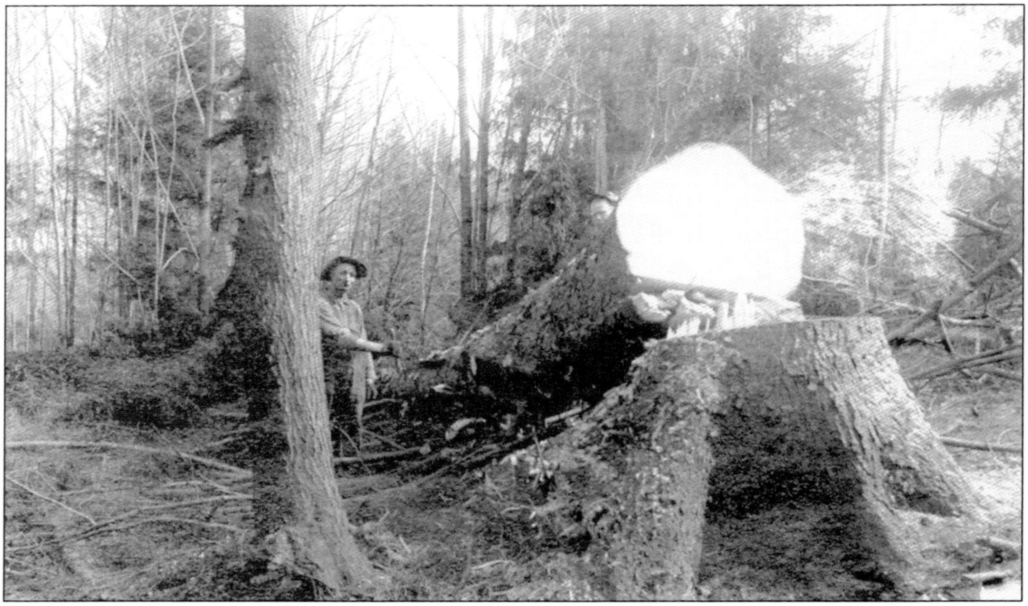

Board Feet. This picture was taken in south Bow in the late 1920s, when old growth trees like this one were plentiful. The pine trunk shown here has no heart rot, which makes for a better quality board and less waste. The two loggers are identified as Dwight Ritchie (left) and R. Legate and they worked for the H. A. Velier Lumber Company. It took some serious muscle to topple these trees with a two-man saw.

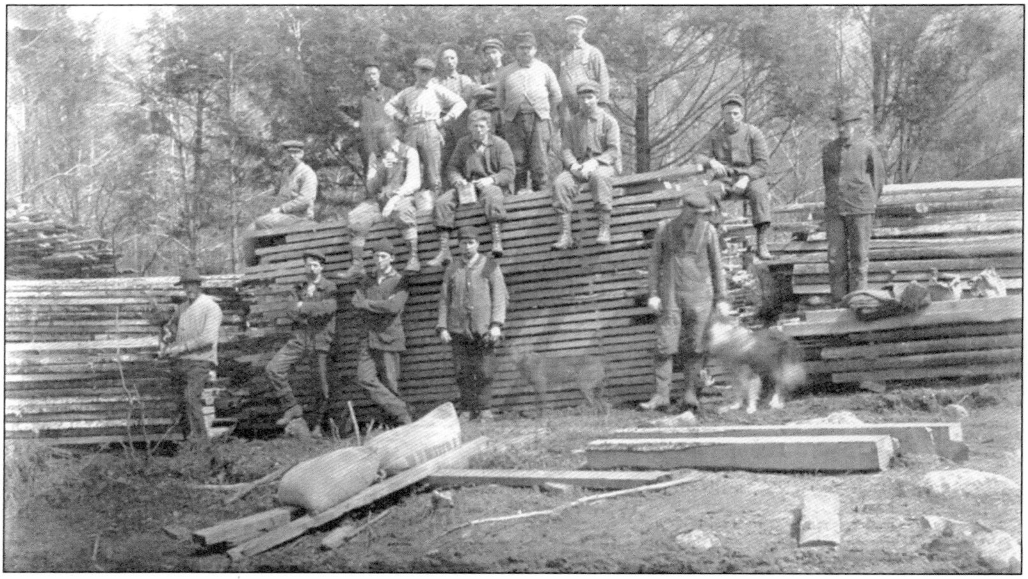

Straight From The Tree. At the day's end, the H. A. Velier Logging crew rests beside the piles of lumber they had produced. Following the 1938 hurricane, there were thousands of toppled trees that needed to be cleared, which resulted in a rebirth of logging and sawmill operations. Many of the men in this photograph, taken at one of the Velier lots in south Bow, are unidentified, but the names on the back include M. Quinn, G. L. Velier, Dwight Ritchie, R. Legate, E. Truesdale, and James Ordway.

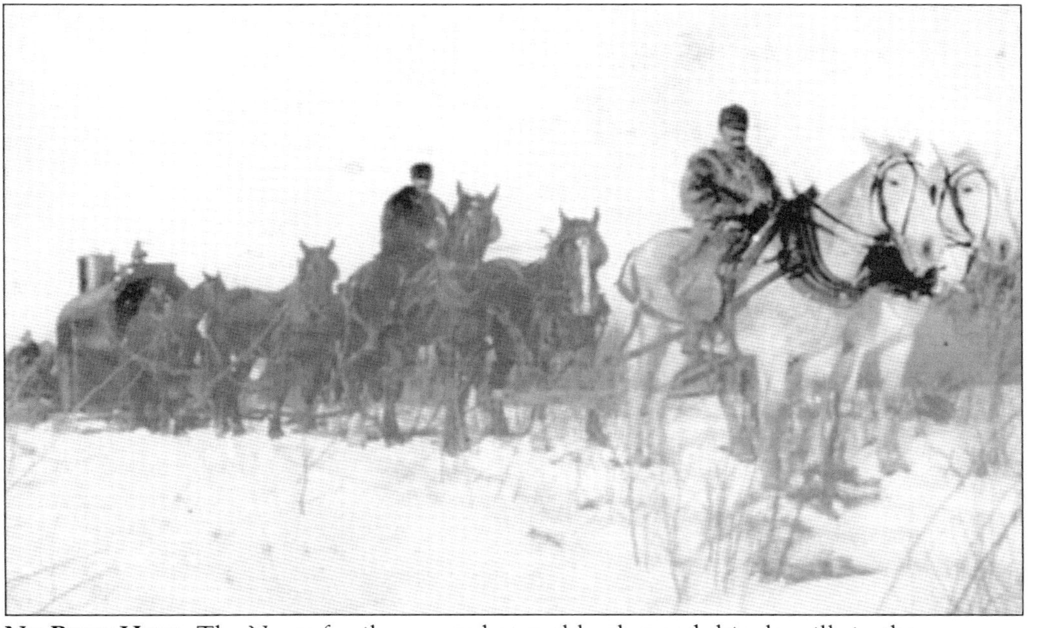

NO RUTS HERE. The Noyes family operated several lumber and shingle mills in the area near the Hooksett town line. Frank Noyes lived on Johnson Road. Lumbermen are seen here moving the portable mill with a team of horses in 1901. Doing this during the winter months made it easier to travel and strained the horses less. No skidder ruts were left behind in the olden days.

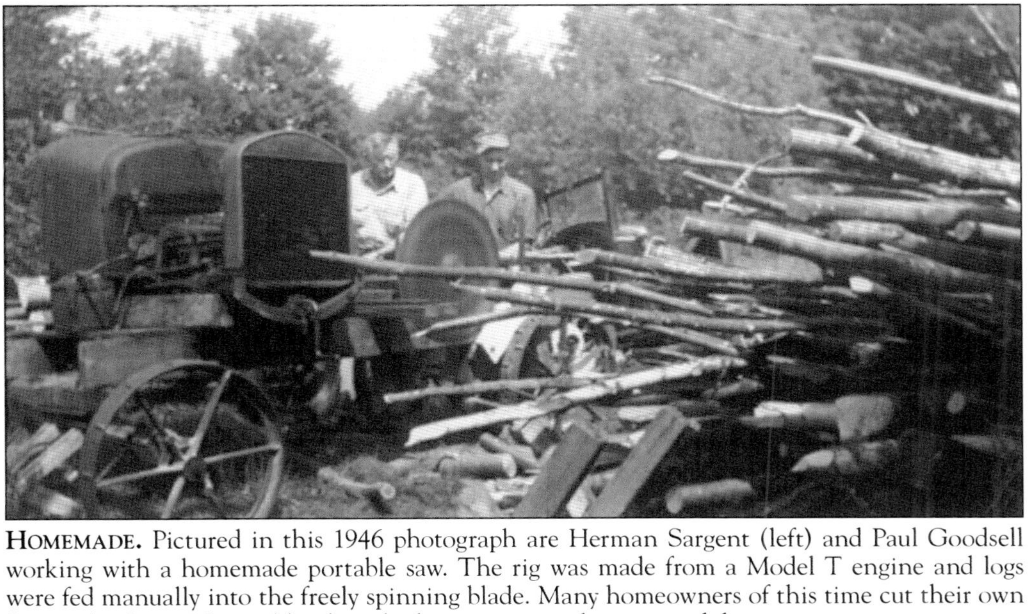

HOMEMADE. Pictured in this 1946 photograph are Herman Sargent (left) and Paul Goodsell working with a homemade portable saw. The rig was made from a Model T engine and logs were fed manually into the freely spinning blade. Many homeowners of this time cut their own firewood, often with rigs like this which were extremely noisy and dangerous.

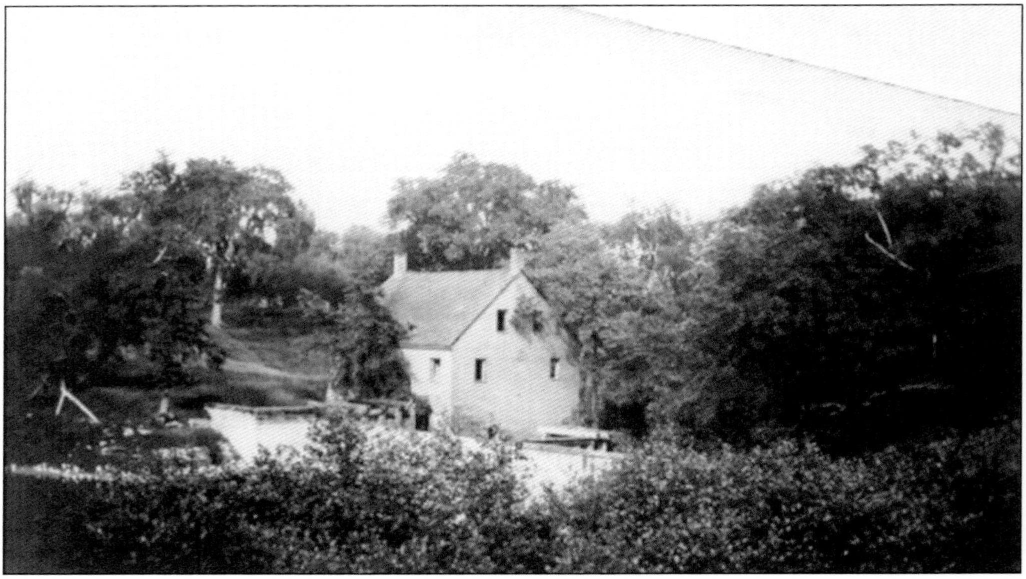

NOT JUST LUMBER. Another of the mills at Bow Mills was the gristmill, located at the lower dam, which formed the "upper pond" seen here. The ponds formed by the dams were popular swimming sites. The Chen Yang Li restaurant currently occupies this site. Above this was the "upper dam" with a small sawmill. There were several dams in this area, the upper and lower dams to the west of South Street, and the middle dam was just east of South Street.

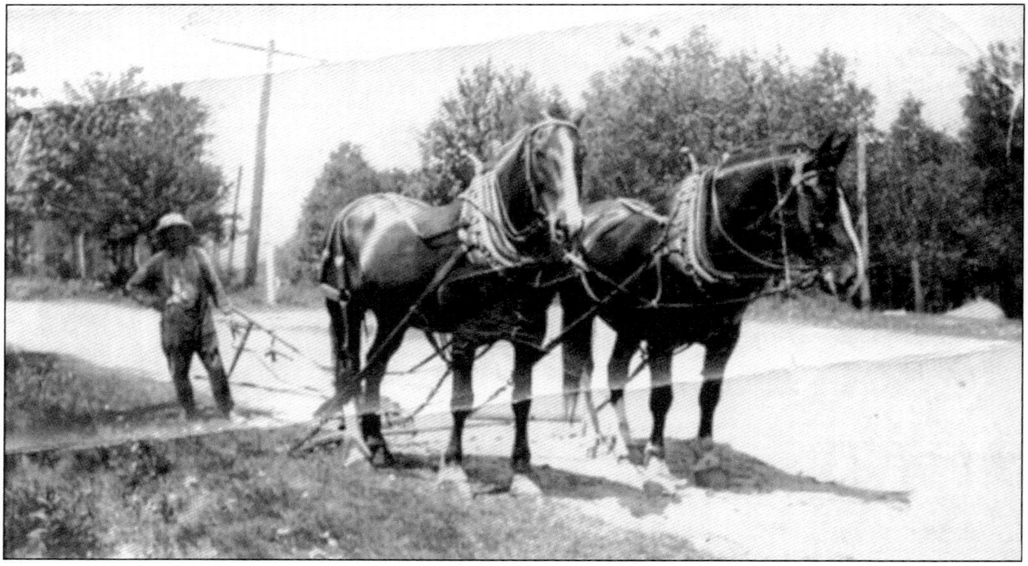

FROM CUTTING TO TILLING. Tom May cultivates land at the intersection of Grandview Road and Route 3-A with Jack and Jerry, horses owned by Earl Voils. There were few cars passing down the still-unpaved Route 3-A in 1915. The Mays' farm is still a private residence.

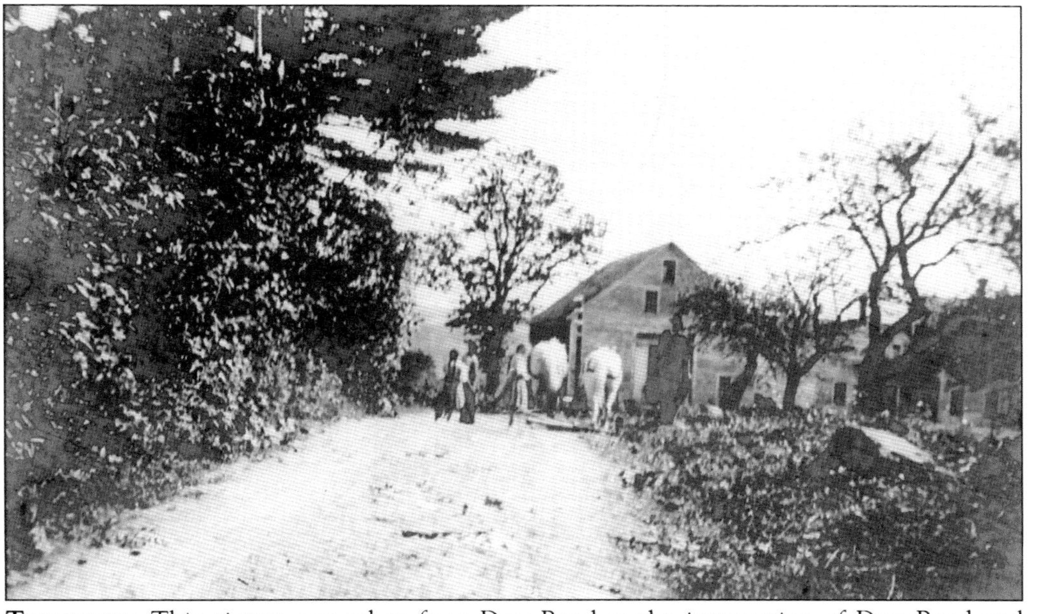

TEAMWORK. This picture was taken from Dow Road at the intersection of Dow Road and the Londonderry Turnpike (now Route 3-A). The barn and farmhouse were owned by Edwin Alexander and conveyed to Burt Alexander and his wife Eva May (Noyes) Alexander. The team of horses was owned by the family and used on the farm. The barn is gone now but the house remains and is currently owned by Arthur Cheney.

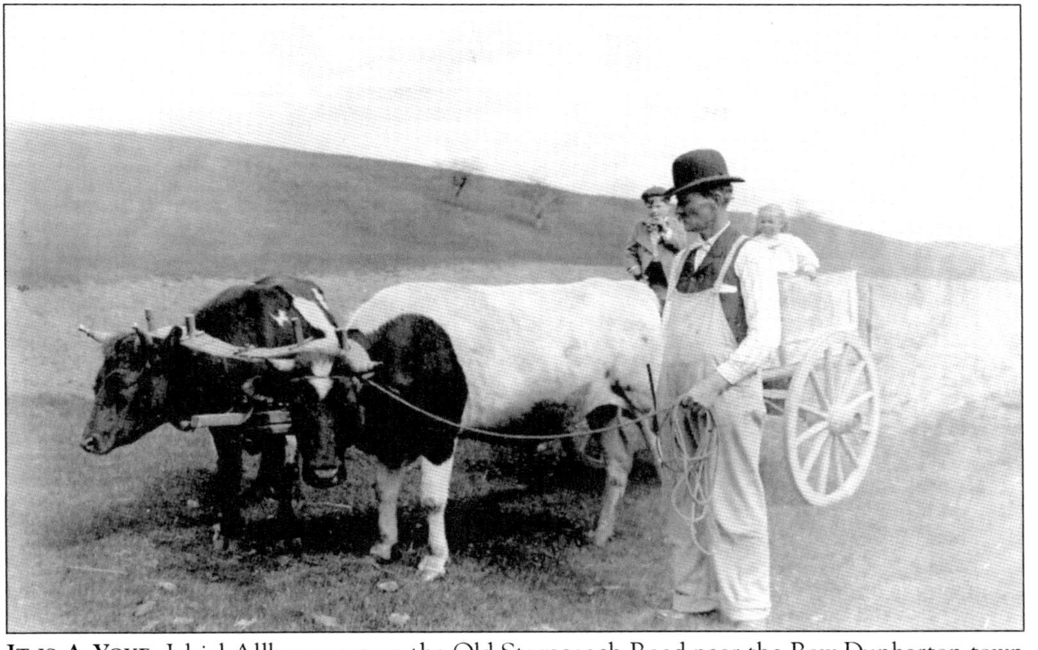

IT IS A YOKE. Jehiel Allbee poses on the Old Stagecoach Road near the Bow-Dunbarton town line with his team of oxen. In the cart are his grandchildren Hiel and Helen. The Allbee family came to Bow in the early 1900s. Allbee and his son George later moved to neighboring farms on Valley Road.

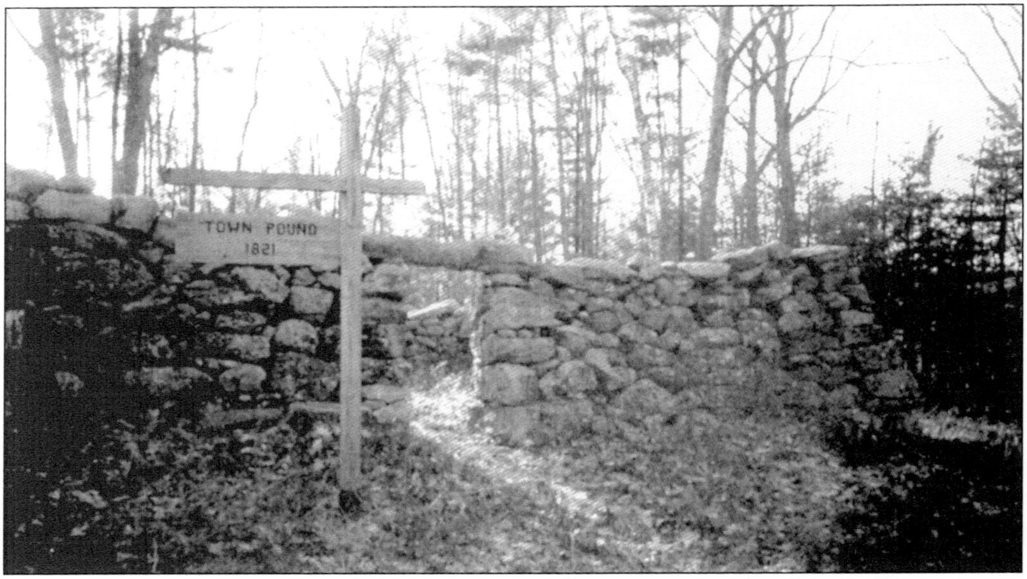

ANIMAL CONTROL. The New Hampshire colonial government mandated the building of town pounds in 1791. The original Bow Town Pound was built in 1768 near Turee Pond. At the second town meeting on April 4, 1768, Bow residents voted Rueben Currier of Bow Mills and Samuel Alexander of River Road as hog constables. These men were charged with impounding all stray hogs, which were a danger to vegetable gardens and grain fields. The pound shown here, near the east branch of the Londonderry Turnpike was built in 1821.

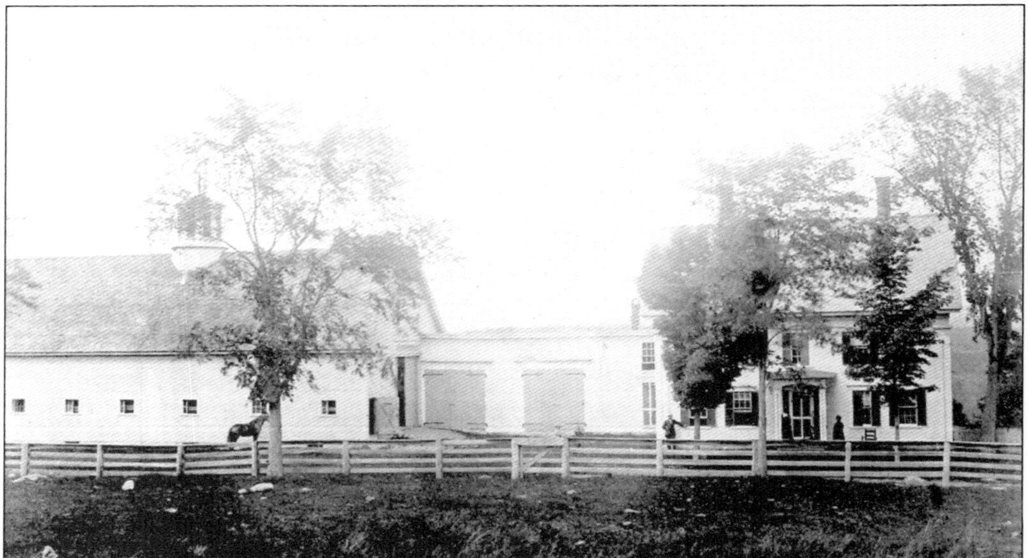

PRIZE WINNING FARM. This farm owned by Henry White and later his nephew D. Waldo White was located on the Londonderry Turnpike and Route 3-A, (the dirt road between the farm and the fence). It was home to a prize winning herd of Jersey cows, and became known for its "White's Jersey Cream." The farm was later sold to the Ordway family, and it continued to be used as a dairy into the 1950s. The barn was damaged in the hurricane of 1938, and razed in the mid-1950s. The house remains today.

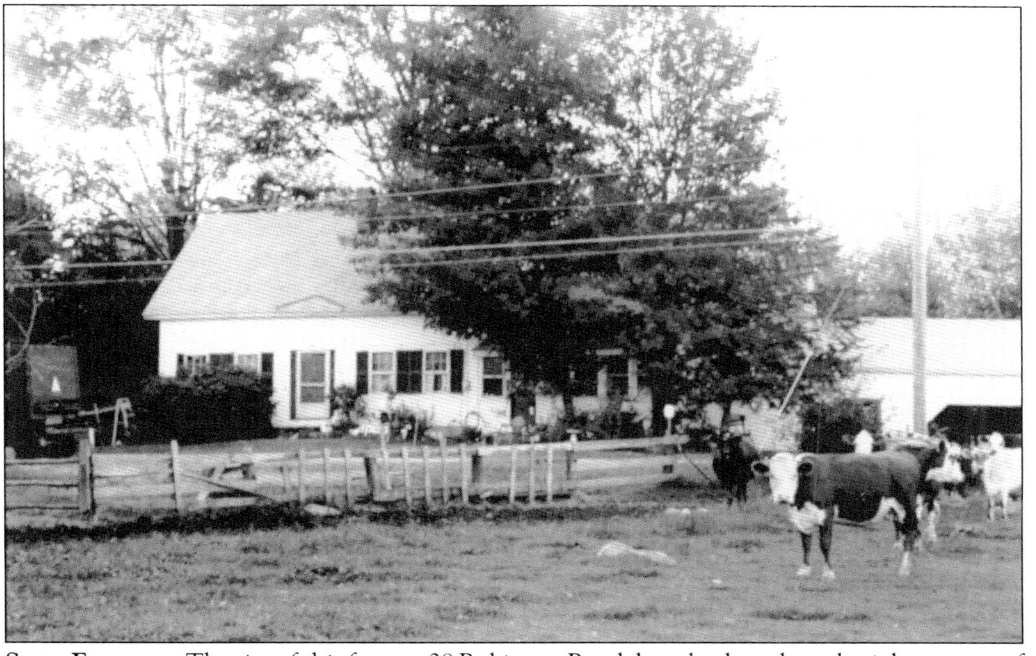

STILL FARMING. The site of this farm at 38 Robinson Road dates back to the colonial governor of New Hampshire, Benning Wentworth. The kitchen, shed, and carriage shed were built between 1750 and 1800. The main section of the dwelling was constructed in 1835 by George Washington Wheeler, who also built the Bow Bog Church. In 1938, Warren and Verna Alexander purchased this farm. Current owners are Linda (Alexander) and Gary D. Nylen.

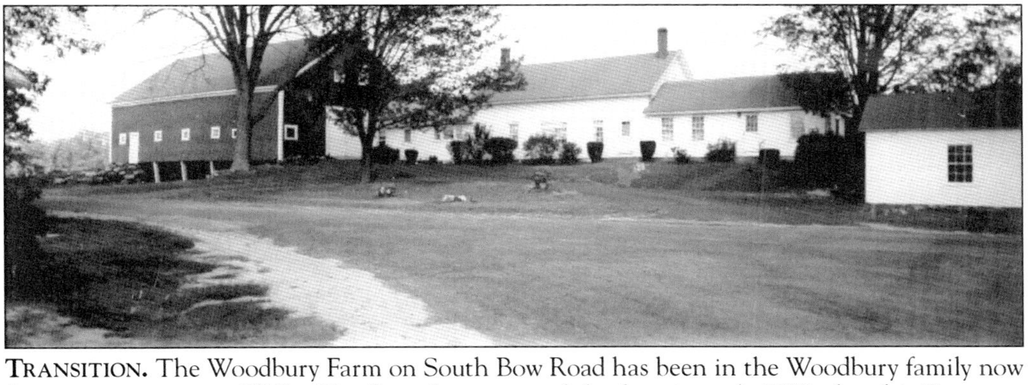

TRANSITION. The Woodbury Farm on South Bow Road has been in the Woodbury family now for seven generations. Willis Woodbury last operated the farm in early 1970 when his Guernsey cows and white leghorn chickens were a full time job. It currently is a Christmas tree farm.

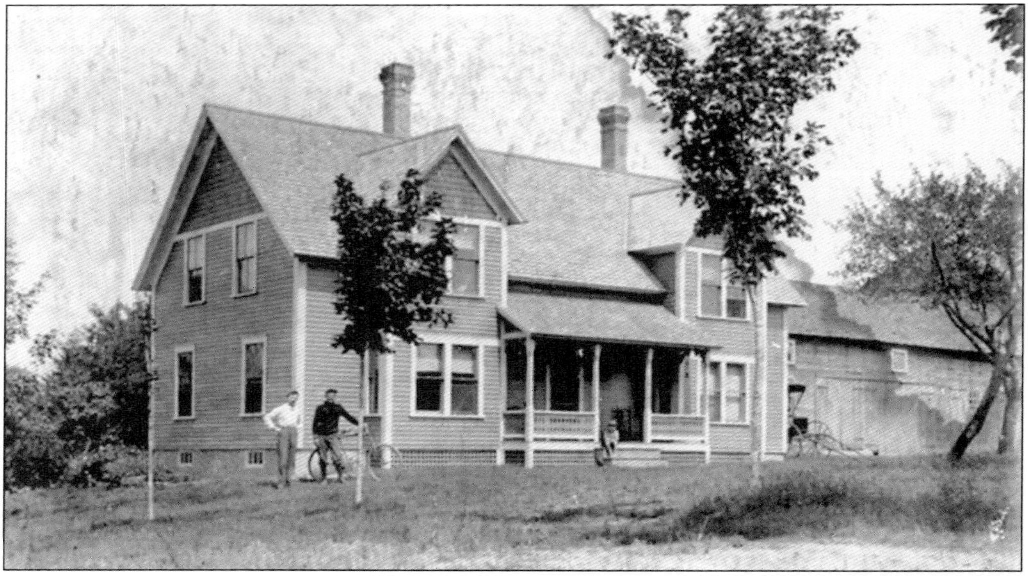

Making Hay. Asa and Rita Morgan and their family were the last of four generations to live on this 110-acre farm. Asa was a selectman from 1933 to 1941. He was an active Grange member for many years, serving as a state master and a national officer. He and his wife spent 10 weeks in India representing American farmers. Asa did all of his farming using his horses, Dusty, Dick, and Dan. The hay raised on the farm was specially cultivated for horses. Wallace Morgan, with the bike, and a friend are pictured here.

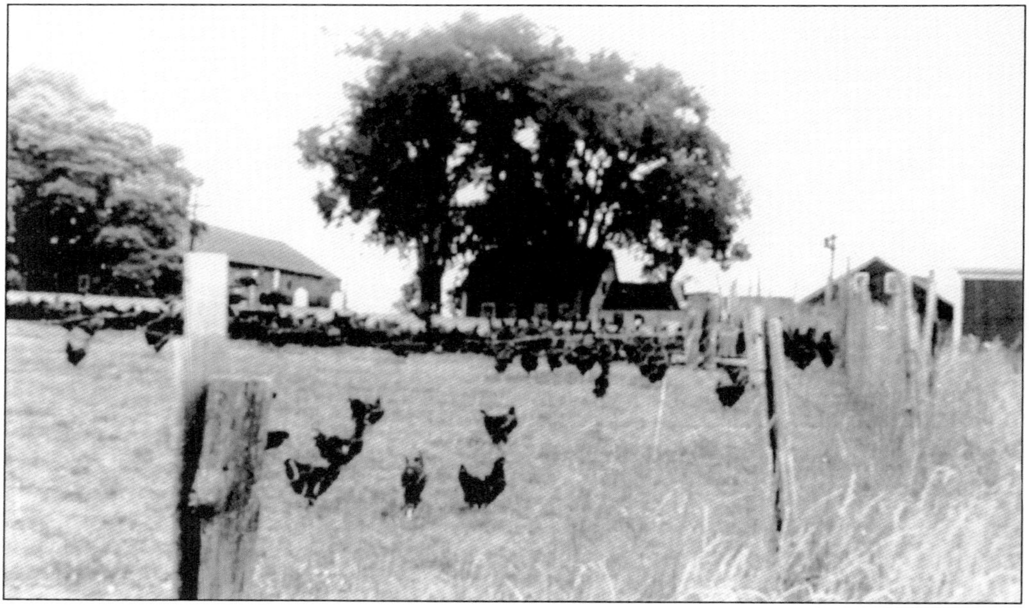

Chicken Anyone? Helen and Henry Cheney raised Rhode Island Red and Black Sex-Link chickens from 1935 to 1980. The poultry was sold and sent to Boston by way of the Boston and Maine Railroad (B&M). This photograph shows the organic free range chickens in the Cheney's field on Woodhill, across from the Woodhill-Hooksett Road. The Cheney family owned the farm from 1925 until 1988.

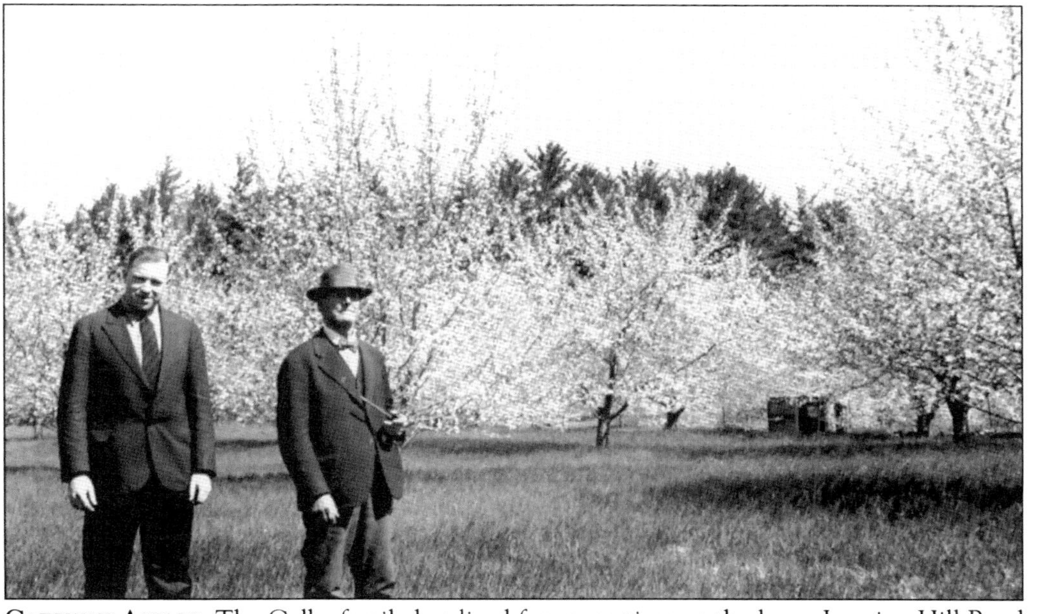

GATEWAY APPLES. The Colby family has lived for generations at the lower Logging Hill Road area. Rob (left) and Doc, seen here, as well as Halstead Colby had orchards on both sides of Logging Hill Road. They primarily sold their apples, as well as other produce, to local markets. This 1940 picture was taken near the location of the present Interstate 89 exit to Bow.

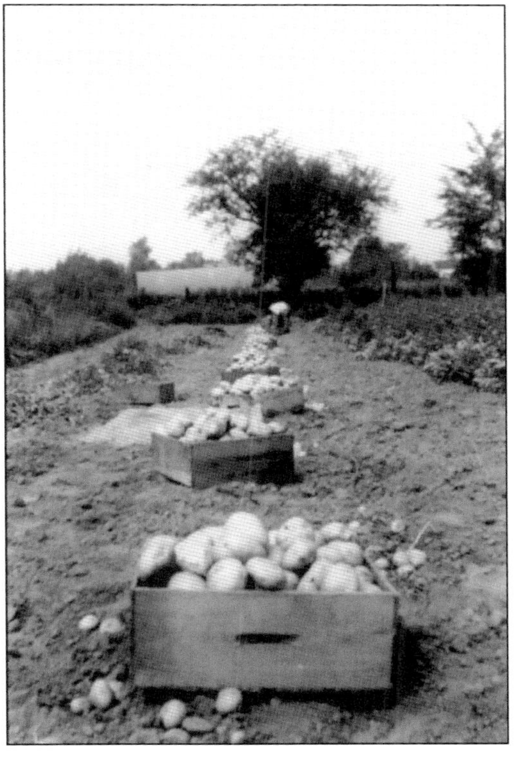

POTATOES AT PITCO. A bounty of potatoes are shown in the fields of the Allbee farm at the corner of Valley Road and Route 3-A. The fields were made fertile by topsoil deposited during the many floods of the Merrimack River. These fields are now home to the Pitco Frialator Company.

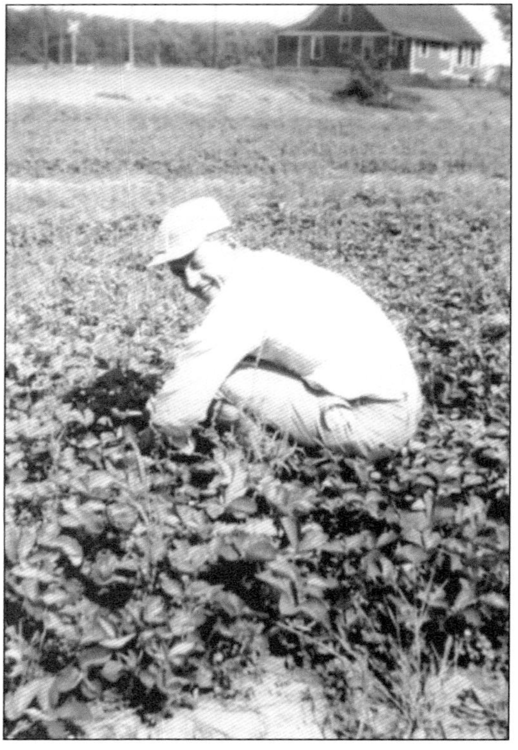

TASTING SWEET. Paul Lindquist picks strawberries at the Allbee Farm, which was on Valley Road near the intersection of Route 3-A. He was later to marry Jane, one of Hiel Allbee's daughters. In 1957, the Allbee home, which can be seen in the background of the photograph, was moved to South Street in Concord.

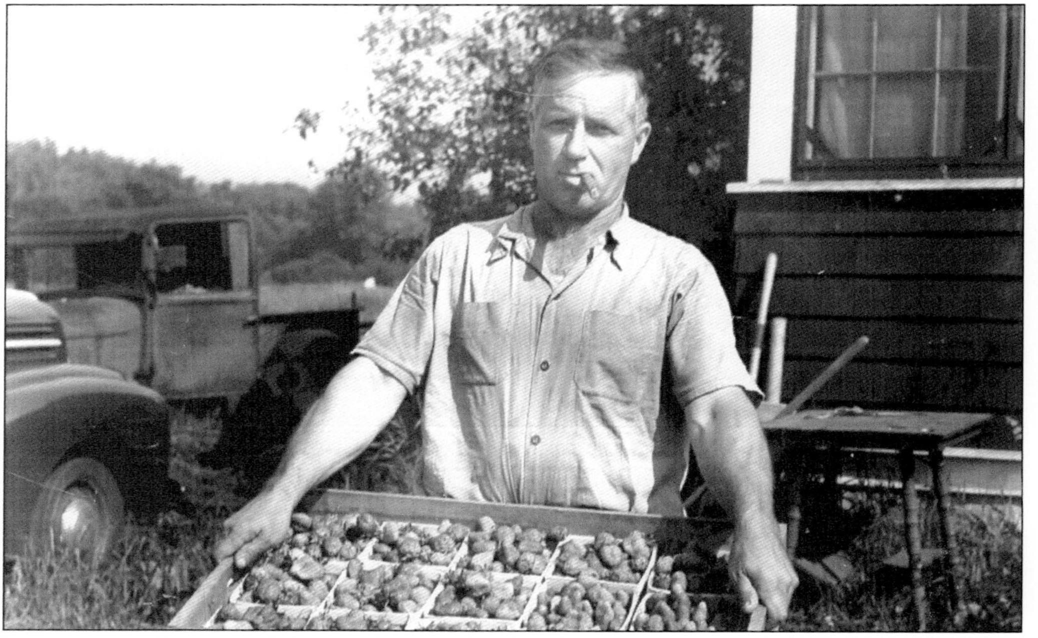

STRAWBERRY KING. Hiel Allbee shows off his fruitful reward in this 1949 photograph. He was a successful farmer, earning the reputation as the "Strawberry King," a title previously held by Joseph Dow in 1892. Many Bow residents can remember picking berries on the farm in the late 1940s and early 1950s. The site is currently the location of Pitco and Interstate 89.

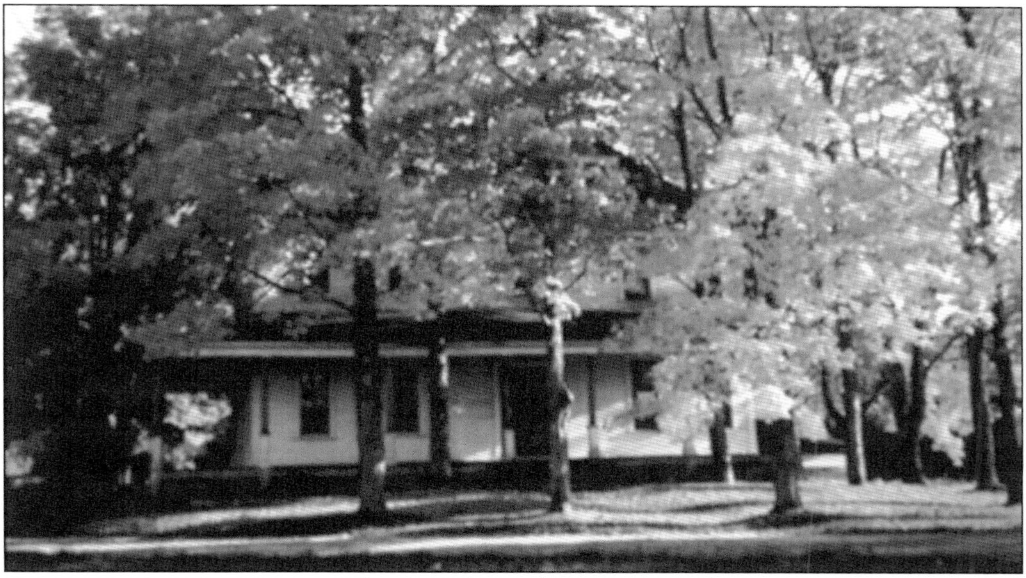

GONE BUT NOT FORGOTTEN. This farm, located on Knox Road just south of the Dow Road intersection, was the home of William R. Parker, a representative to the New Hampshire legislature and a Bow selectman in 1827, 1828, and 1832. Parker was also a member of the militia, becoming a major general of the 1st Division in 1849. The home was later bought by Sherman Saltmarsh, a lawyer from Massachusetts, who used it as a summer residence. The barn, which was located across the street, and the house were burned to the ground in the early 1970s.

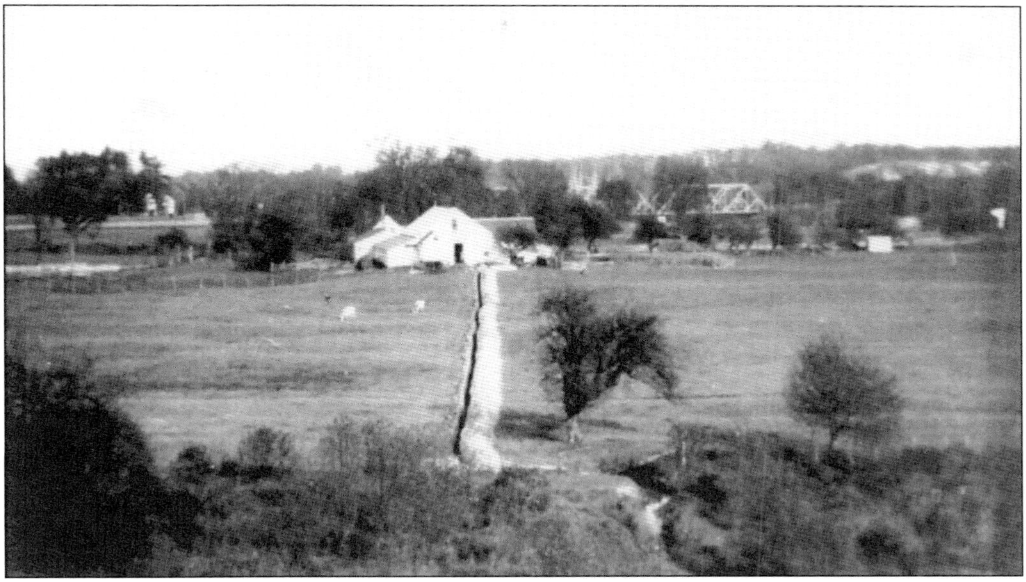

LOOKING DOWN. This is a view from the hill, looking down towards the Cote farm and the fertile fields of the Merrimack River Valley. Tom and Grace Cote were the owners of the land but allowed their neighbor, George Allbee, to use their barn and farm the fields. Grappone Ford and Interstates 89 and 93 interchanges now occupy this site. This shot was taken from the current location of the Hampton Inn. In the background, the steel railroad bridge over the Merrimack River can be seen.

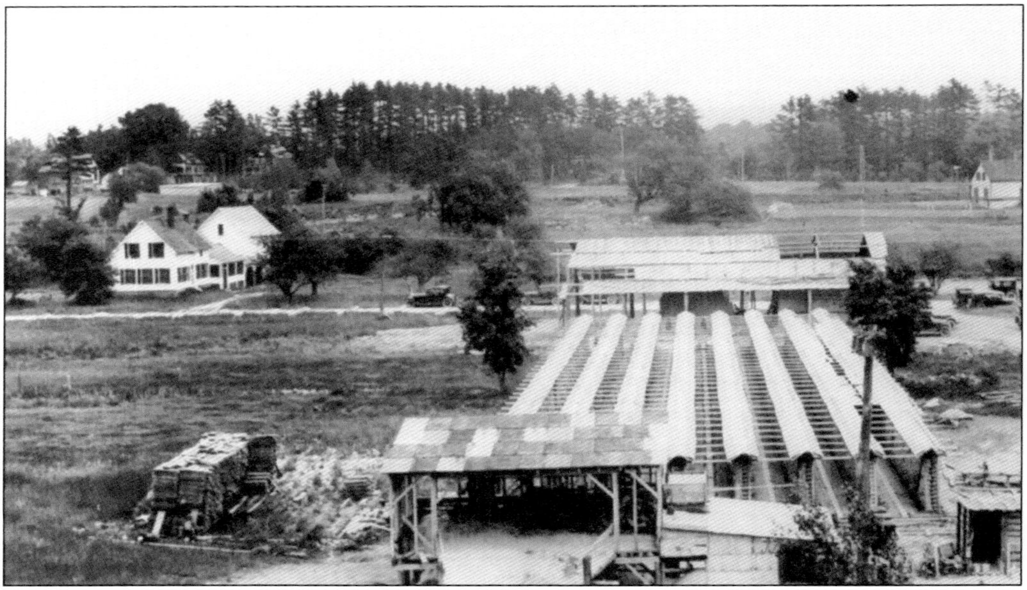

BRICKS OF CLAY. Located across Route 3-A from Ma Willey's Pond, north of Merrimack Farmers Exchange, is the brickyard. Bricks were usually manufactured during the summer from clay found adjacent to the riverbank. Farmers brought wood during the winter for the next season's firing. The brickyard was in operation between the late 1800s and 1938. This site is currently occupied by Grappone Auto Dealers.

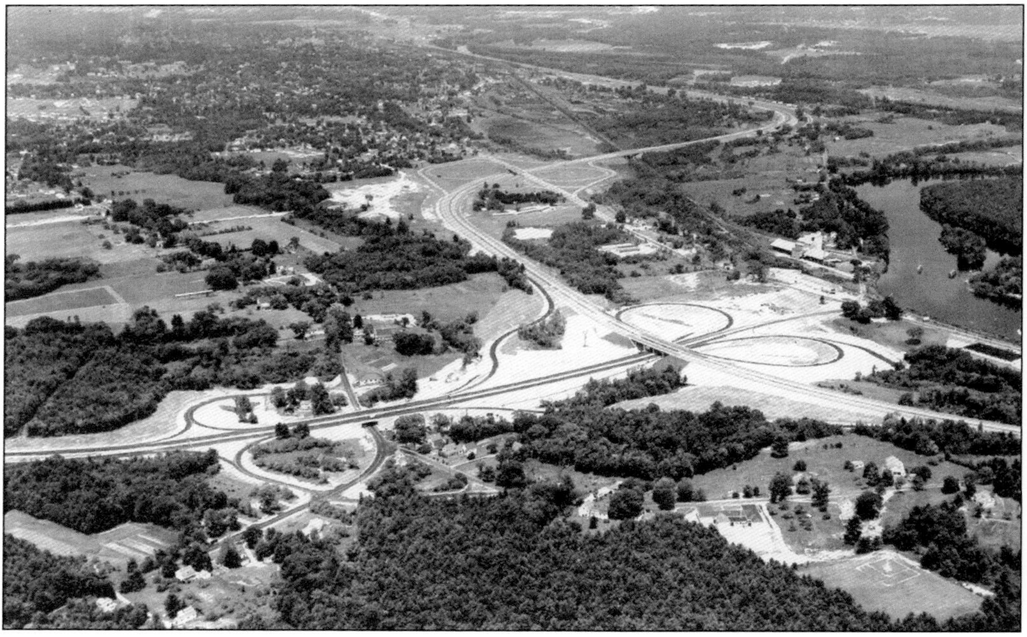

THE GROWTH OF ASPHALT. This aerial photograph taken of Interstate Highways 93 and 89 in July 1959, reflect the changes that consumed the farms and gardens of the valley and the Bow Junction section of Bow. Some early business and industry facilities shown here are Merrimack Farmers, Evans Radio, and Grappone Companies.

Three

MOVING ABOUT

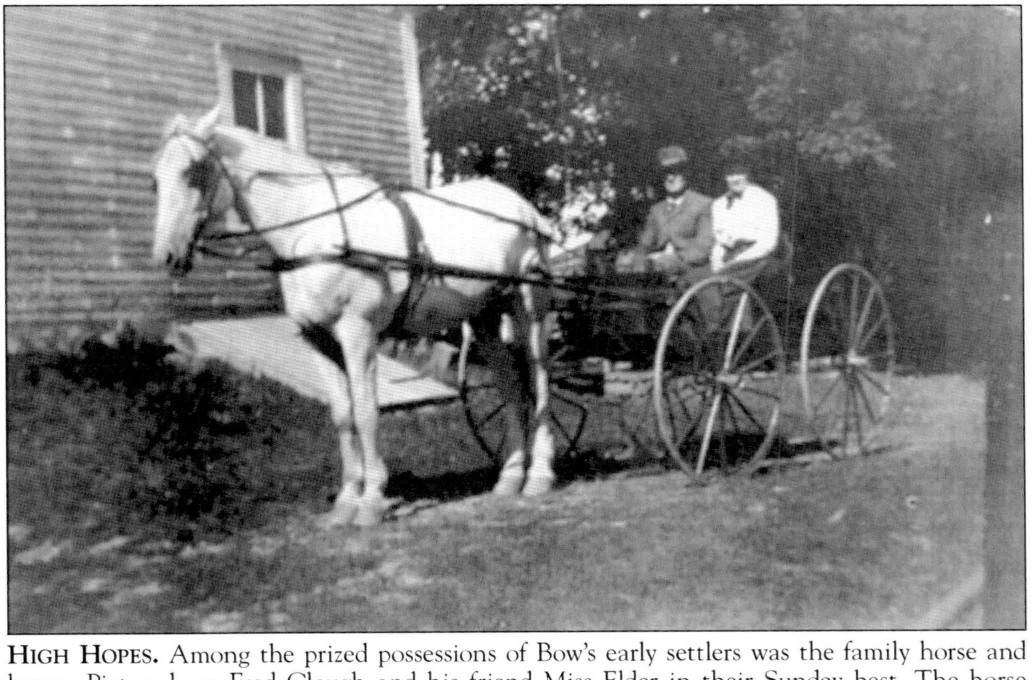

HIGH HOPES. Among the prized possessions of Bow's early settlers was the family horse and buggy. Pictured are Fred Clough and his friend Miss Elder in their Sunday best. The horse and buggy were a luxury around 1900. Gradually the planning and construction of a modern road system developed from the well-worn neighbors' foot paths to dirt and gravel roads. A stage route that ran from Hanover to Boston passed through town. The use of ferries to cross the Merrimack River, canal boats on the Bow Canal, and railroad lines were all considered state-of-the-art transportation. In 1911, with high hopes, Bow residents voted to repair and expand the bridges at Bow Mills, north Bow, and the Bog. New concrete bridges were constructed following the monetary gift from Mary Baker Eddy's estate. In the late 1950s the interstate highway system came to Bow.

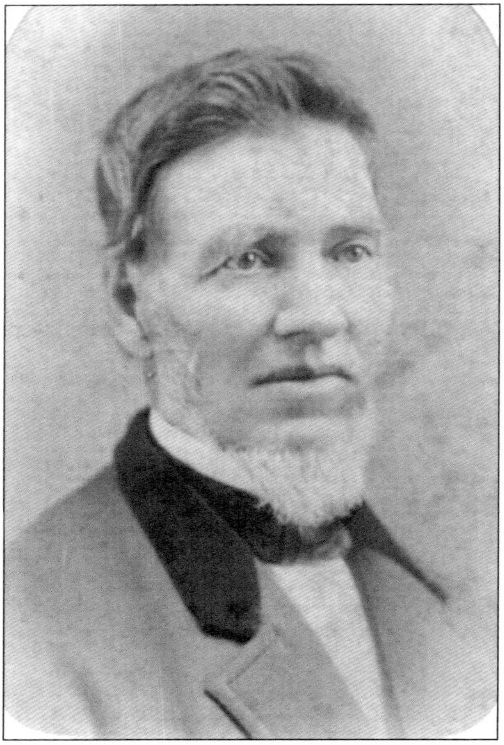

Noyes Ferry. Capt. Benjamin Noyes received a permit to operate one of the three original ferries to cross the Merrimack River from Bow to Suncook in 1791. Records indicate the crossing was established at the earlier date of 1764. The ferries shuttled passengers, wagons, carriages, goods, and livestock across the river from Bow to Suncook, Pembroke, and Hooksett. Noyes Crossing is located on River Road at the intersection of Johnson Road and is on the town's historical marker list.

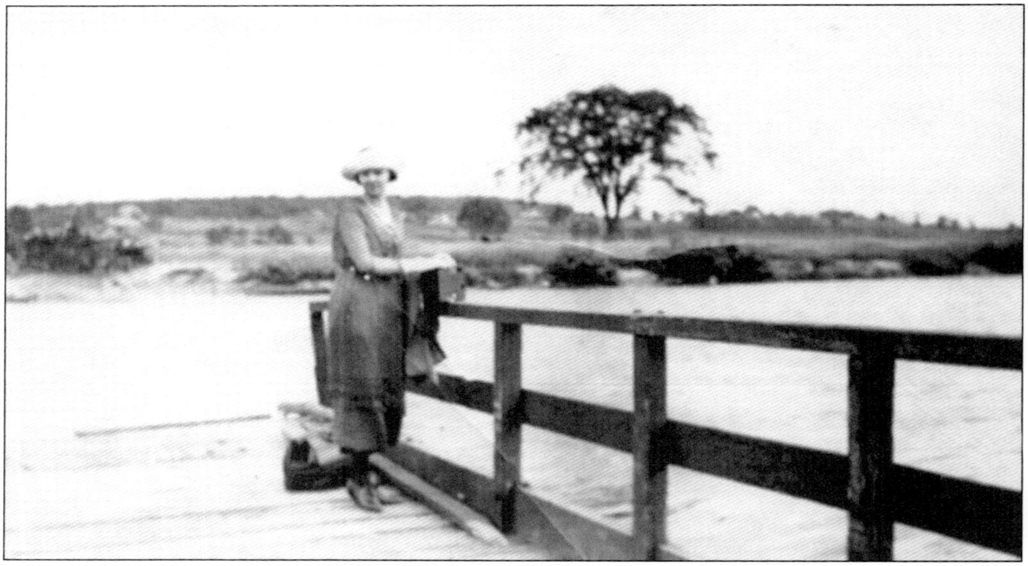

Ferry Boats. Lottie Morgan stands at the rail, awaiting the departure of the ferry at Noyes Crossing in 1921. During the 18th century there were four known ferry operators in town: Benjamin Noyes, as mentioned above; Jonathan Dix, who operated at a similar Merrimack River location; John Robertson, who operated further north up the river; and John Bryent who ran his ferry above Garvins Falls.

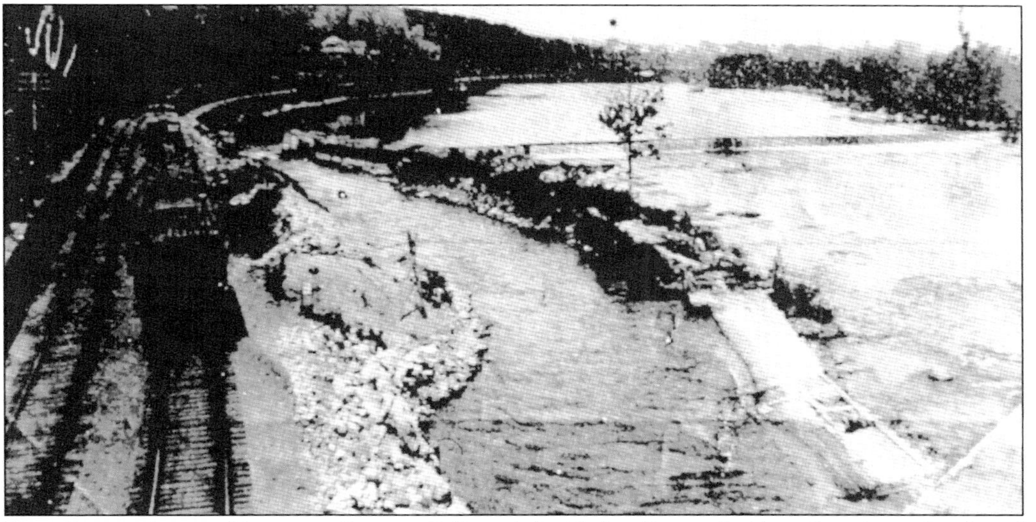

BOW CANAL. Located between Garvins Falls and the Turkey River, the Bow Canal was developed as a means of linking Concord and points north with Boston. The first craft from Boston passed through on June 23, 1815. The opening of the canal had a positive effect on the local economy, bringing new markets to and for the farmers. During the last of the canal's 38 active years, only lumber was being transported. Improved roads and the newly developed railroads were making the canal system obsolete. The Bow Canal consisted of four locks running over a three-quarter-mile course. Sections of the canal are still visible.

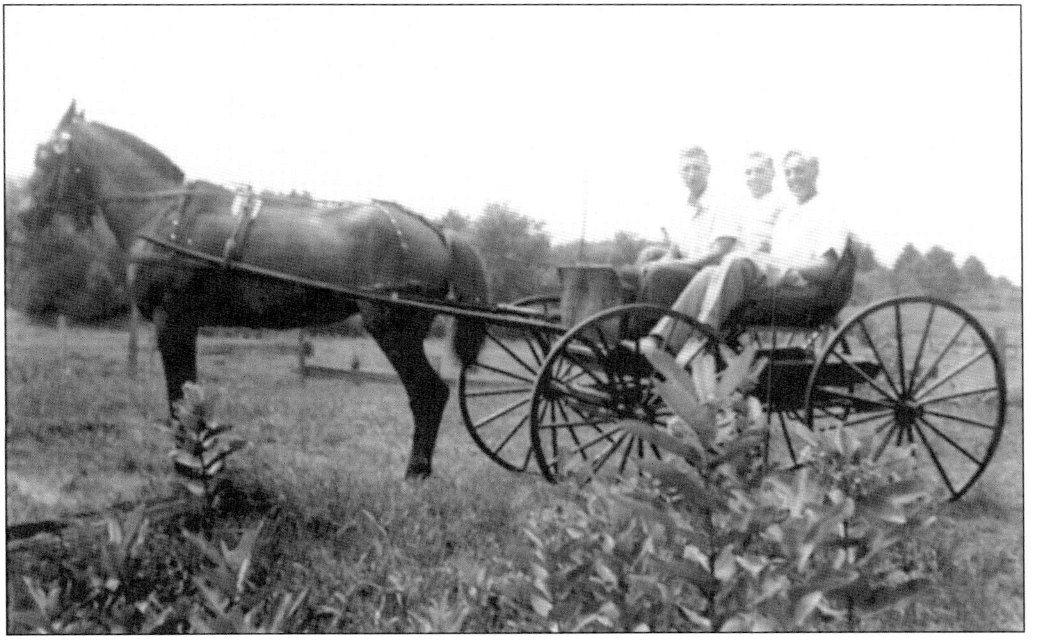

SUNDAY DRIVERS. Edwin Luce and Allen and Hollis Furbush are out for a drive with Luce's horse Lady. The Luces were farmers who lived on Johnson Road. The Furbushes worked in the summer on their grandparents, the Allbees', farm on Valley Road. Sadly, Luce and Hollis Furbush were both killed in World War II.

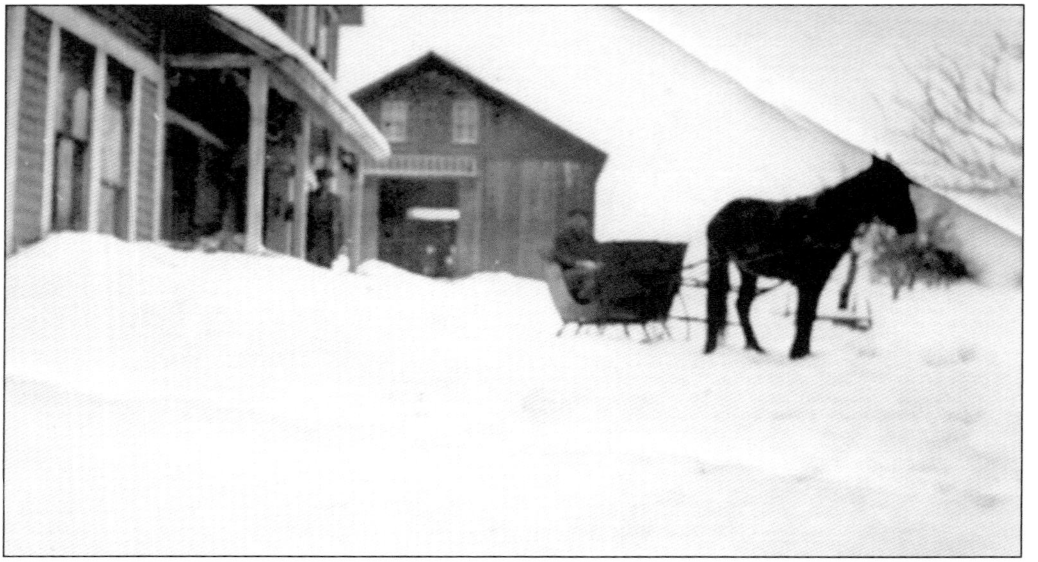

One Horse Open Sleigh. A horse and sleigh wait to leave after a visit to the Morgan homestead at 155 Bow Bog Road in 1900. At this time, sleighs and wagons were the prevalent mode of travel for neighborhood socializing. The house and barn are still standing, and have been completely restored and modernized.

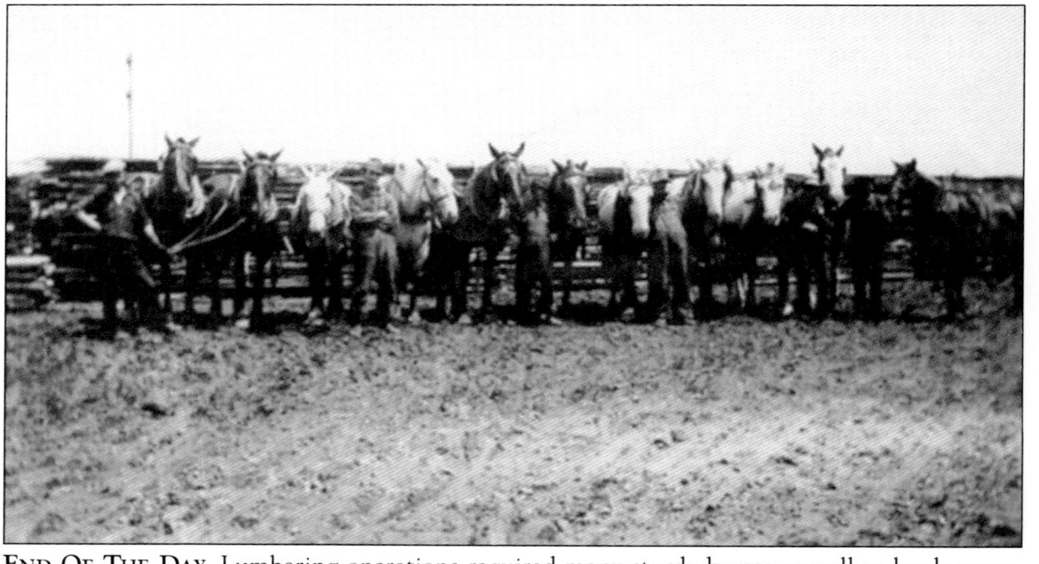

End Of The Day. Lumbering operations required many sturdy horses as well as lumberman. Here teams of workhorses stand for a group photograph after a hard days work in the south Bow woodlots in the early 1930s. The many stacks of logs seen in the background are a testament to their labor. It was not until after World War II that tractors and other mechanized vehicles replaced horses in the woods of Bow.

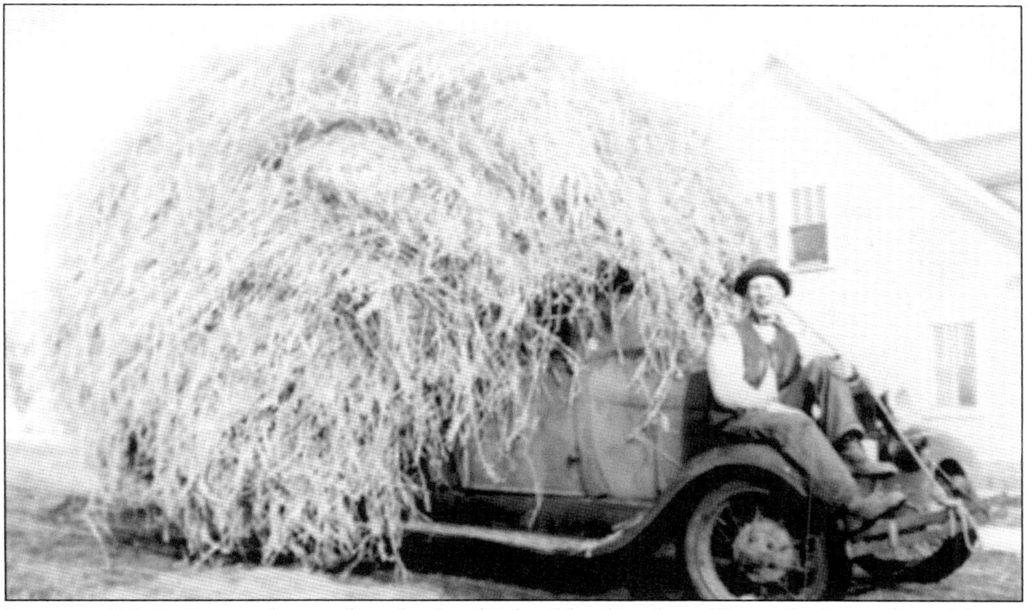

LOADED. Edwin Luce relaxes after the hard job of loading hay. He worked as a farm laborer for Hiel Allbee, who mowed hay on fields all over the Valley Road area and the Londonderry Turnpike area. The truck was used for every chore on the farm, from hauling milk to the creamery on South Spring Street in Concord, to bringing young farm help for a trip to Pine Island Park in Manchester.

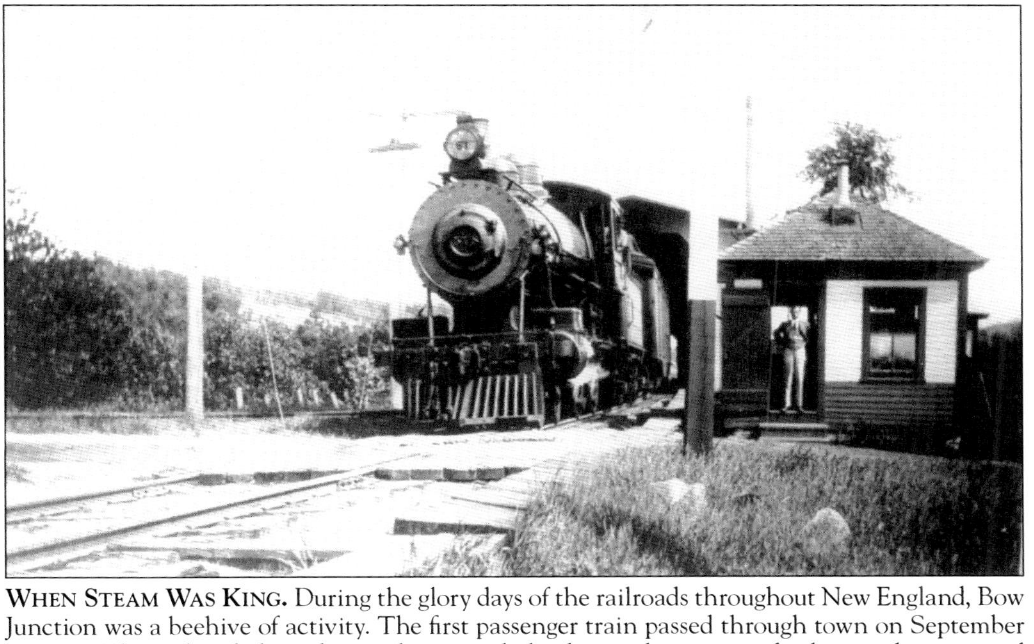

WHEN STEAM WAS KING. During the glory days of the railroads throughout New England, Bow Junction was a beehive of activity. The first passenger train passed through town on September 6, 1842. The railroads brought employment, helped grow businesses, further settlement, and expanded tourism. The lines seemed to go everywhere. Seen here is the signalman's shack at Bow Junction, located off Hall Street. One rail line continued over the Merrimack River to Suncook, the other curved off and continued along the west side of the river to Boston.

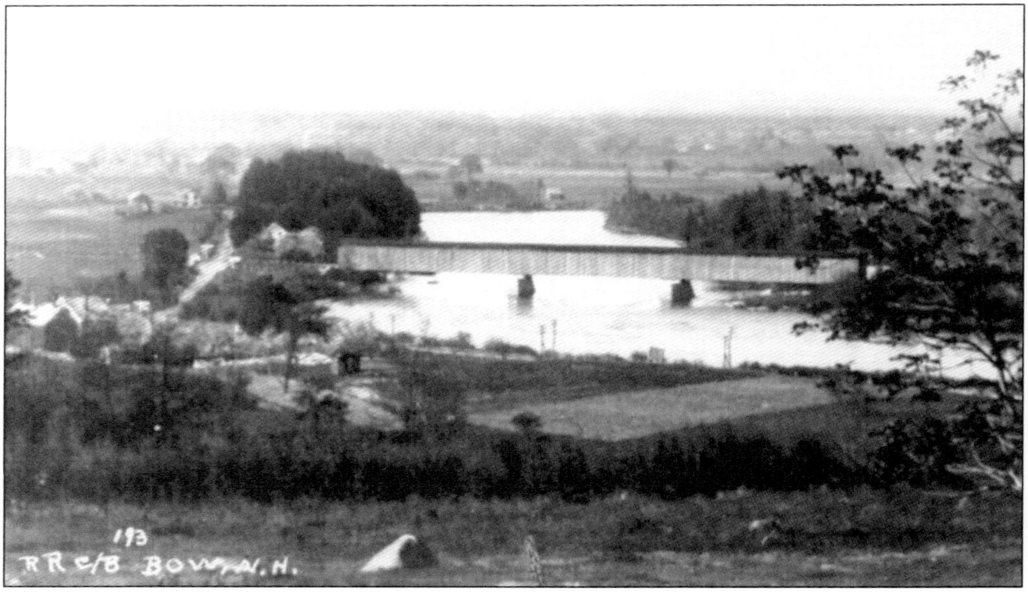

BOW'S COVERED BRIDGE. The Suncook Loop and Concord and Manchester Electric Branch Railroads used this covered bridge to cross the Merrimack River. The dates of the bridge's existence are unknown, other than it washed away in one of the many floods of the river in the 1920s.

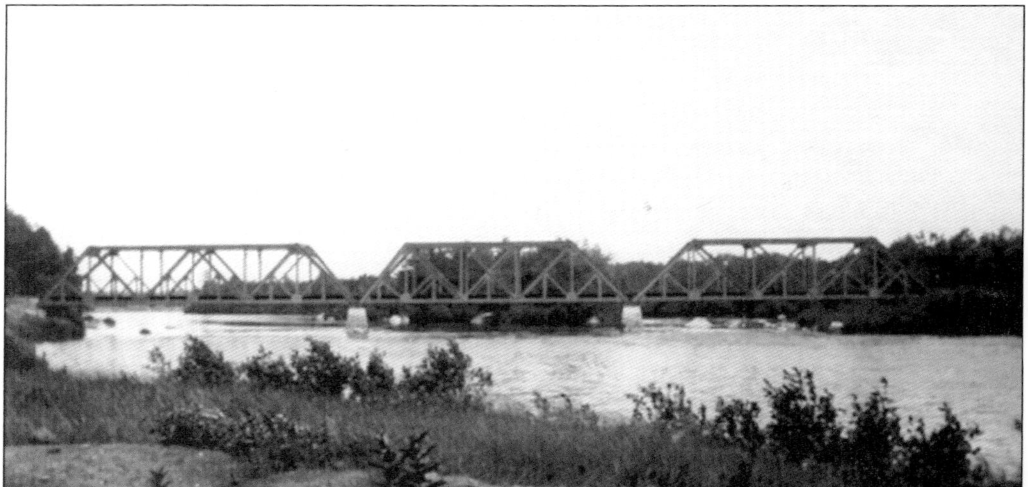

STEEL SPAN. After the covered bridge was washed away, it was replaced by a modern steel two-rail span bridge. As the use of railroads declined, the route across the Merrimack River was abandoned. The structure was deemed to be too valuable to leave and was dismantled in 1952 and sold for scrap. Only the abutments are visible today.

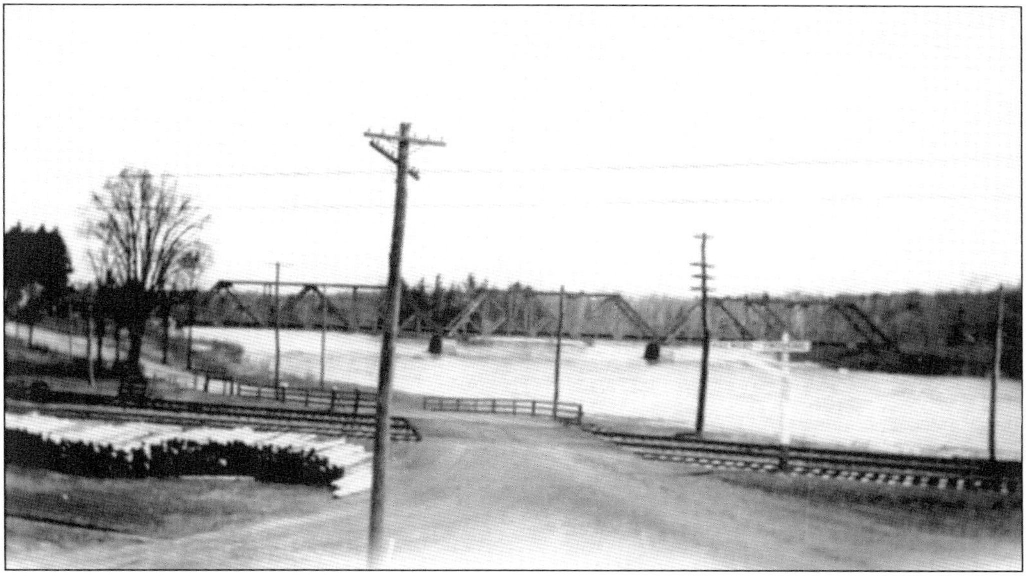

RAILROAD CROSSING. The B&M crossing at Hall Street is seen in this 1924 photograph, which was taken from the roof of a home which stood at what is now the intersection of Interstate 89 and Route 3-A. The Bow Junction Station was a short distance north from this point. Boards from the Upton Sawmill can be seen in the foreground awaiting transport by rail.

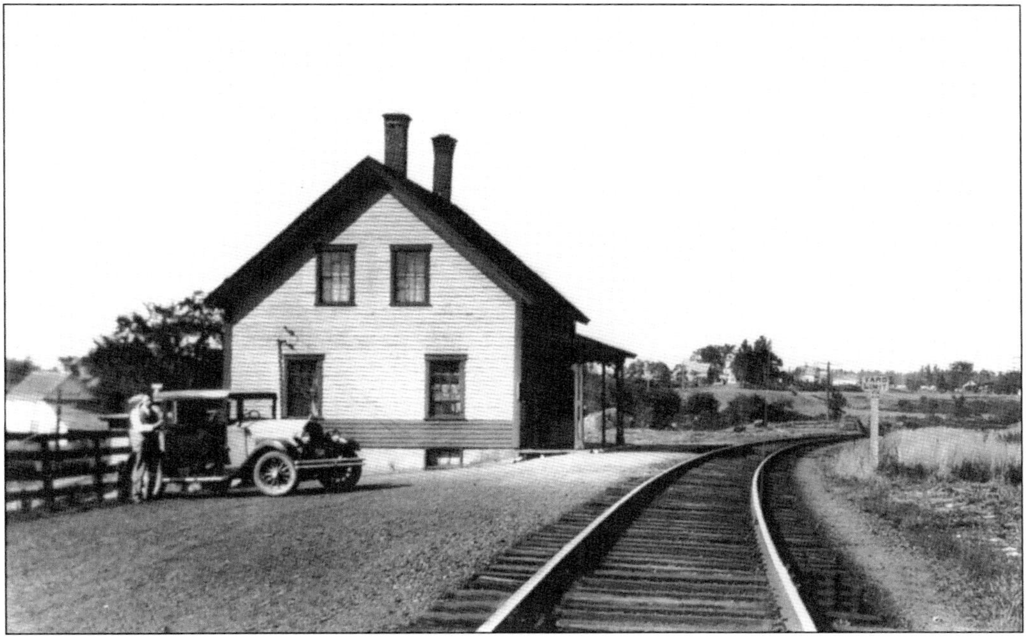

NEXT STOP BOW. The Bow Railroad Station is shown in the early 1920s. The station was located off Hall Street, behind what is now Grappone Honda. As the use of the railroads declined and businesses at the junctions took over, the station was moved around the corner, becoming a private residence.

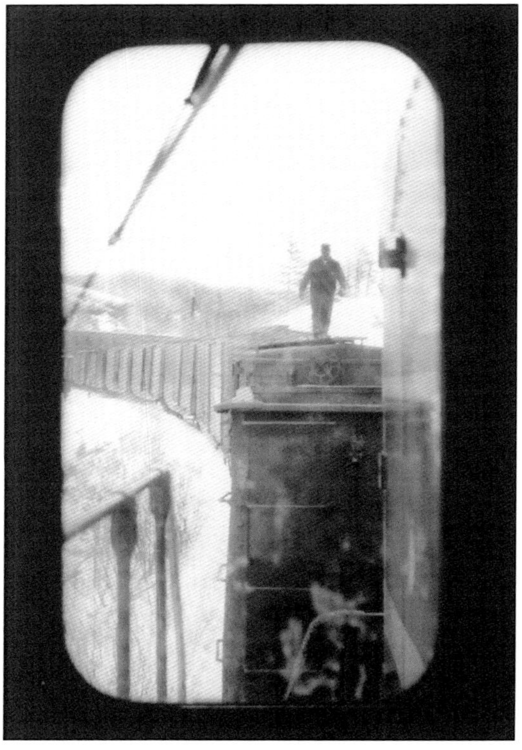

Working The Railroad. Morris Foote Sr. is shown in 1964 walking atop a freight car as it passes through town. He was one of many residents employed by the B&M. Foote was active in town affairs, most notably serving as selectman from 1968 to 1971.

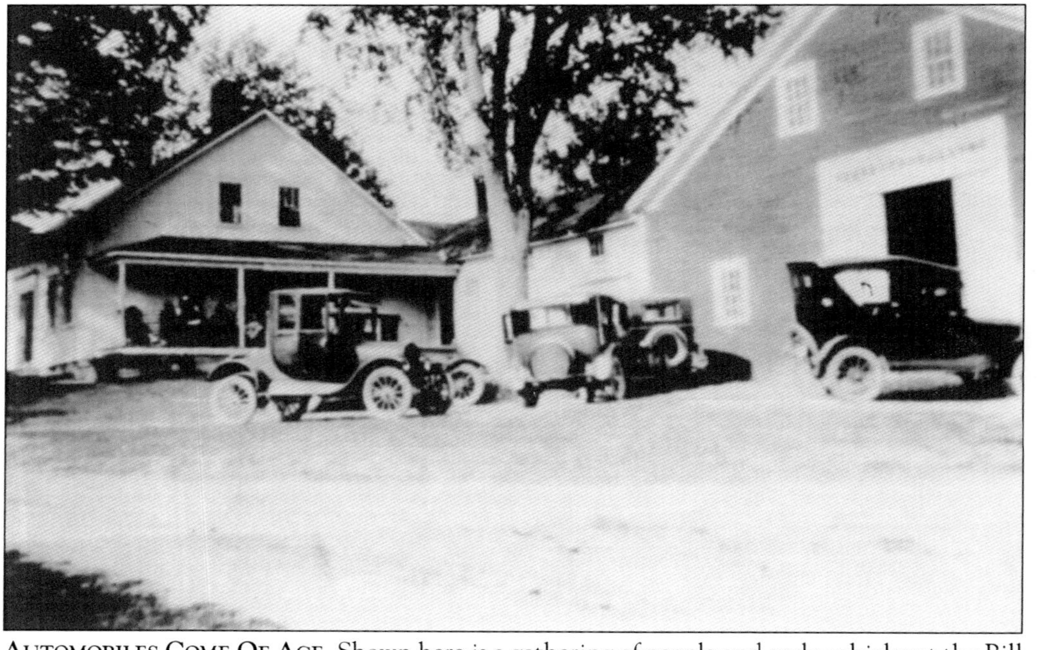

Automobiles Come Of Age. Shown here is a gathering of people and early vehicles at the Bill Colby house at the corner of Woodhill and Woodhill-Hooksett Roads. During the 1930s Bow's roads were greatly improved. This made the use of automobiles more practical.

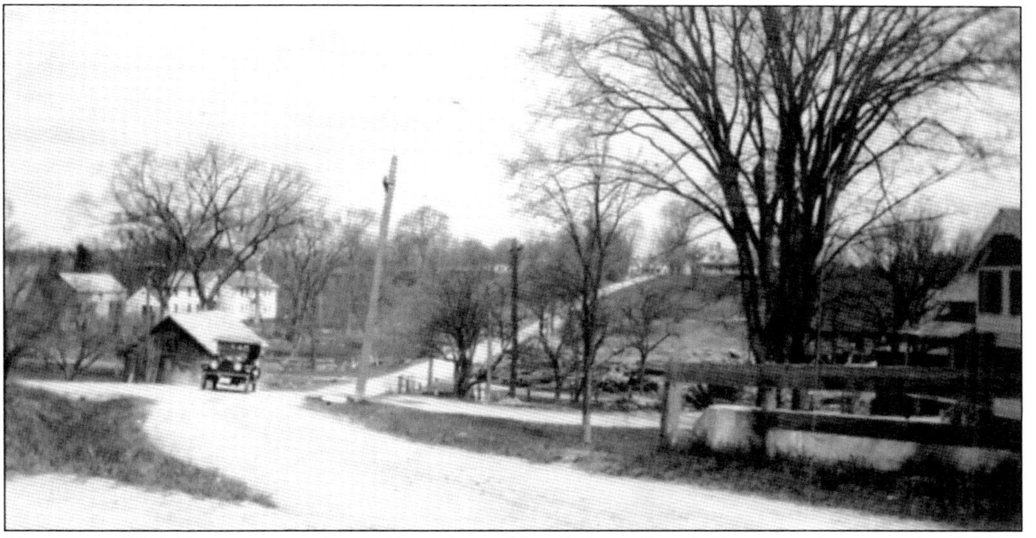

TOURING. Phil Sargent travels up Grandview Road from South Street in his new Ford. The Colby Blacksmith Shop is directly behind the car and the Perley Wheeler farm can be seen on the left. The farms of R. Herbert White and Arthur Case can be seen in the distance at the top of the hill. At the bottom of the hill on the right are logs in the Upton Mill Yard and the corner of Upton's Store.

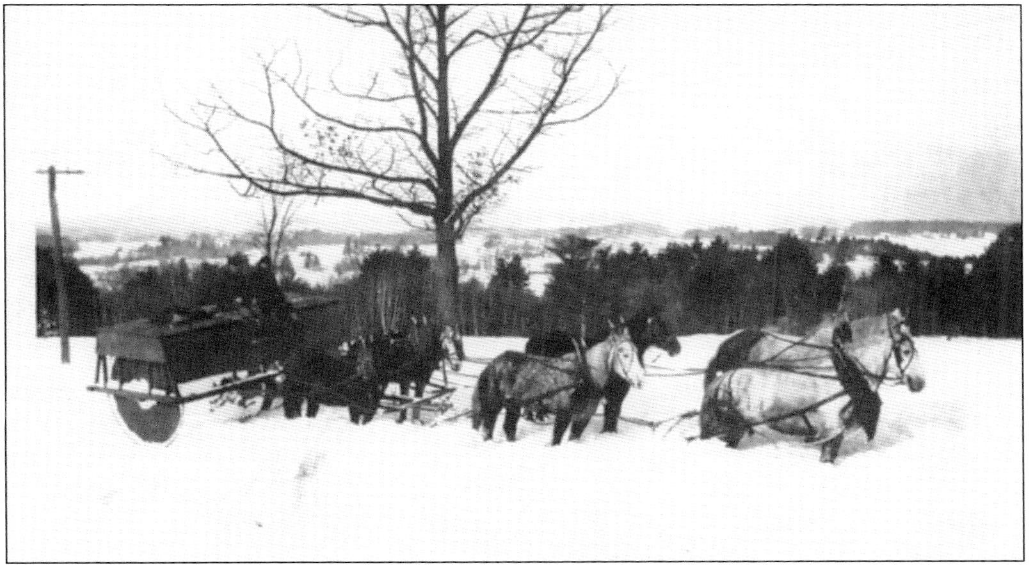

SNOW ROLLER. Before the wide-spread use of the automobile and before paved roads, the roads were rolled in the winter to pack down the snow. This allowed for traffic to continue by horse-drawn sleigh or wagon. In this 1920 photograph, Philip Sargent is shown driving his six horse team to roll the snow along Grandview Road. Paving in Bow started between 1923 and 1925. South Street and the Bow Mills area were the first to be paved, with many roads soon to follow. This made the snow roller obsolete as mechanized snow plows came into use.

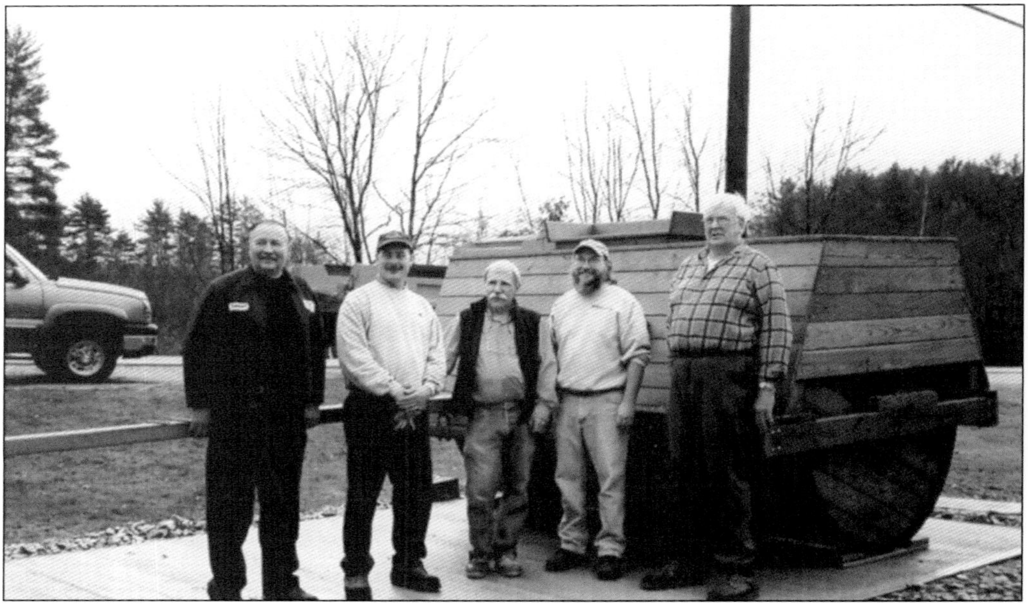

SNOW ROLLER REBORN. A replica of a Bow snow roller sits on its pad at the Bow Center Schoolhouse historic site. This was rebuilt by Dick Welch, a master craftsman, from the original wheel frames and a few other metal pieces. From left to right are Lenny Virgin; Tim Sweeney; Chum Cleverly of the Department of Public Works; Andy Young of Young's Furniture, who donated his vehicle hauler for the transport; and Dick Welch.

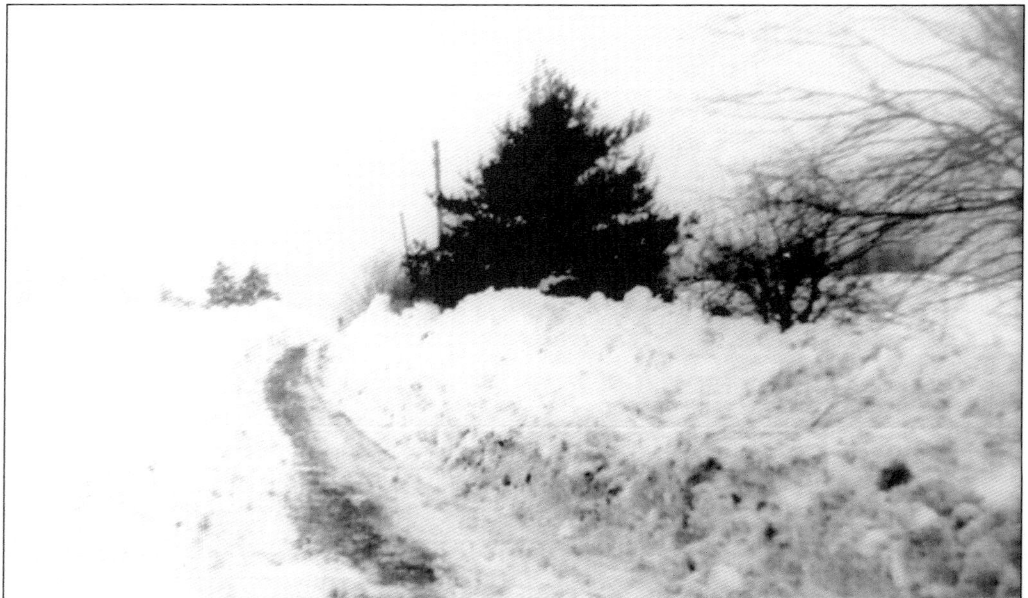

WHAT ROAD? The transition from rolling the snow to plowing it with a treaded tractor and V-shaped plow did not result in the clear roads of today. This photograph was taken at the top of Page Road just beyond the intersection with White Rock Hill Road. Fortunately there were not many cars on town roads in the 1940s, as the travel lanes seem pretty narrow.

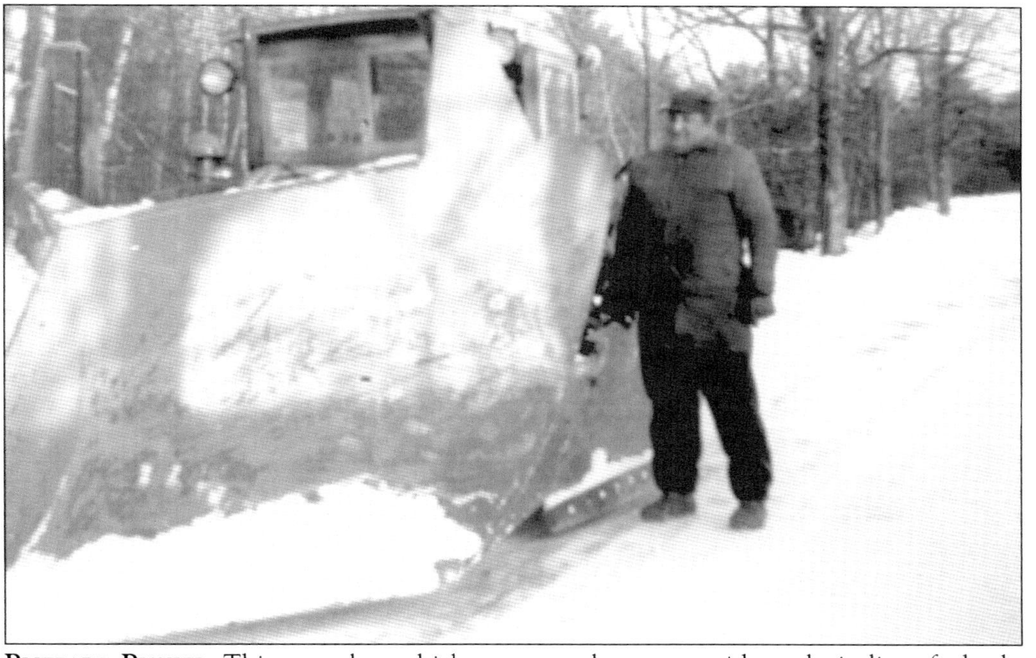

BLIZZARD BUSTER. This snowplow, which was a crawler tractor with tracks in lieu of wheels, was utilized by Ted Downs in 1958 to open the snow-clogged roads. Downs was a longtime employee of the Bow Highway and Police Departments.

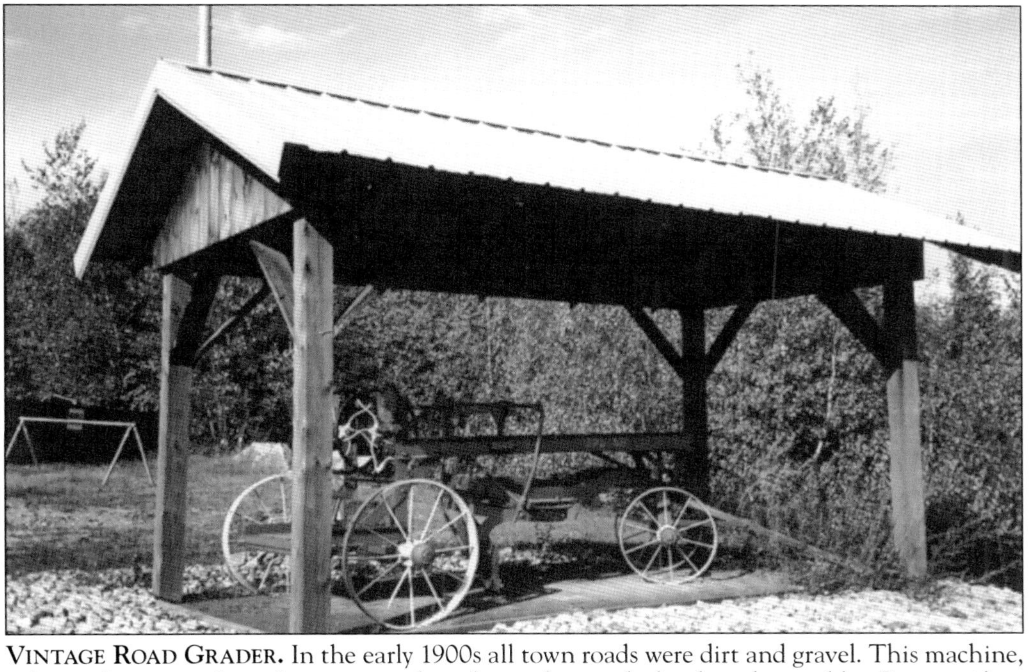

VINTAGE ROAD GRADER. In the early 1900s all town roads were dirt and gravel. This machine, a horse-drawn road grader, was used to keep the roads level and passable. Bow resident Tim Sweeney restored the grader in 1996. It is on display at the town highway garage on Robinson Road.

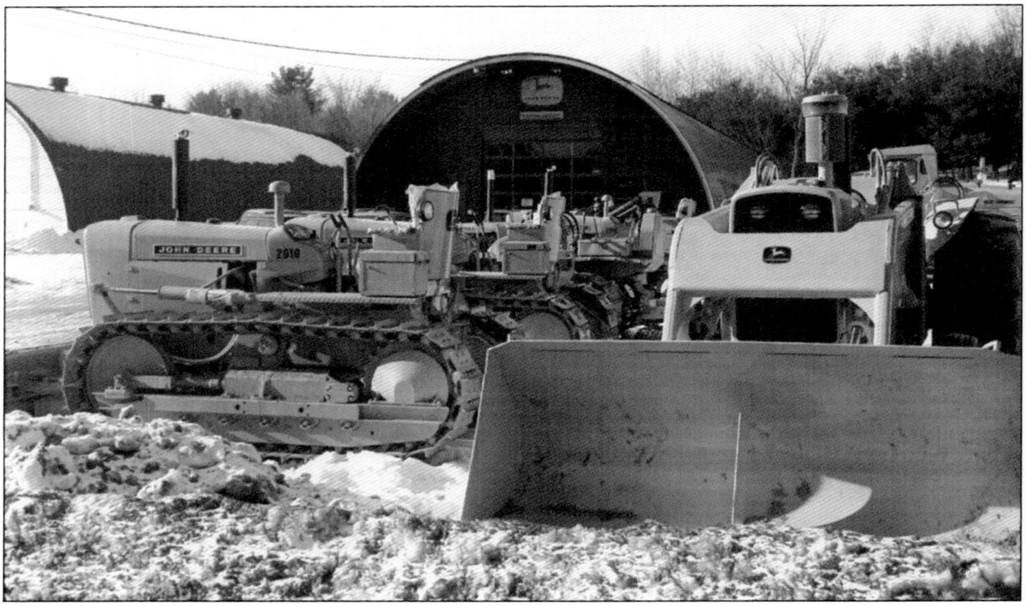

OH DEERE. John Grappone Industrial Equipment Company was located in the vicinity of the old brickyard on Route 3-A, and it was one of the first commercial businesses in Bow. The company would evolve from selling construction equipment out of Quonset huts, seen here, to a sprawling complex of automobile dealerships. Grappone companies have been very active in supporting many local and town projects.

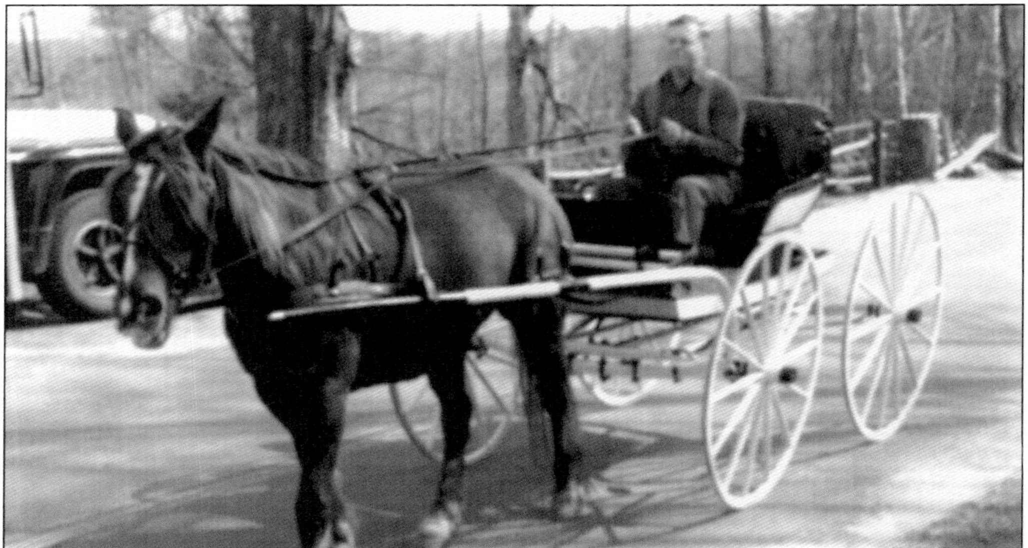

FROM 727 JETS TO HORSE AND BUGGY. Ron Askin, who lived on Dow Road, takes Lady for a stroll around the block. This picture was taken in front of the Alexander Farm on Robinson Road in the early 1970s, when Bow's roads were not as heavily traveled. Water, oats, and hay at the farm kept Lady busy while Askin visited Mike and Verna Alexander, the farm's owners. Askin, a pilot who flew 727 jets, was active in town affairs and served as selectman from 1970 to 1974.

Four

Reading, Writing, and Arithmetic

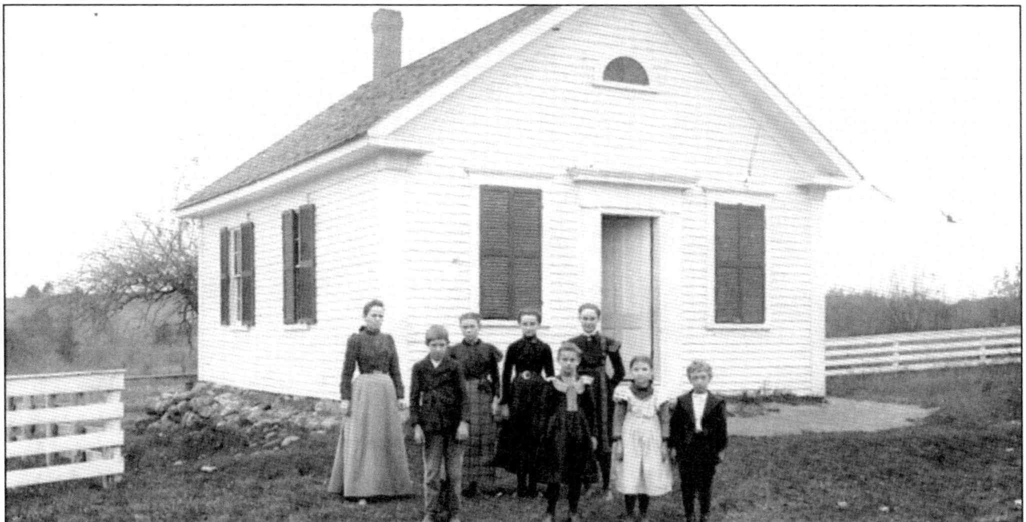

One-Room Schoolhouse. In 1878, Bow had 14 one-room schoolhouses scattered around town. Only four exist today—the former White School (in session until 1937); the Woodbury District School (in session until 1938); the Wood Hill School (in session until 1920), which has been converted to a residence; and the Bow Center School (in session until 1945), which has been preserved by the town as a historic site. This photograph of the Wood Hill School shows the second of two school buildings in the Wood Hill District. Originally organized in 1790, the school was first located on the corner of Wood Hill and Dunbarton Center Roads. The second school was built further south on Wood Hill Road. Later it was moved across the road and closed in 1920. The building was purchased and made into a residence. This photograph dates from the early 1900s.

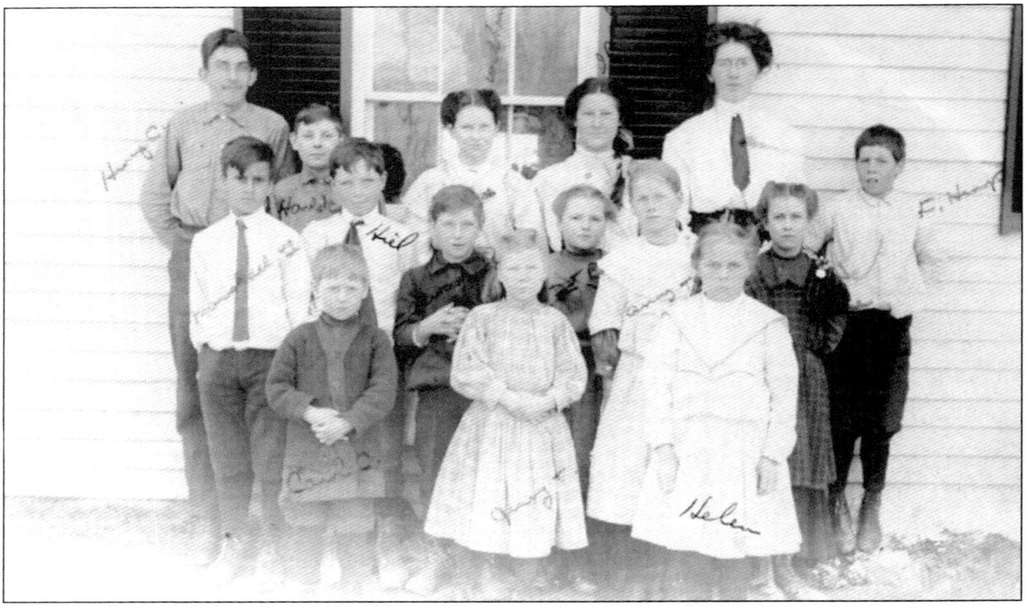

WOOD HILL SCHOOL. In this 1908 photograph, the students of the Wood Hill School are shown. From left to right are (first row) Carroll Colby, Jenny Tenny, and Helen Allbee; (second row) Marchall Goodhue, Hiel Allbee, Edward ?, Dorothy Colby, Amy Tenny, Elsie Colby, and Earl Hemphill; (third row) Henry Cheney, Harold Colby, Whilhelmina Warren Clough, Isabel Downing, and teacher May Calden.

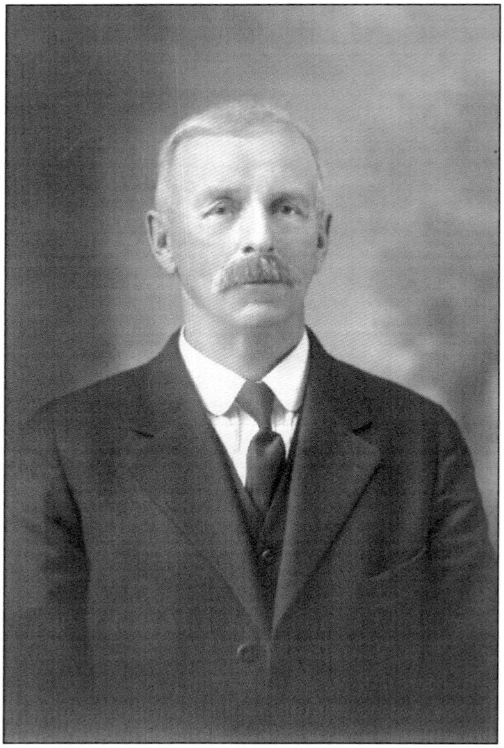

EDWIN COLBY. Edwin Colby was a popular and longtime educator, teaching for a total of 68 terms. He was known for his ability to handle difficult students and took in many high school scholars. Colby also served as selectman, representative to the legislature, and as a member of the Bow Board of Education.

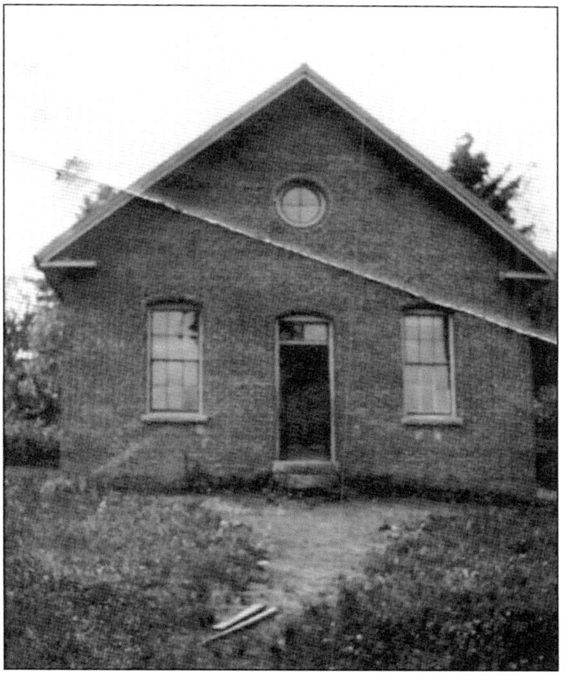

BOW MILLS BRICK SCHOOL. This photograph shows the red brick Bow Mills Brick School, which was located at the foot of Logging Hill Road in District No. 14. It was open from 1878 to 1927. It was converted to a residence and eventually demolished when the interstate highway was built. Previously, a school in the mills area was located on Valley Road in 1848.

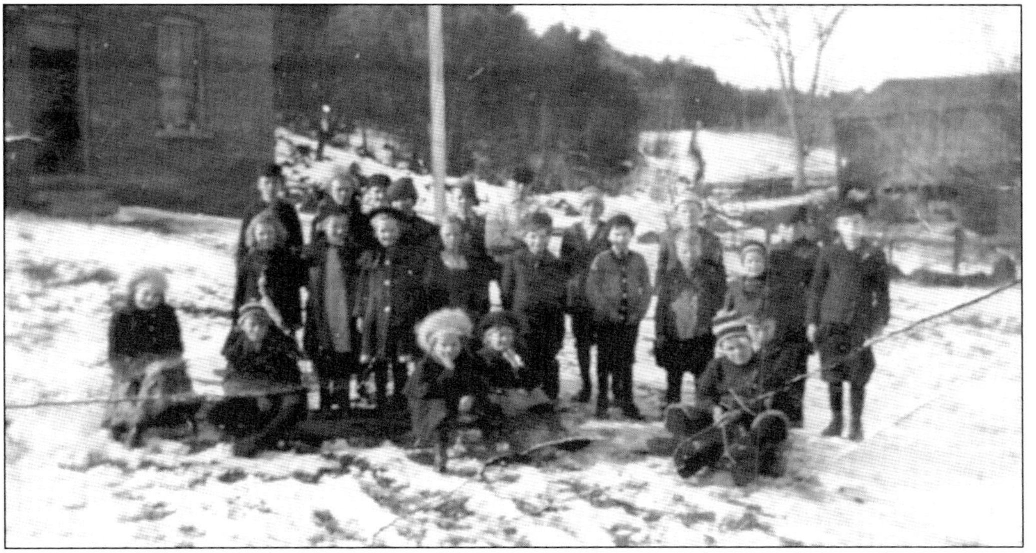

RECESS TIME. Students of the Bow Mills Brick School pose with their sleds and toboggan at recess time. Perley Wheeler's barn can be seen in the background and the tall tree, a sycamore or plane tree, still stands today across from Bow Mobil Station and inside the Interstate 89 ramp loop. The toboggan is currently on display at the Bow Center School Museum.

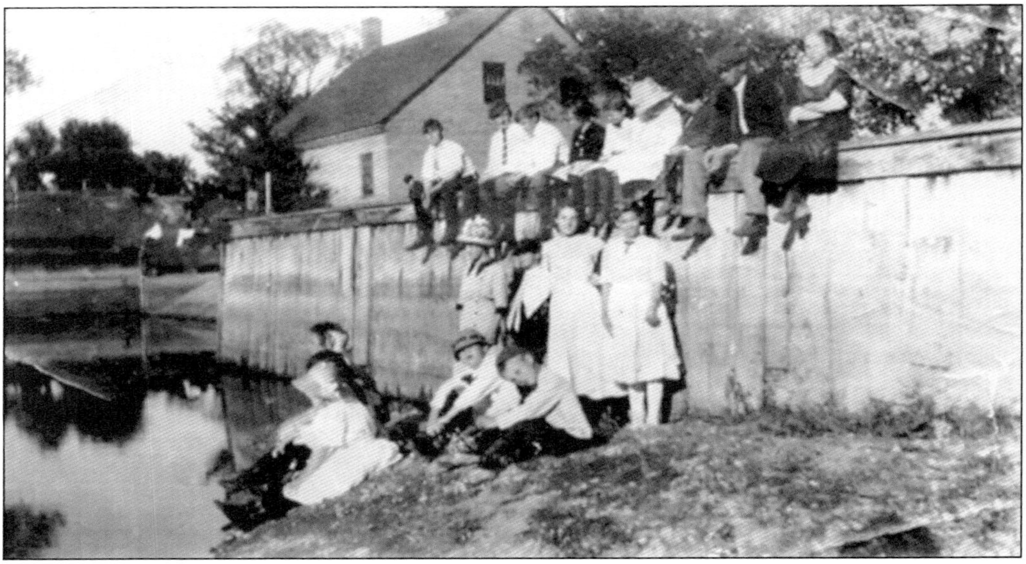

SCHOOL OUTING. Schoolchildren from the Bow Mills Brick School sit on and around the gristmill wall in this 1912 photograph. Identified here are Doris Clark, Lester Sidelinger, Albert Drew, Florence Drew, Flavius Harris, Bea Shreve, Priscilla Noyes, Oscar Hanson, George Foote, Arthur Hanson, Grace Clark, Enos Foote, and Elizabeth Foote.

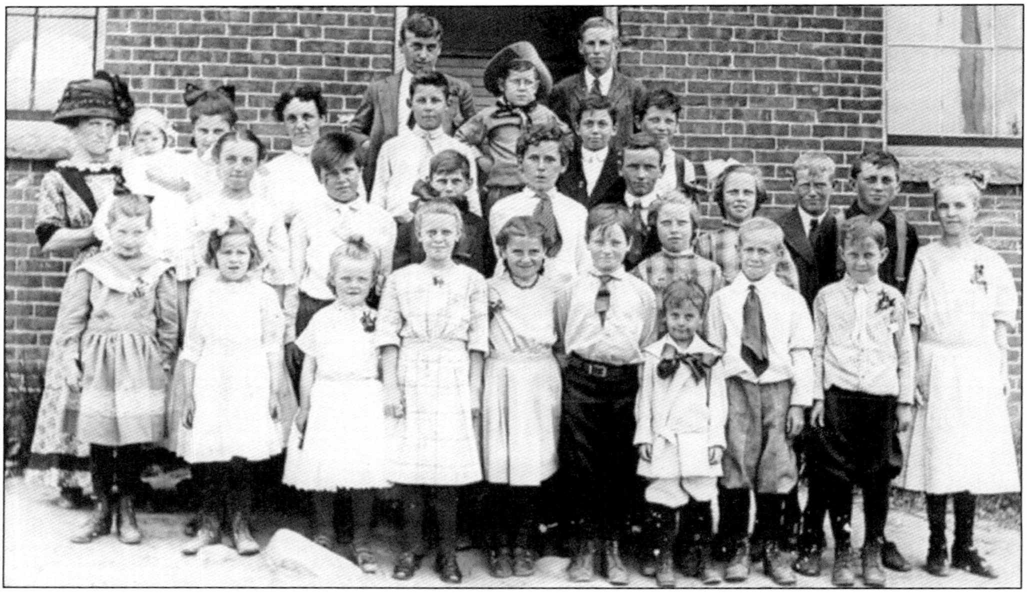

BOW MILLS BRICK SCHOOL STUDENTS. Students in the 1909–1910 school year are shown here. From left to right are (first row) Ruth (Gordon) Wheeler, Ruth Clark, Gladys Silver, Ruth Bernard, Hilda (Sargent) Morgan, Herman Drew, Raymond Drew, Ronald Clark, Harold Hanson, and Anna (Ordway) Nordine; (second row) Maude Hanson with Orissa (Lee) Armstrong, Florence (Flanders) Drew, Oscar Hanson, Arthur Hanson, Solon Colby, George Abbott Foote, Elizabeth Foote, Grace Foote, Levi Clark, and Herbert Drew; (third row) Iva (Nordine) Clough, teacher Ellen Hobbs, Dewey Humphrey, Lester "Tom Mix" Newell Sidelinger, Flavius Harris, and Chester Drew; (fourth row) Parker Morgan and Charles Clark.

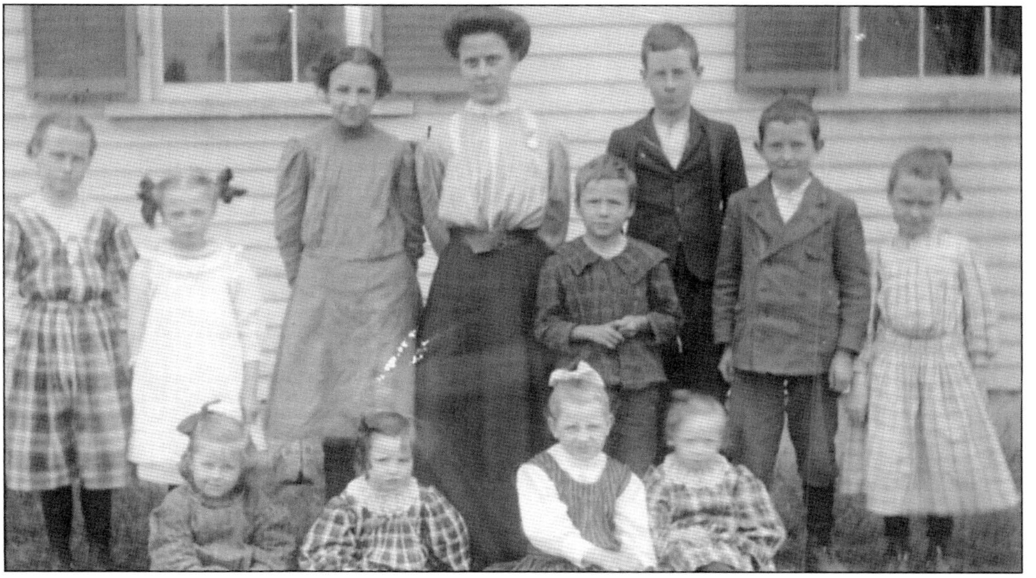

River Road School. Pupils of the River Road School class of 1910 pose in front of the schoolhouse. The building was located in District No. 4 on the west side of the River Road, just before the railroad bridge, and operated from 1792 to 1939. Later it was converted to a residence and has since been demolished. Students attending school that year included Stewart Astiles, Herbert Alexander, Gladys Alexander, Canra Chagnon, Harvey Fowler, Beulah Fowler, Beatrice Morin, Eva M. Tappan, Marion L. Tappan, and France E. Tappan.

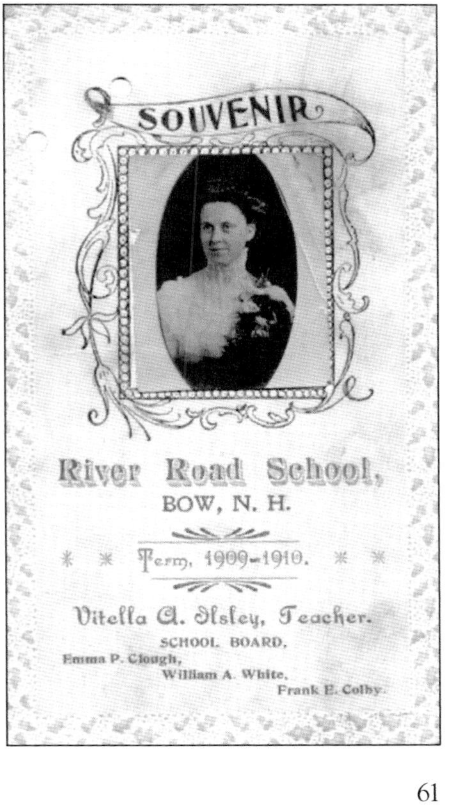

School Day Memories. Vitella Isley taught at River Road School from 1910 to 1912. She was paid a salary of $30 per month. Souvenir cards such as this were printed to commemorate important events in one's life, such as school graduation.

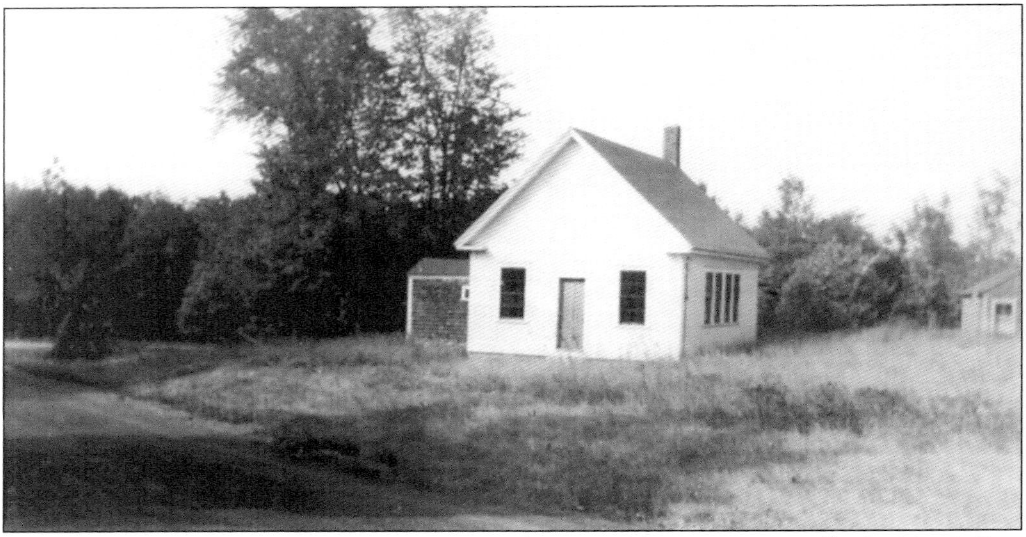

Bow Center School. The Bow Center School, pictured here, was originally the North Bow School. The building was moved in 1924 from the lower end of Page Road, using teams of horses, to the present location at the intersection of White Rock and Bow Center Roads. Maude Putney was the teacher at the school. The school was closed in 1945 and the building was sold to the Baptist Church. Sunday school was taught here until the 1960s, after which the Town of Bow again assumed ownership. Volunteers worked to refurbish the school for the town's 250th anniversary celebration in 1977.

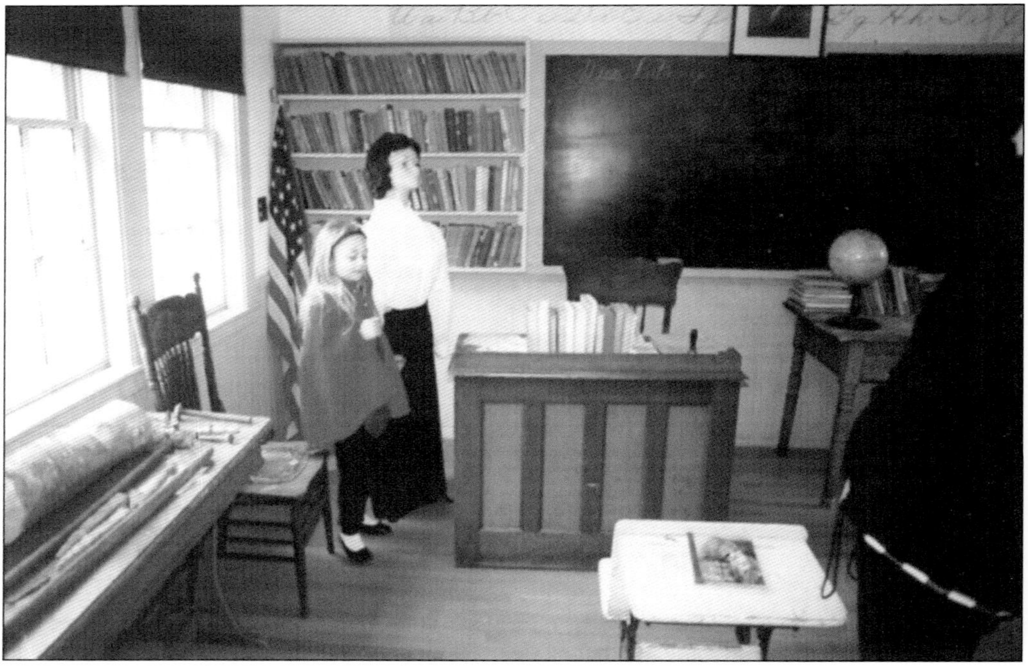

School Visits. The Bow Center School is currently open to visitors on an as-requested basis. Students periodically visit as part of the Heritage Commission's Historic Building Tour. Here a student pretends to be talking to a teacher during an open house held in 1996.

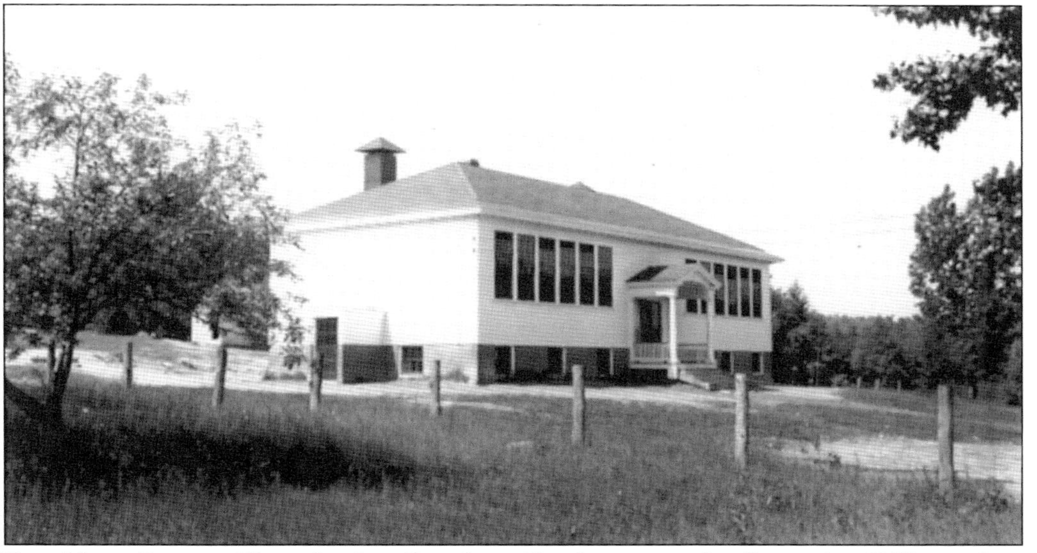

Bow Mills School. This school on Grandview Road was opened in September 1927 to replace the brick schoolhouse at the bottom of Logging Hill Road. This school gradually became the largest in town and by 1945 was the only school in operation in town. Much needed rooms were added in 1948 and 1949 as wings to the main building. Until 1963, students in grades one to eight were here. When the Memorial School was completed, grades one to four remained at Bow Mills. The school was closed in 1970 when the new wing at the Memorial School was completed.

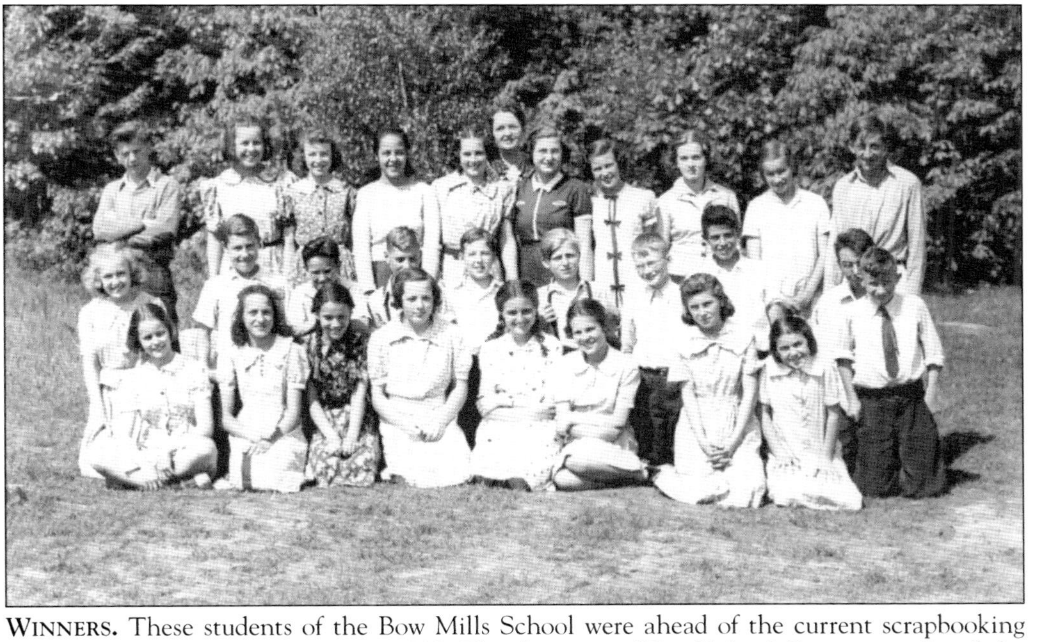

Winners. These students of the Bow Mills School were ahead of the current scrapbooking craze by winning a state contest in 1938. The theme was "Our Federal Constitution" and the contest was sponsored by the Commission in Charge of the Celebration of the Sesquicentennial of the Constitution. The leader of the group, Marion Smith, seen in the third row at the center, was a longtime and well-loved teacher at the school.

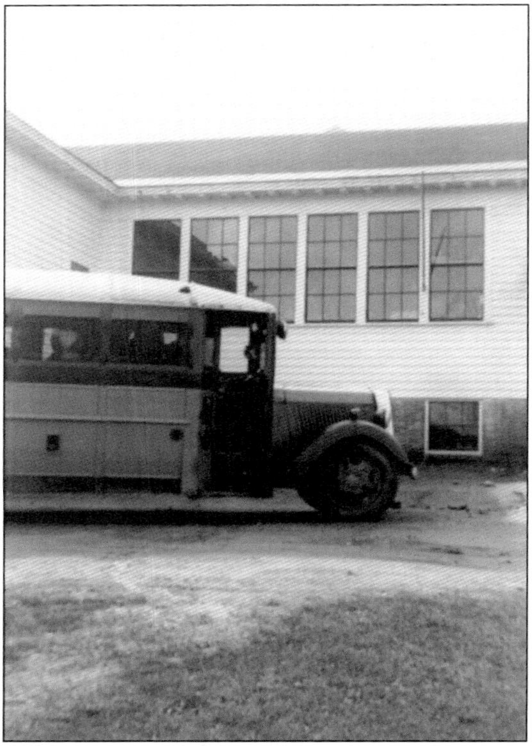

Let's Ride. Bow's first official school bus is seen parked outside the Bow Mills School. In the days of one-room schoolhouses, it was the responsibility of the student's family to get them to school on time. With the consolidation of the schools, the town took over this responsibility.

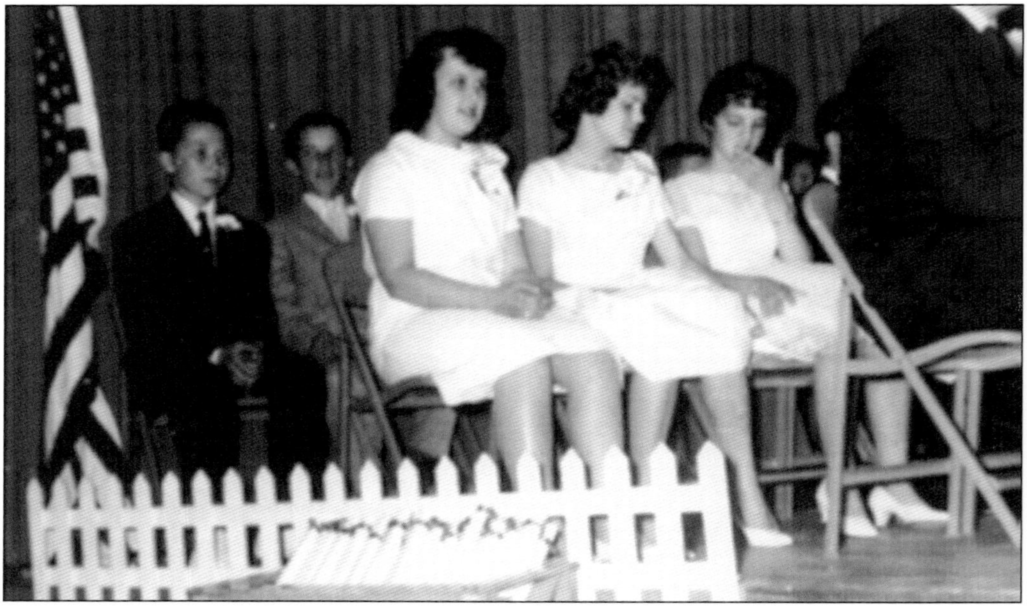

Graduation Day. Students patiently wait to receive their diplomas at the eighth grade graduation ceremony at Bow Mills School in 1960. This stage was downstairs where the current Planning and Economic Development Office is at the Municipal Building. Graduates are, from left to right, (first row) Lorraine Whittier, Sandra Godbout, and Beverly Heath; (second row) Robert Goodsell, and Robert Young.

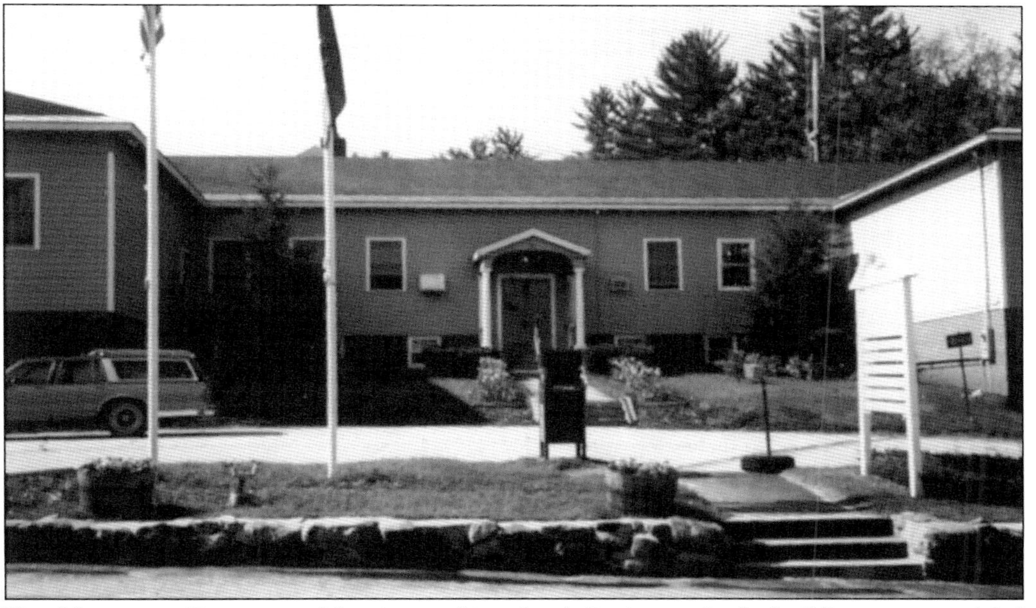

THE MUNICIPAL BUILDING. After it served its school district needs, the building was remodeled to house the town offices and the police department. The police department later relocated to the Hews Building on Robinson Road. A preschool operates in a few rooms of the building. Most of the building is used for town officers and staff, town committee board meetings, and storage.

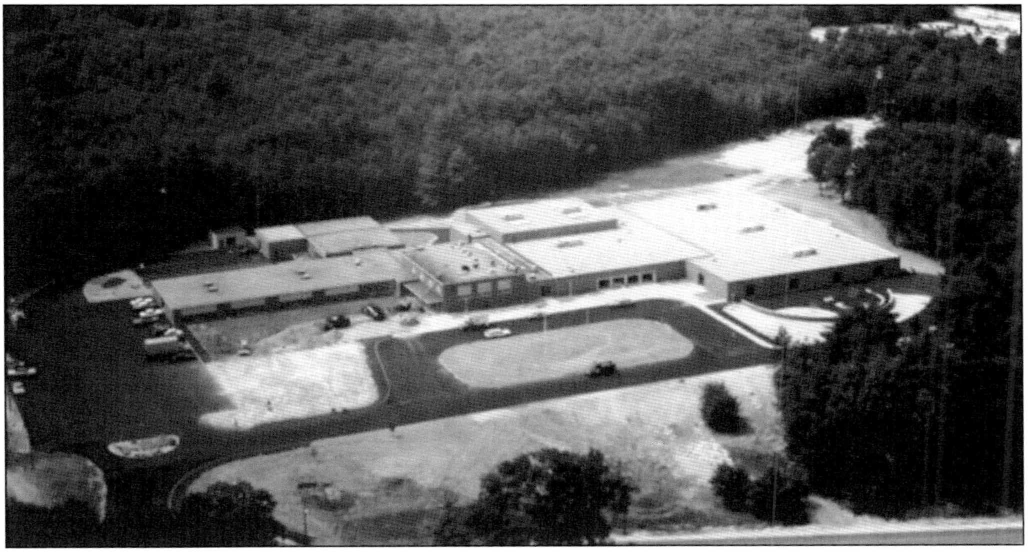

BOW MEMORIAL SCHOOL. This is an aerial photograph of the Memorial School, after the completion and dedication of the new wing on August 8, 1970. The darker roofed buildings on the left were originally home to grades five to eight. After the addition was built, kindergarten to grade six were in the newer part, and grades seven and eight in the original building, which had been built and dedicated on August 30, 1974. In 1974, grade nine was also educated here and continued here until the completion of the high school. Currently the building is home to grades five to eight, with kindergarten to four at the elementary school and grades nine to 12 at the high school.

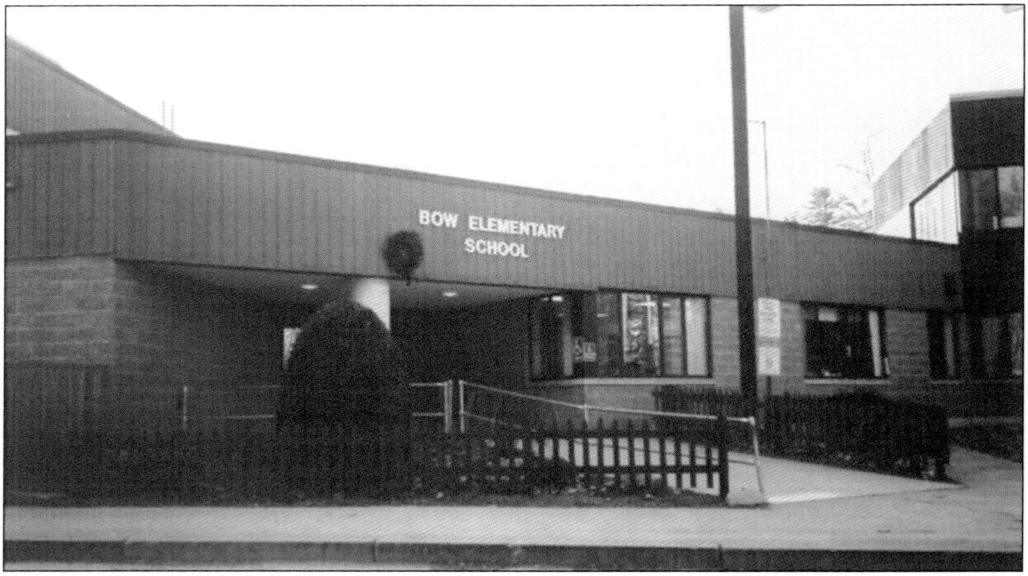

BOW ELEMENTARY SCHOOL. At the Bow School District meeting of April 13, 1978, it was voted to construct an elementary school building. In September 1979, the new school was dedicated. Due to the continual growth of the town, a major renovation was approved to add a new kindergarten wing and additional fourth grade classrooms upstairs. The addition, along with a new gymnasium and complete office renovation, was opened in January 1992, with every available space filled and fully functional.

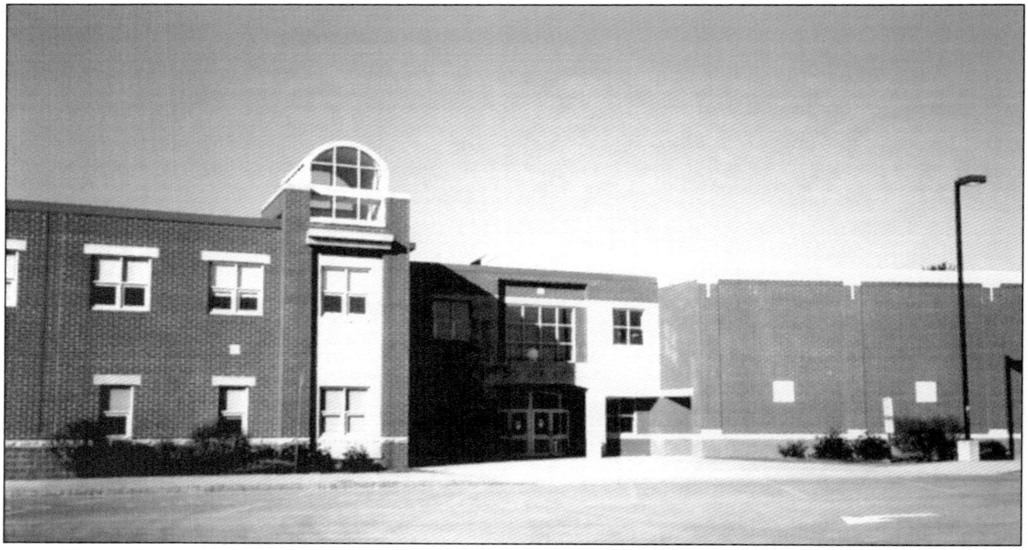

BOW HIGH SCHOOL. Residents voted at the 1994 town meeting to build its own high school by 1997, at which time Bow tuition students would no longer be accepted by the Concord School District. At this time, the town's population was continuing to rise from 5,500, according to the 1990 census, to 7,136 in the 2000 census. Previously Bow voted to leave the School Administration Unit No. 19, which included the towns of Weare, Dunbarton, Goffstown, New Boston, and formed its own school district. The school opened in 1997 and is today considered one of the finest in the state.

Five

YESTERDAY AND TODAY

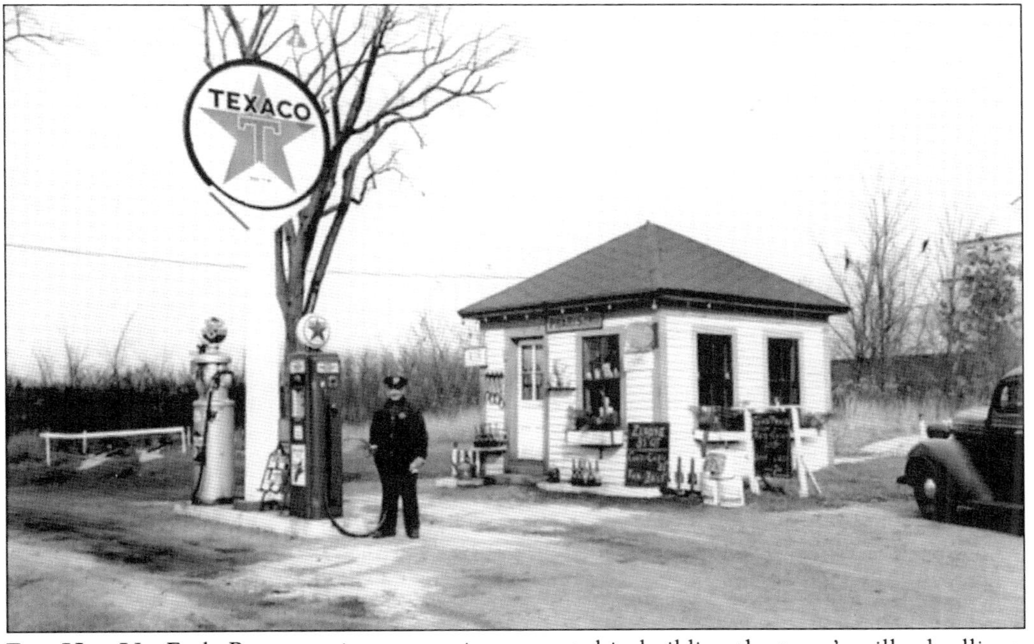

FILL HER UP. Early Bow proprietors were instrumental in building the town's mills, dwellings, and businesses. South Street was the gateway to Bow Center with its mills, orchards, and store. Bow Junction was where the railroad and trollies provided transportation for workers, passengers, and commercial goods. Londonderry Turnpike (Route 3-A) was also the home of many early businesses. As one moves from yesterday to today one sees that those images of the early businesses mirror the geographical locations of the businesses. One of those early Route 3-A Bow Junction businesses was the service station, shown here in 1945, operated by Bill Rollins from the 1940s to the mid-1960s. The building was a former signalman's shack that had been moved from the Bow railroad stop. The filling station was originally on the site of what is now Pitco's warehouse. It was later moved a short ways down the road to a spot opposite the current Park and Ride lot.

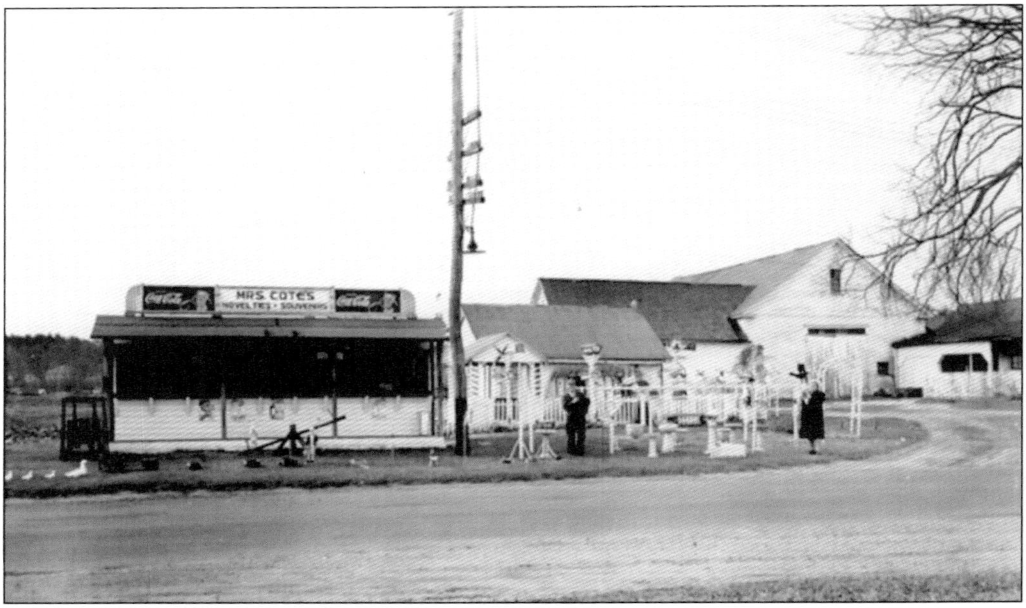

COTE'S SOUVENIR STAND. Mrs. Cote's souvenir stand was built around 1940 at Bow Junction near the present site of Pitco Frialator Inc. Grace Morgan Cote and her husband Tom sold penny candy, novelties, and handmade lawn ornaments from their stand. Grace was very active in the Grange and donated land for the Women's Christian Temperance Union hall and Bow Mills United Methodist Church. Grace died in 1955 and the land was sold to the Pitco Frialator company.

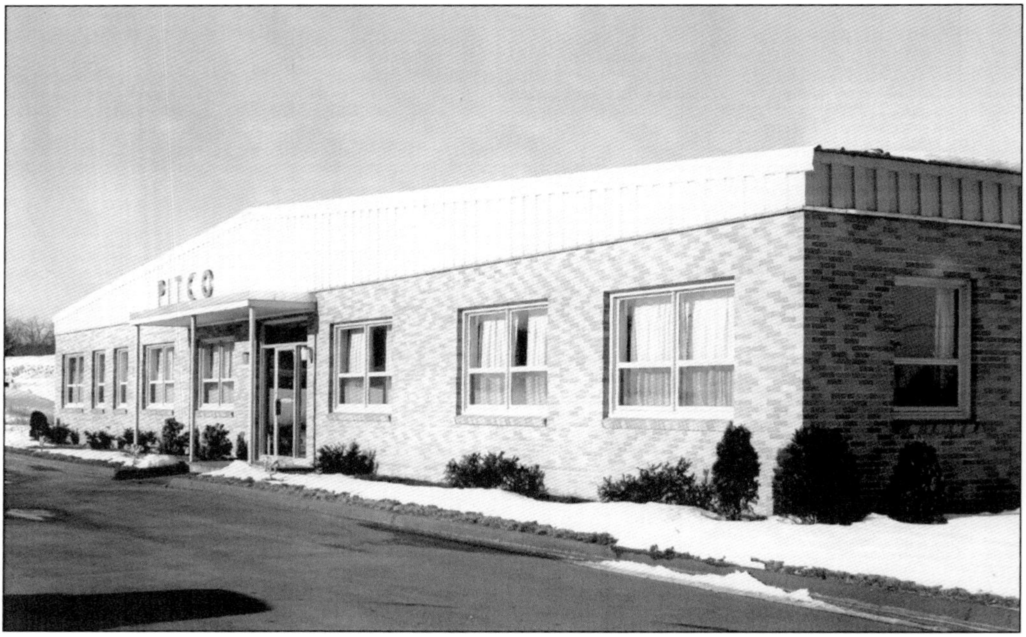

QUICK FRY, PITCO FRIALATOR INC. This very successful enterprise is at 509 Route 3-A, just north of the intersection with Interstate 89 and Hall Street. On the east side of Route 3-A, the warehouse was part of Merrimack Farmer's Exchange, now Blue Seal Feeds. The other building in the foreground is on the west side and on the site of Cote's stand.

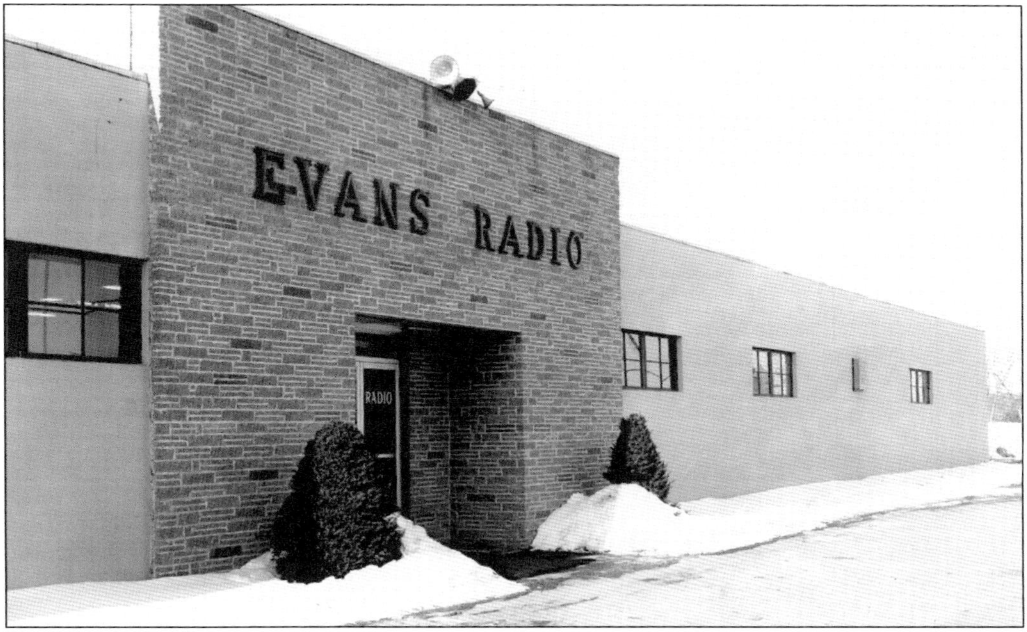

EVANS RADIO. This complex was built in the 1960s on Route 3-A by Carl Evans, on the present site of Grappone Toyota. Evans was a true pioneer in early radio and as a young amateur radio operator was instrumental in setting up communications during the 1927 floods and the 1938 hurricane. The complex served all aspects of radio and electronics.

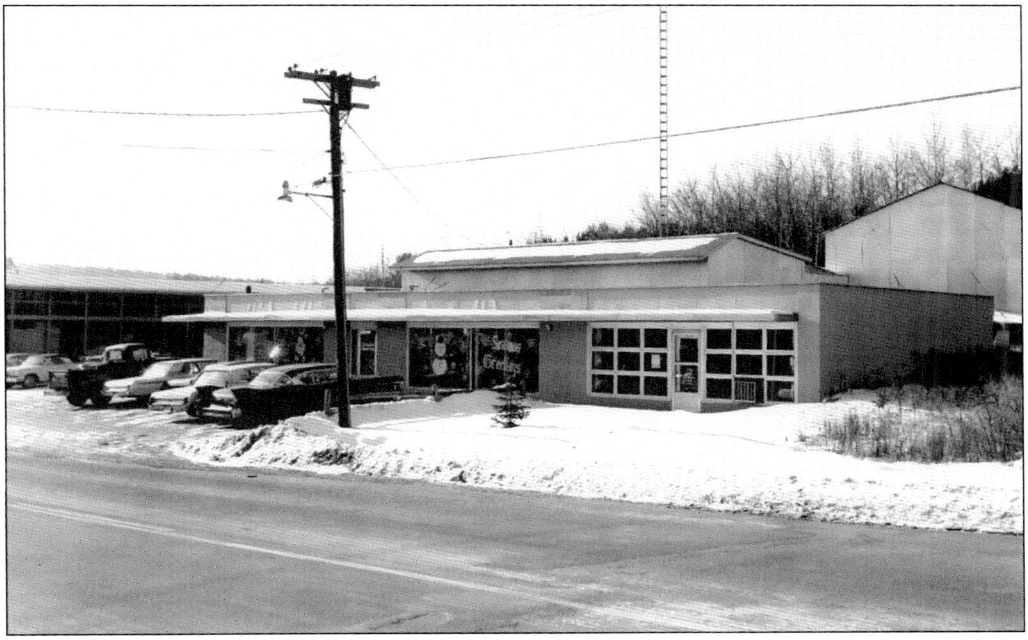

SUBURBAN LUMBER COMPANY. The lumber and building supplies company was located on the west side of Route 3-A on the current site of the Irving Gas Station and Blue Canoe Convenience Store. Suburban Lumber was one of the new industries opening since the 1960s and was owned by John Amrol. The property was transferred to the Irving Oil Company in 1994.

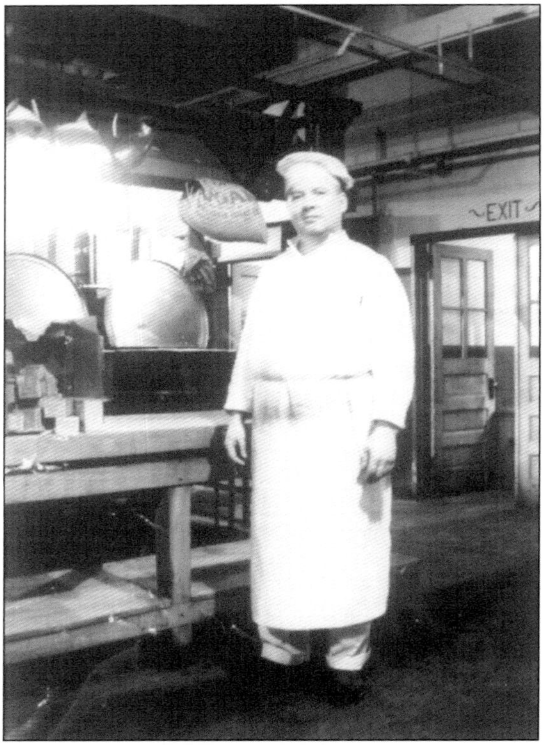

QUEENIE BOISVERT. Arthur "Queenie" Boisvert operated a small store at the corner of Old Road Hill and Route 3-A as one of the handful of businesses in the 1930s. The store was lost down the Merrimack River during the 1936 flood. He got his name from also selling Queens Bread door-to-door.

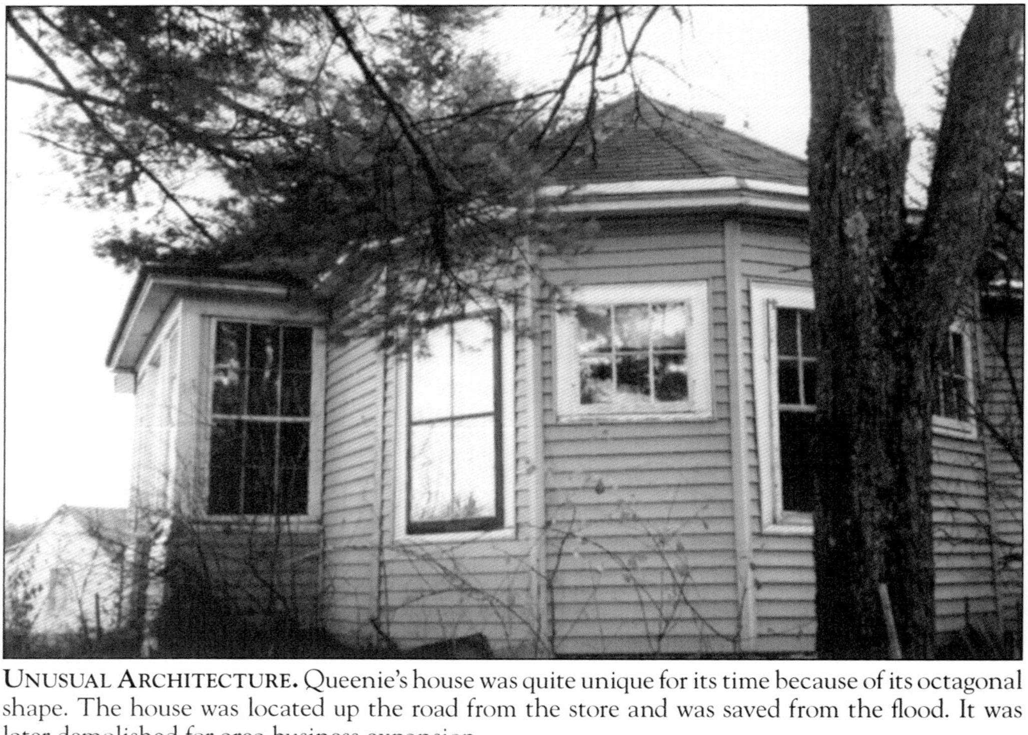

UNUSUAL ARCHITECTURE. Queenie's house was quite unique for its time because of its octagonal shape. The house was located up the road from the store and was saved from the flood. It was later demolished for area business expansion.

UPTON'S STORE. This store was located at the intersection of Valley and Grandview Roads in the Bow Mills section of town. The house was the residence of Mark and Clara (Kendall) Upton, the store was in the lower section and faced out onto Valley Road. Mark Upton also served as postmaster for many years until rural delivery took over.

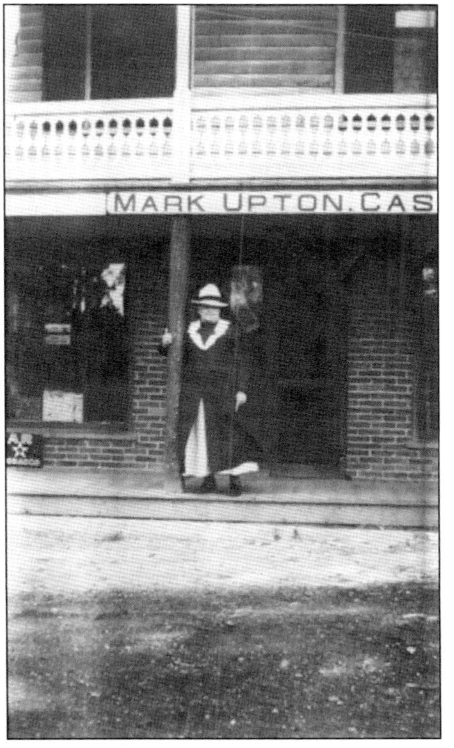

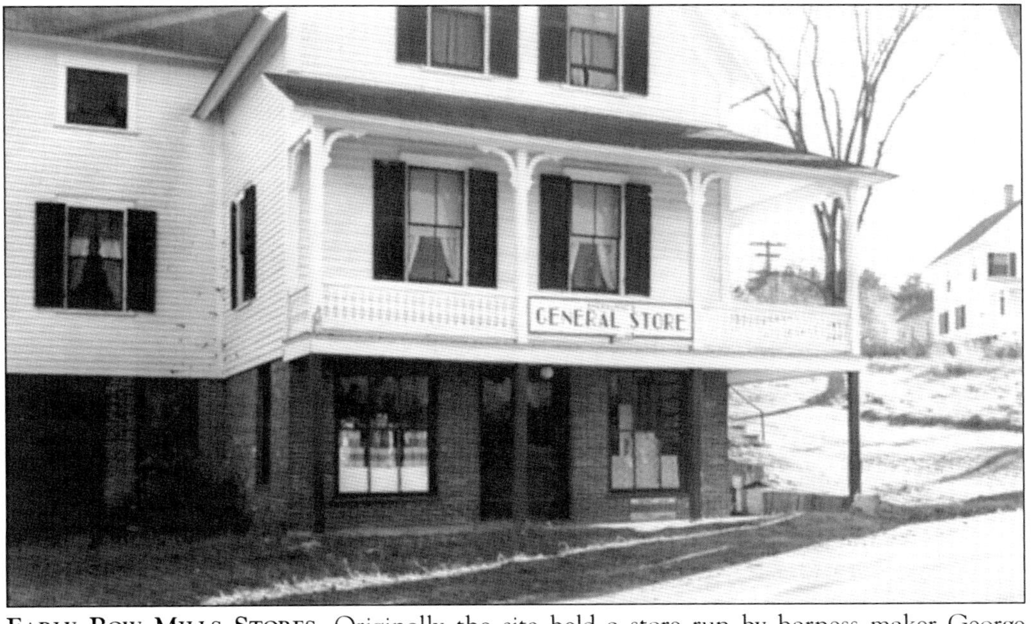

EARLY BOW MILLS STORES. Originally the site held a store run by harness maker George Elliot, which burned in 1869. Then a store was built on the same site by George Batchelder to complement the Upton Mill. The general store had many interim owners, the last being Harold and Winnie Wood, who closed the store in 1971 after operating it for over 17 years. The building is currently owned by Kenneth Blevens.

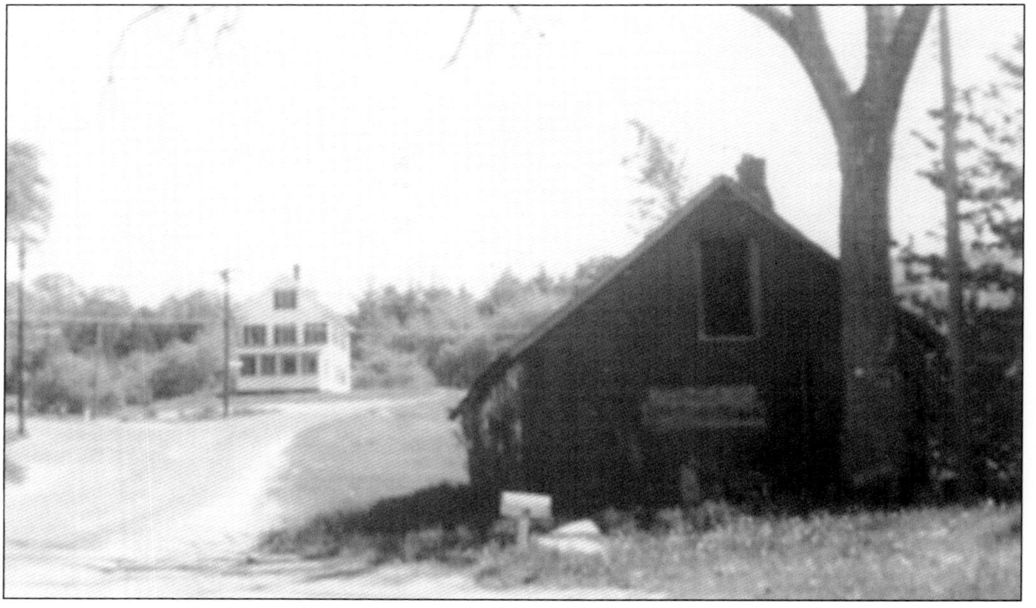

COLBY BLACKSMITH SHOP. This photograph shows the blacksmith shop at Bow Mills, operated by Willaby Colby. The shop was on the west side, at the foot of Logging Hill Road, as shown in 1958. In the background is the Frank Colby family home. Grandview Road goes off to the left and Logging Hill Road to the right. It was opened in 1860 and was in operation into the 1920s. The area is now part of the Interstate 89 loop.

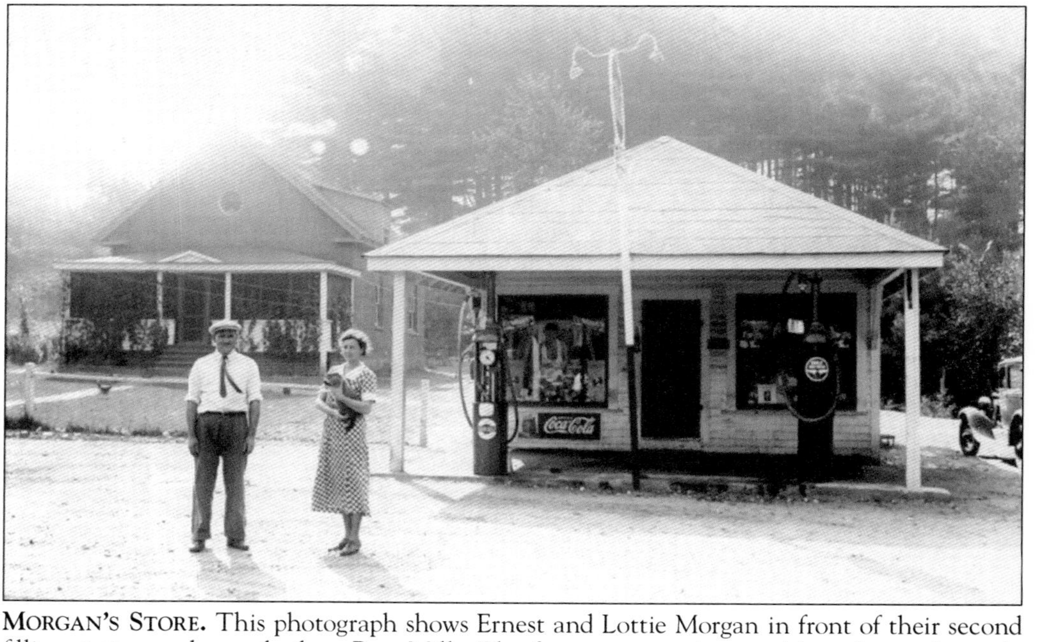

MORGAN'S STORE. This photograph shows Ernest and Lottie Morgan in front of their second filling station and store built at Bow Mills. The first store was destroyed by a fire in the early 1930s. This building was later used as the town's first fire station. The building on the left is the former Bow Mills brick one-room schoolhouse, which was converted into the Morgans' home. This area all became part of the Interstate 89 overpass.

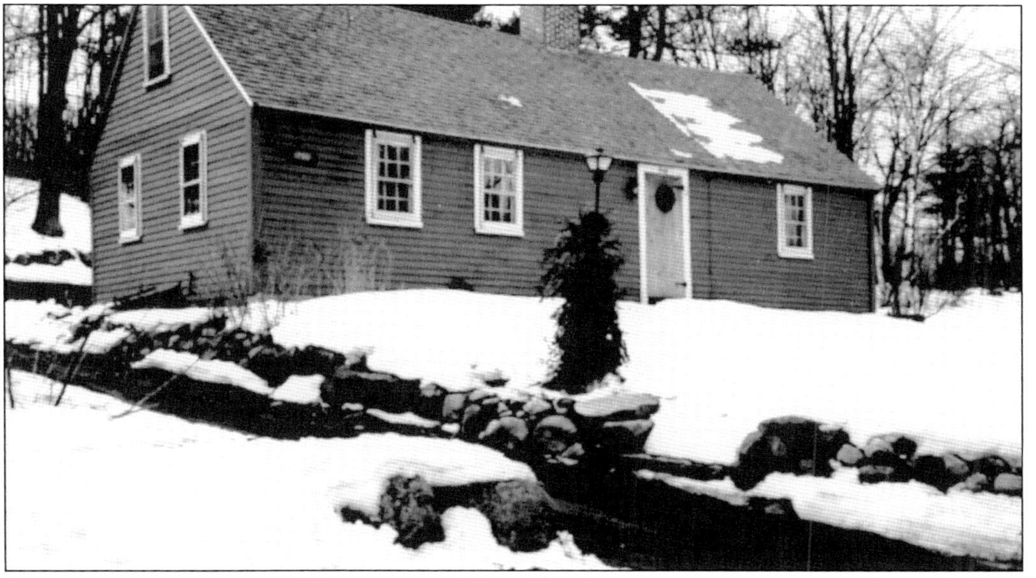

GIDEON MORSE TAVERN. This is one of the oldest houses in town, built in the mid-1700s. Gideon Morse opened the house to serve liquor to the public in 1807 and it was one of the most prosperous taverns in town. It operated until about 1830, when prohibition groups became a major force in town. The house is located on 40 Grandview Road and is now a private residence.

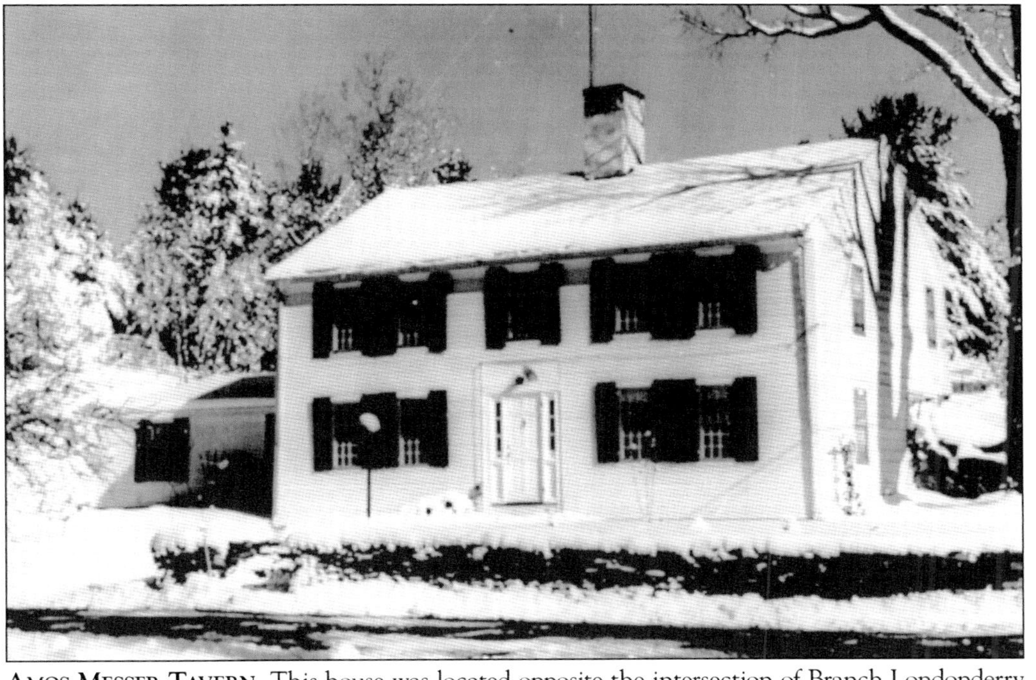

AMOS MESSER TAVERN. This house was located opposite the intersection of Branch Londonderry Turnpike West and Page Road. It served as a tavern for many years beginning in the early 1800s. Amos Messer was the owner of record in 1818. Messer also owned a sawmill in the same vicinity. The Londonderry Branch Turnpike Corporation frequently met in this building. The house was also thought to have been used as part of the Underground Railroad, it is now a private residence.

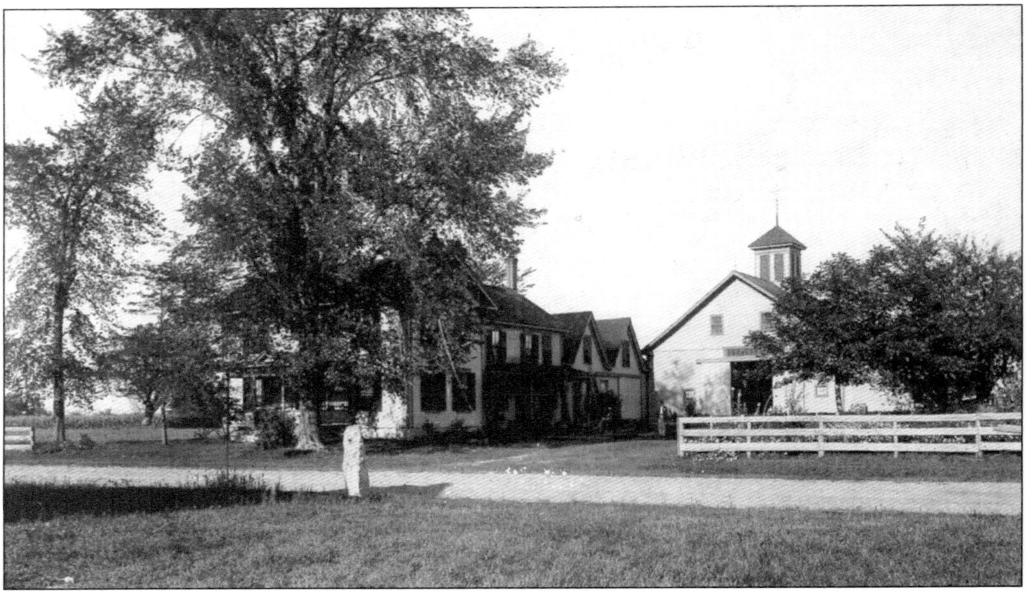

Henry M. Baker Residence. The South Street homestead of Henry M. Baker is seen in this 1892 photograph. Baker was born on January 11, 1841. During his lifetime of 71 years, he was a mill operator and became a successful lawyer. In 1912, he donated funds and part of his land for the construction of the Baker Free Library. The home eventually was demolished, making room for the New Hampshire Automobile Dealers Association building.

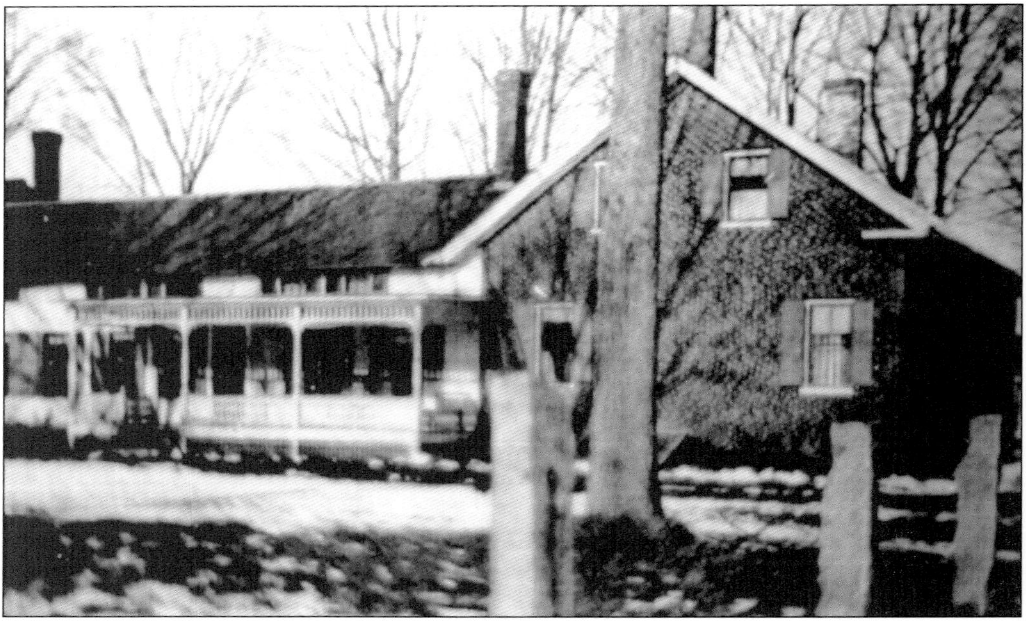

Arthur Chadwick Home, 502 South Street. This home was built by John B. Dustin, who operated a sawmill and gristmill at the Bow Mills site. It is thought to have been the home of Archibald Stark when he was a representative to the legislature from 1852 to 1853, and a selectman in 1856. Chadwick served on the school building committee in 1926 and on other town committees. He sold his property to the Concord Group Life Insurance Companies in 1997.

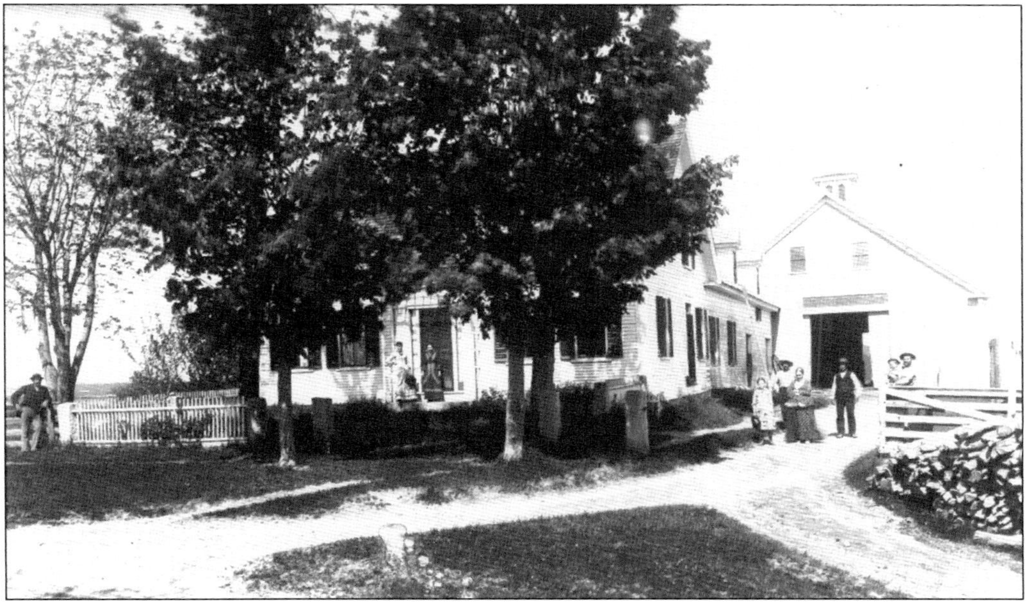

White-Stevens House. Rufus Herbert and Millie White pose with their family on their South Street farm. White was a successful farmer and also served as selectman from 1908 to 1911. The home was previously owned by John Brown who operated the brickyard on Route 3-A. The Whites sold the farm to the Stevens family in 1959. Eventually the property was sold and became the site of the Hampton Inn.

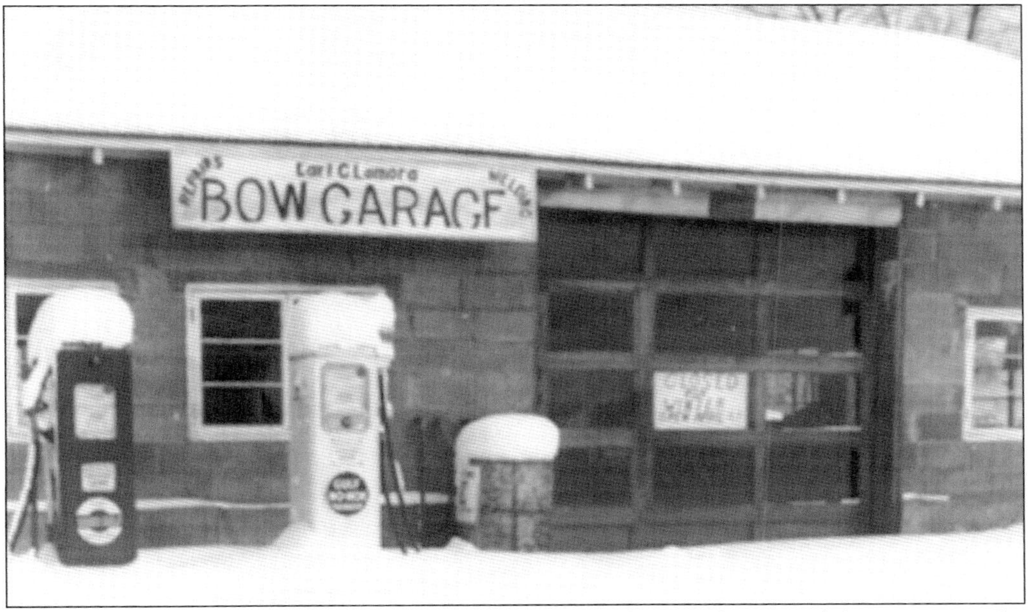

Grease Anyone? After Earl Lamora returned from World War II he opened this garage on the corner of Valley Road, at 521 South Street. Lamora's Garage was popular with Bow residents for over 30 years. This photograph, taken in the winter of 1957, shows when the garage was closed for the season, while the Lamora family vacationed in Florida. The garage is now operated as Dick's Service Center.

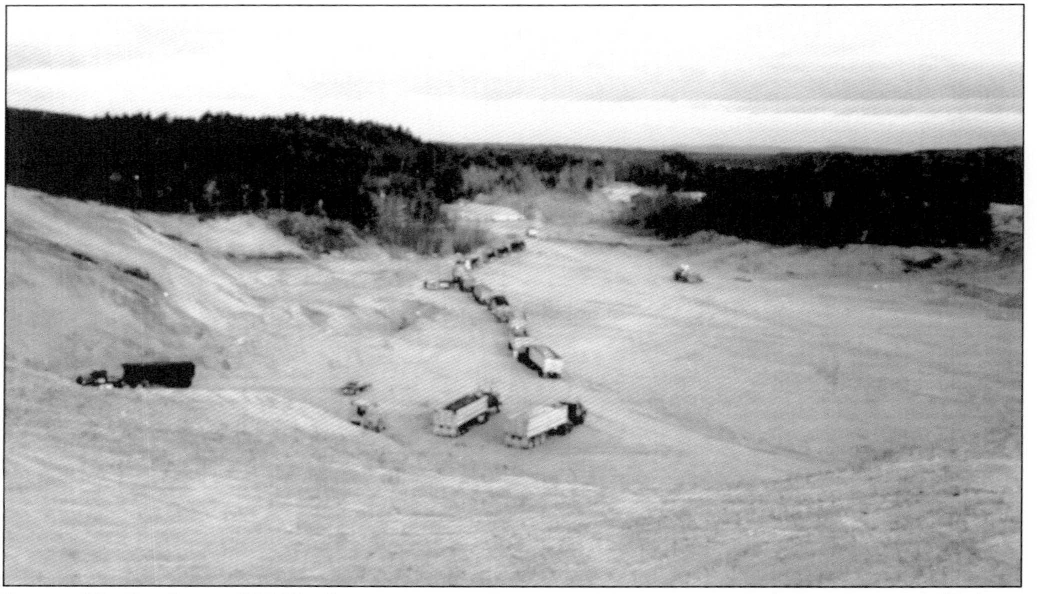

LINED UP. In the mid-1980s the runways at Logan airport were extended using sand fill from Bow. The Perini Corporation hauled hundreds of thousands of cubic yards of material from this sandpit, by both truck and rail. This picture was taken at the sandbank off Johnson Road, west of the railroad crossing.

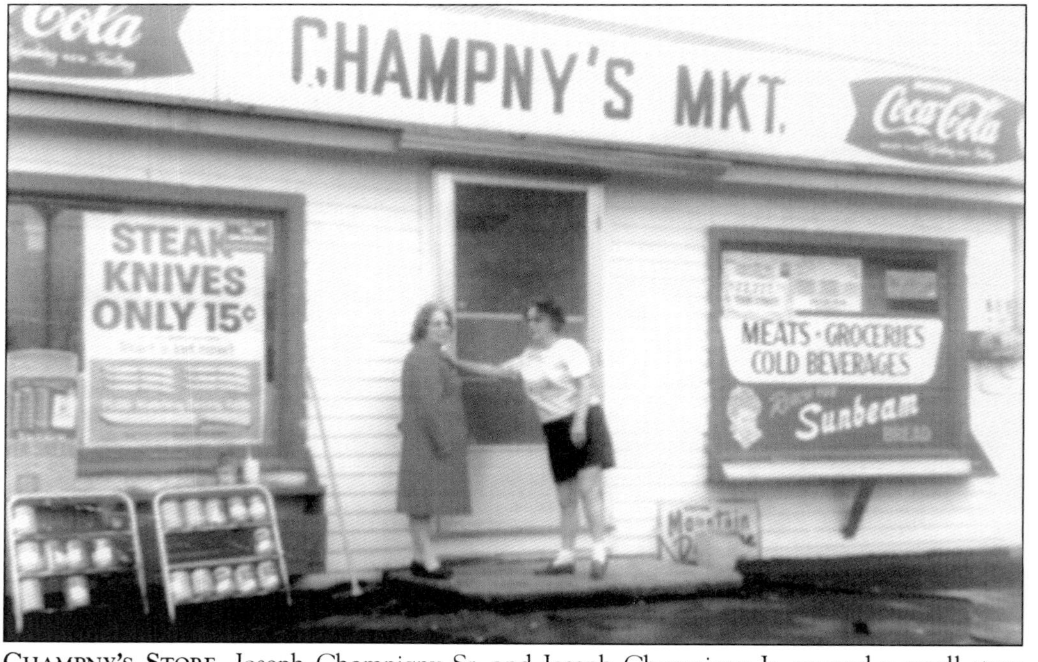

CHAMPNY'S STORE. Joseph Champigny Sr. and Joseph Champigny Jr. opened a small store on Route 3-A north of Garvins Falls Road in the late 1930s. They sold groceries, snacks, and gasoline. This store was sold to Frederick Lund who continued to operate it as Freddy's Store until the mid-1970s. The Champignys opened a larger store on Route 3-A, just south of Robinson Road, selling meat, groceries, sandwiches, and produce grown in the gardens behind the store.

Six

Look About

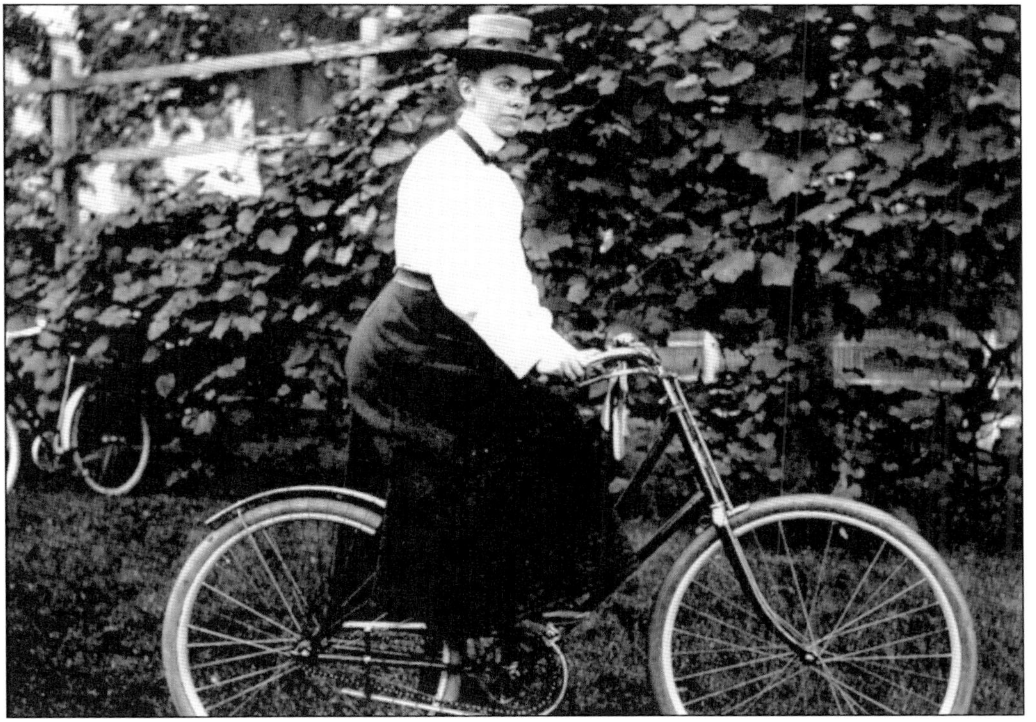

Pedaling About. During the 1920s and 1930s, traveling about the network of dirt roads by bicycle became quite common during the summer months. In this photograph is Doris Tilton Johnson pedaling about the Bow Bog area. The Johnson family owned a factory in Connecticut and spent summers at their home on Bow Bog Road. In 1949, the house was purchased by Ernest and Lottie Morgan. Vacationers and summer residents from the New England area were not uncommon. Bow had much to offer—quiet country hills, colonial homes, clean air, and a more relaxed pace of living. As one looks about, one observes interesting places and people who make up the historical profile of Bow.

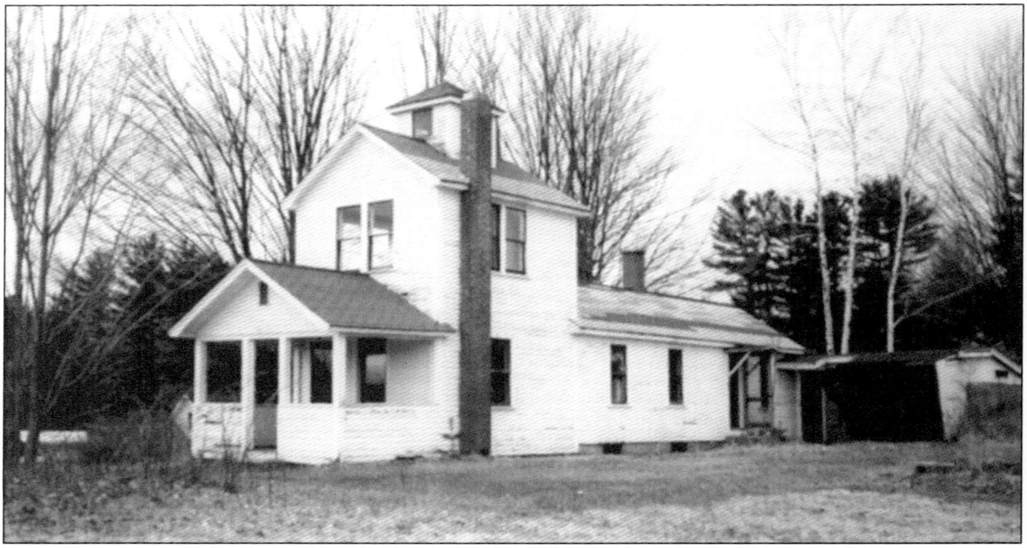

OBSERVATION. The Bow Observation Tower was built in 1942 on the high ground of Carl Ogden's farm on Bow Bog Road. The tower was staffed by volunteers 24 hours a day during World War II. Hilda and Laura Sargent, members of the Army Air Ground Observation Corps, were two of those volunteers. They received extra gas coupons in order to drive from their homes to watch for enemy planes. A warning siren was mounted on top of the Bow Mills School (currently the Municipal Building). The observation tower exists today on private property.

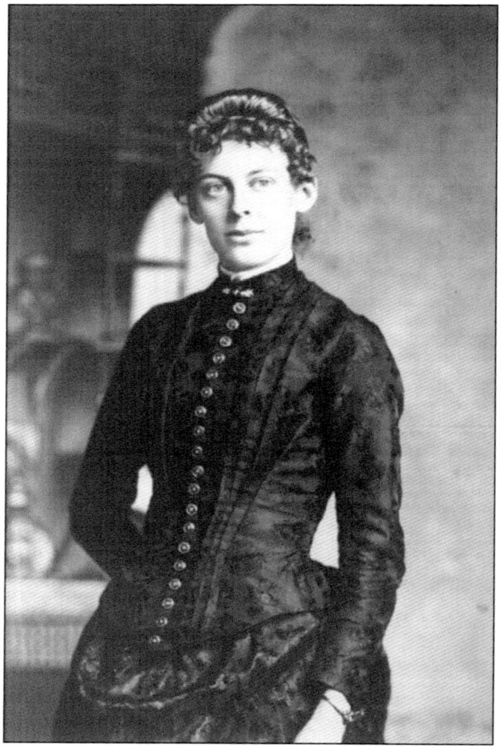

SUNDAY BEST. The Gault family came to Bow in the 1700s, purchasing land from one of the original Bow proprietors, colonial governor Benning Wentworth. Seen in this photograph taken around 1900 is Mrs. Andrew Gault in her Sunday best. She lived on a farm on Route 3-A which was, until recently, owned by Elizabeth Alexander Bailey.

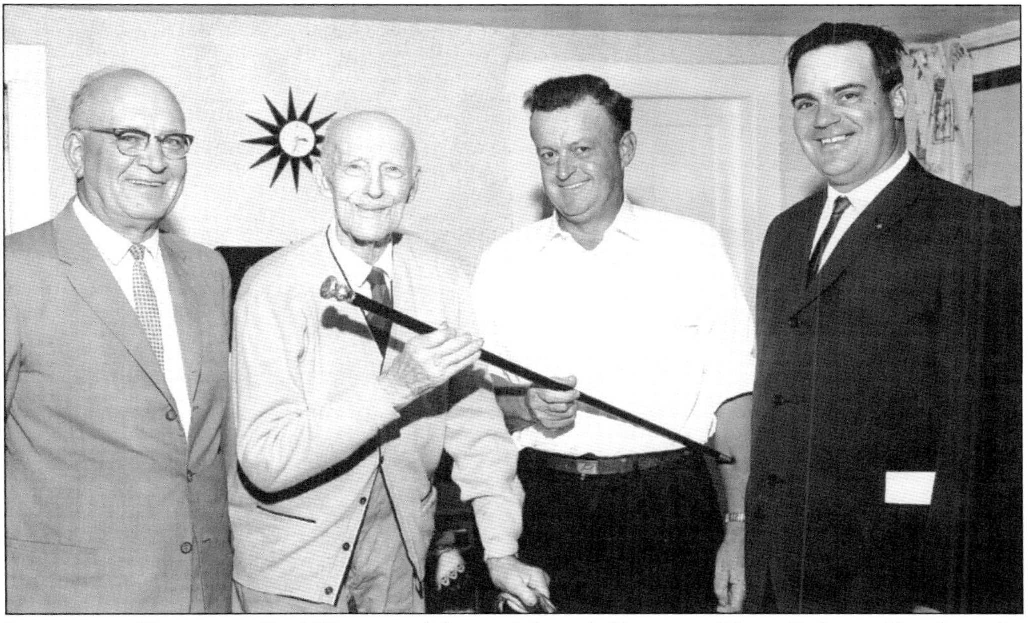

Longevity Prevails. Fred Hammond (second from left), at age 96, smiled proudly when the Boston Post Cane was presented to him in 1964. The selectmen, from left to right, were Norman Ordway, Paul Lindquist, and Richard Hanson. Presentation of the cane to a town's eldest citizen is a small but important way of recognizing valuable members of the community.

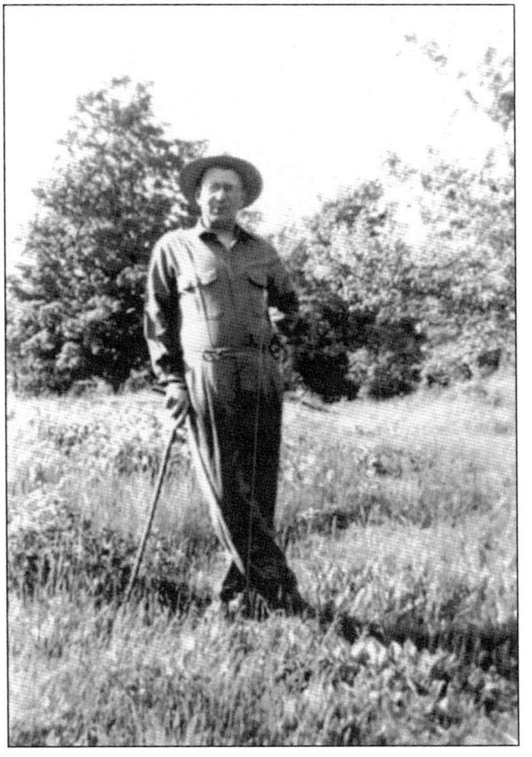

Popular Guy. James Arthur "Pop" Knauf was a joker, often stating he was "known coast to coast, from one side of the Merrimack river to the other." Pop began repairing and installing water pumps at the age of 16. He operated his own water and well business in the 1940s. In 1984, he was presented the Boston Post Cane for being the oldest resident. He lived to a ripe old age of 95 and a half years.

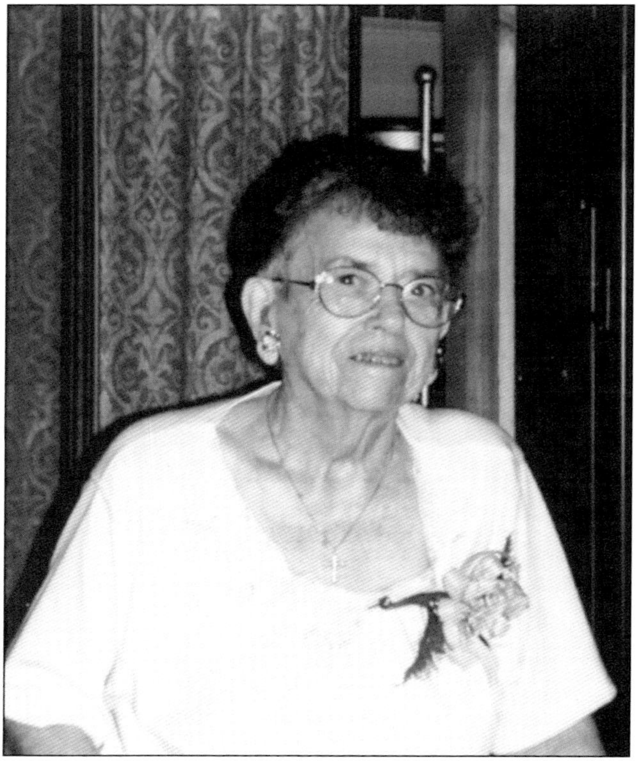

Hilda Morgan Sargent. A native of Bow, Hilda Sargent was born on June 19, 1903, at the family farm on Bow Bog Road. When she was three, the family moved to 5 Grandview Road, where she lived for the next 99 years. Over her lifetime, Sargent was active in just about every social club and event in town. Sargent was the last known person from Bow to have spoken directly to Mary Baker Eddy. She was the holder of the Boston Post Cane from 2002 to 2005.

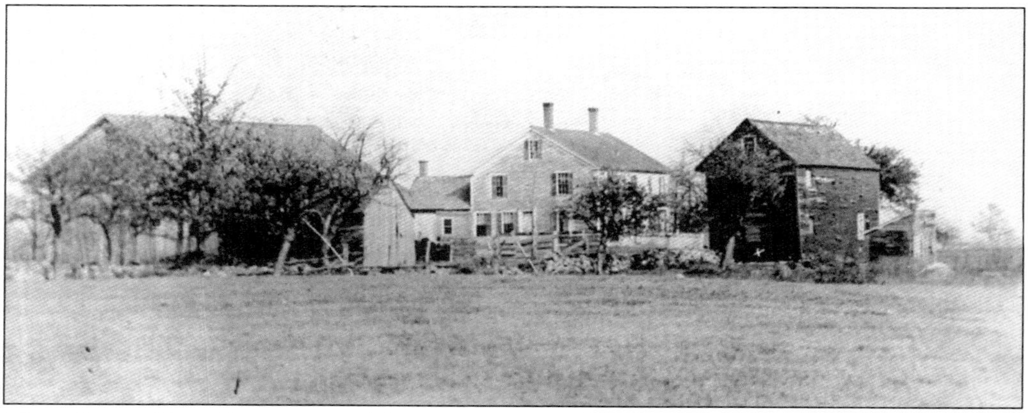

Mary Baker Eddy Birthplace. Three generations of Bakers—James, Aaron, and John—lived on this farm, which was on the west side of the Londonderry Turnpike (Route 3-A) just south of River Road. This was the home in which Mary Baker Eddy was born. This photograph was taken in 1868. The entire farm burned in 1910 and the site is marked today with a plaque and stones outlining the original buildings.

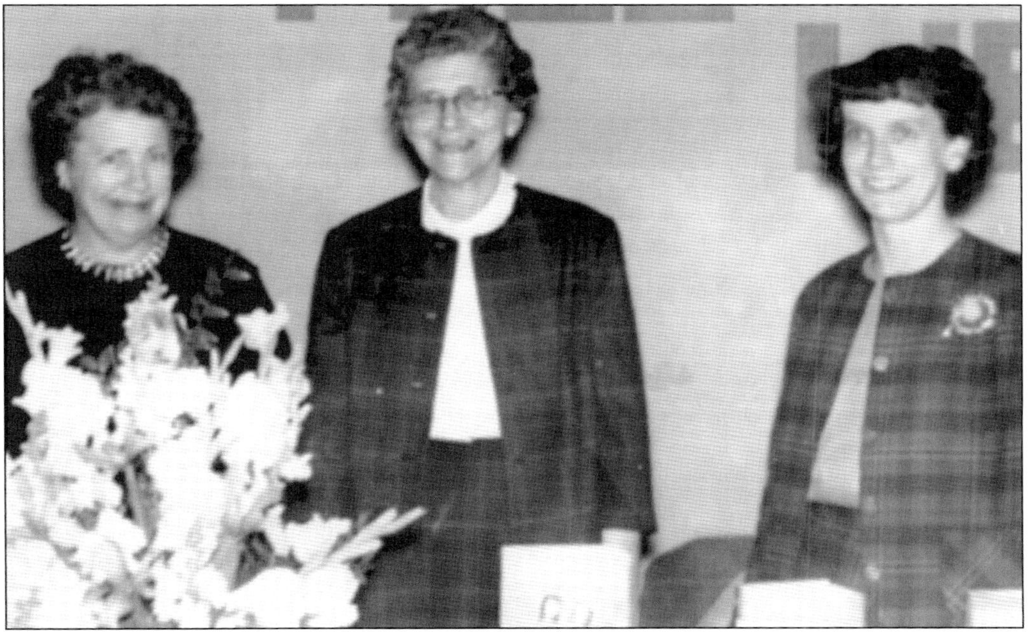

BOOK WORMS. From left to right, Virginia Brown, librarian Helen Howe, and Helen Robinson discuss new additions to the Baker Free Library collection at the March 1966 Voting Day. At the town meeting, a warrant article requesting that money be set aside in the Captial Reserve Fund for an addition was approved. The addition was completed in 1967.

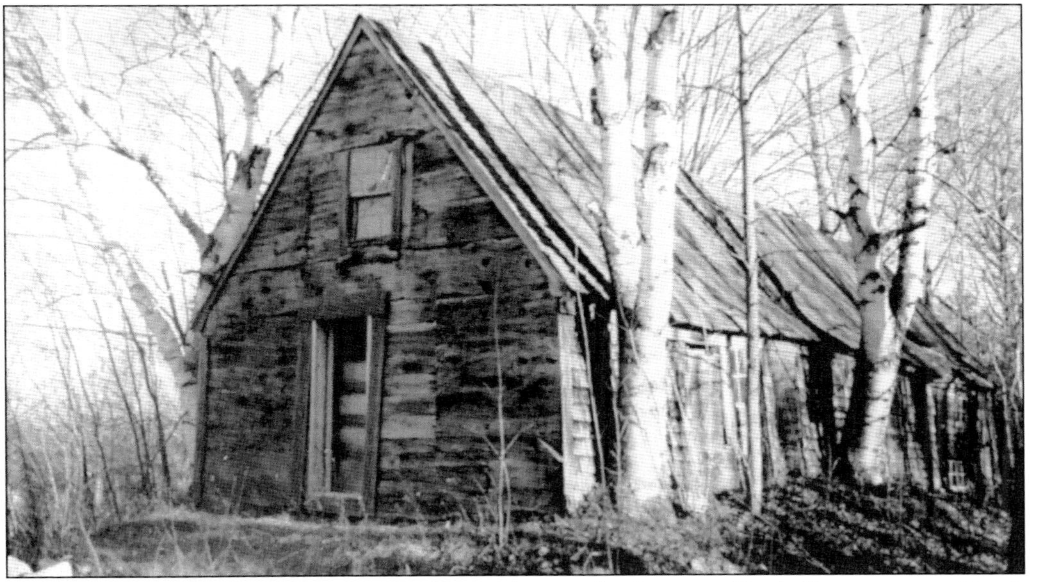

NINETY-NINE BOOKS ON THE SHELF. Shown here is the Bonneau Book Depository on South Bow Road, where numerous books once served as a library for families of south Bow. This building, built in 1896, now abandoned, has empty shelves and a few National Geographic Magazines. Leon Bonneau lived next door where the Murray family now lives. His print shop was across South Bow Road. Dennis Ordway worked there as a teenager. It is now Merrill Crossing, a development of 12 new homes.

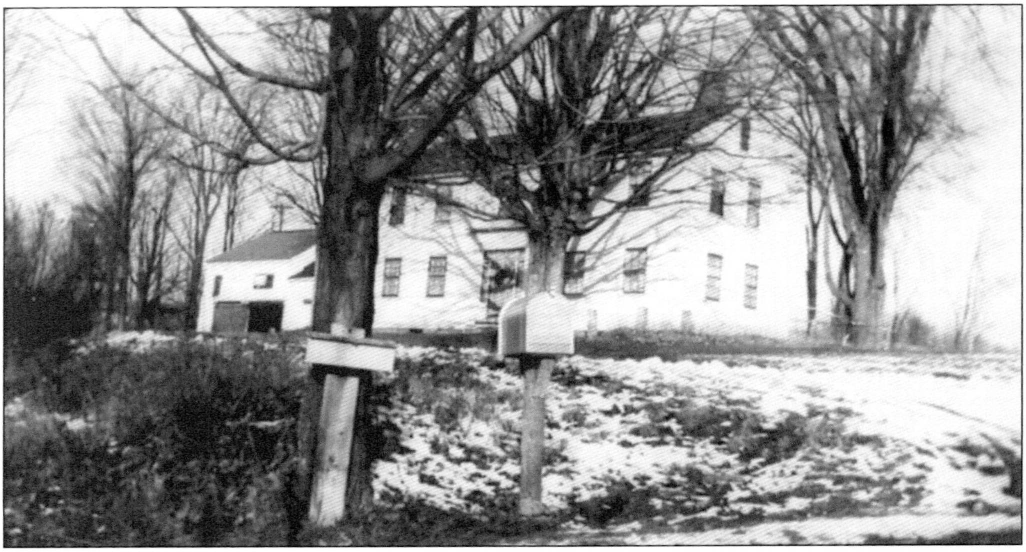

STAGE COACH STOP. This house located on Branch Londonderry Turnpike West, at the corner of Bow Center Road, was Bow's first US Post Office, with Isaac Clough as Postmaster. It was one of Bow's first stores and stagecoach stops and many early 1800s meetings were held here. Abolitionist Obed Gault, lived here until 1851. It is now a private residence owned by Alna and Dick Stevens and is on the Historical Marker Map and List.

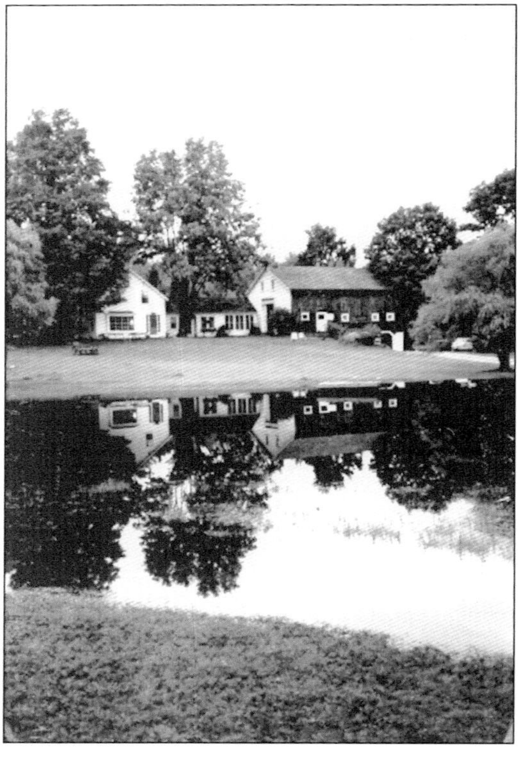

MORE THAN FIVE. A typical farmhouse, with trout pond, at number 10 Ordway Lane has seen over five generations of Ordway families. It is thought that Robert Ordway, born 1797, his wife Sarah "Sally" Colby, and their 11 children were the first Ordway generation at this site. Brickyard Brook flows through the property and feeds a fine pond. In 1962, Bow children had swimming lessons there, taught by Jet Jennings, for a program organized by the Bow Women's Club. Jacquelyn Dey Langenfeld Jennings currently owns the property and calls her 100 acres Bowsprit.

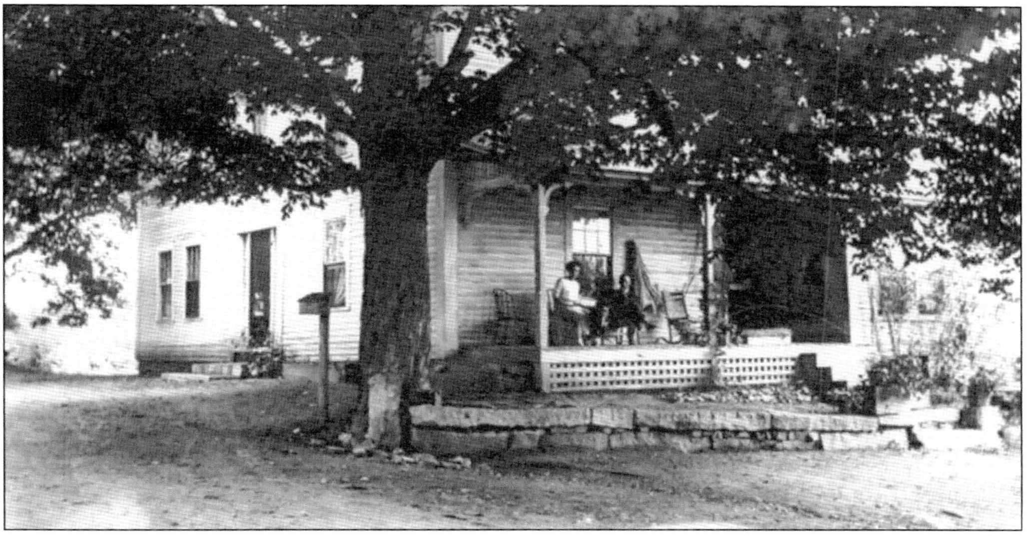

WHITE FARM. This farmhouse was built sometime prior to 1810 by Isaac White who settled the land between the Londonderry Turnpike (Route 3-A) and the Merrimack River in 1777. White's grandson, also named Isaac, was a prosperous farmer, winning awards for his dairy cows, butter, and Concord grapes. The farm stayed in the family, first owned by Frank, a popular surveyor and town selectman, and then by his son William. The property was purchased in 1959 by Paul Lindquist. The home is now owned by David and Eva Lindquist.

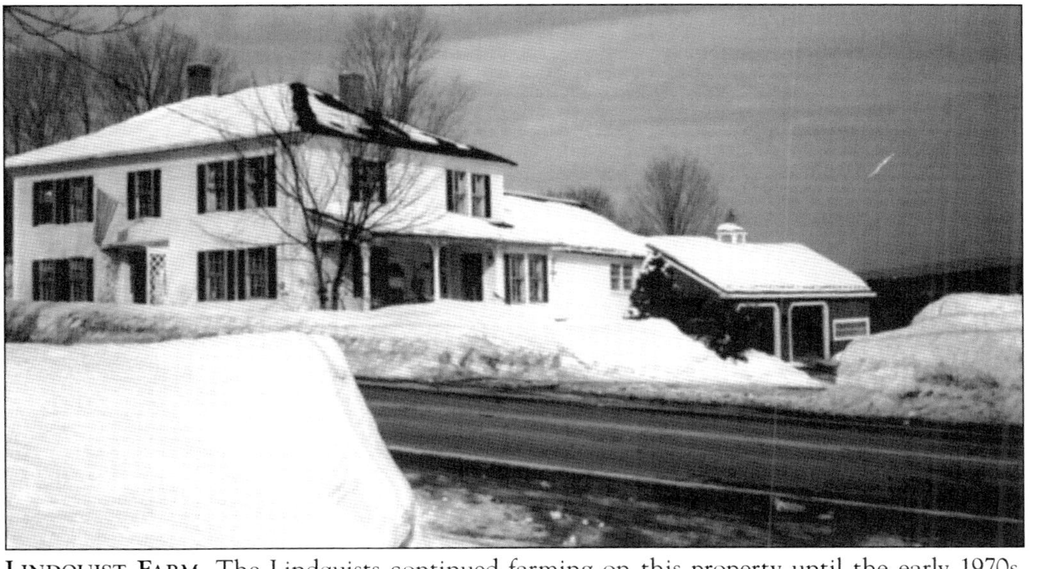

LINDQUIST FARM. The Lindquists continued farming on this property until the early 1970s, raising dairy cows, chickens, pumpkins, corn, and strawberries, and running a farm stand from their home. Paul Lindquist worked many jobs, including at the Garvins Falls Hydroelectric Plant, as a home builder, town road agent, town building inspector, and selectman. His wife Jane worked for the town as a school bus driver and was a member of the Heritage Commission.

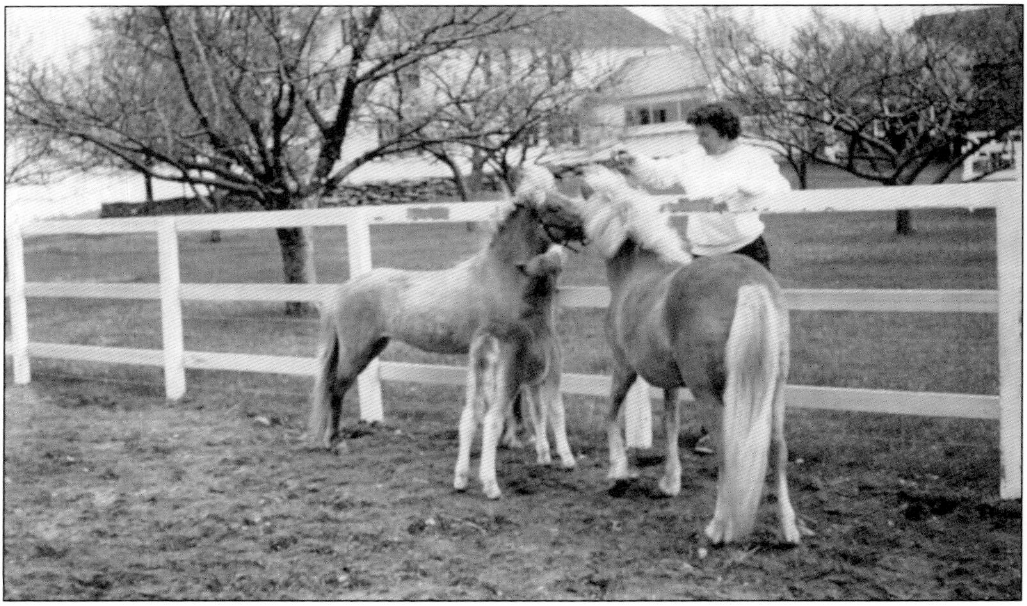

Brown Hill Pony Farm. The farm atop Brown Hill was built in the early 1800s, home to four generations of the Clough family and later the Jamesons. The Brown Hill Pony Farm was established in 1954 by the next owners, Archer and Stevie Leary. Their most successful pony was Solitaire Dickie, who won championships all over New Hampshire. Jane (Langley) Strablizky worked on the farm and exhibited the ponies. She remembers the many people who would visit, have a picnic, pet the ponies, and go on pony rides.

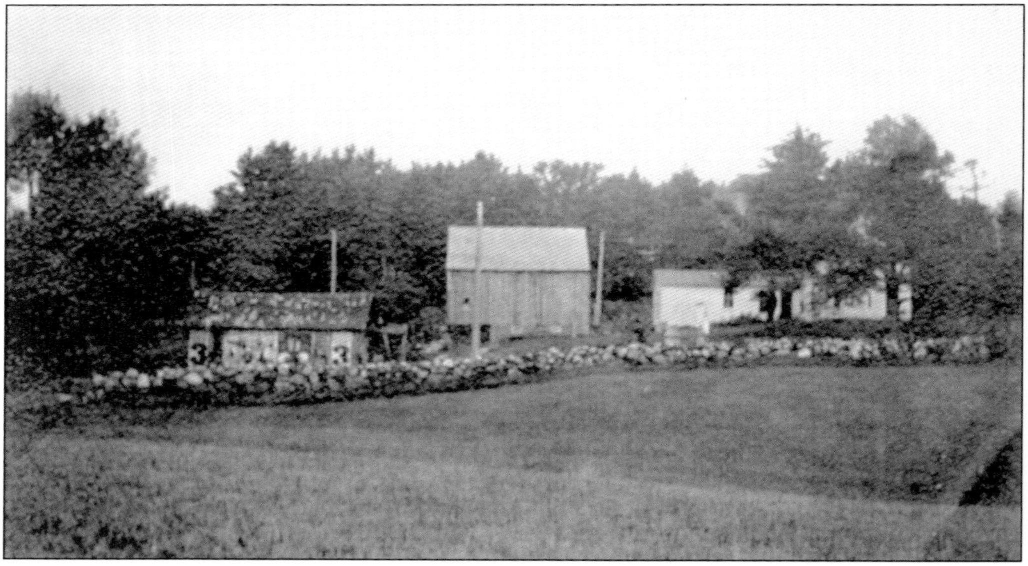

Anderson Family Homestead. Eric Anderson's family has owned the property at 4 River Road for over 100 years. His grandparents lived there, and now he and his wife Cherilyn live there. Until a few years ago, the property contained approximately 46 acres. Anderson's great grandparents lived at 3 Grandview Road, and his great-grandparents were also from Bow. A blacksmith shop was located to the left of the property.

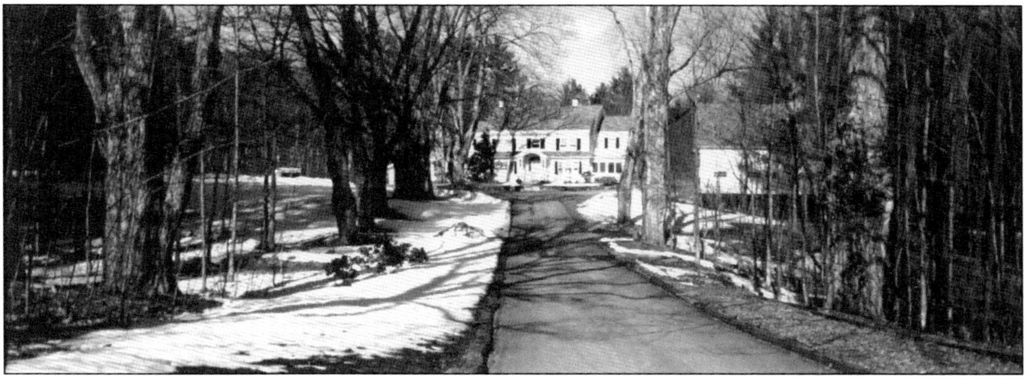

THE DOCTOR'S HOME. The beauty of Bow is reflected in the home of Dr. Robert Boucher at 70 Bow Center Road, called the Maples. This home was originally built in 1924 by Red Murray for Anne and Harry Clough. Many townspeople visited the Bouchers' home at Christmas season for an open house when it was beautifully decorated for the holiday. The Boucher family had a small maple syrup operation and gave tours to school groups. The home is now occupied by Mary Boucher.

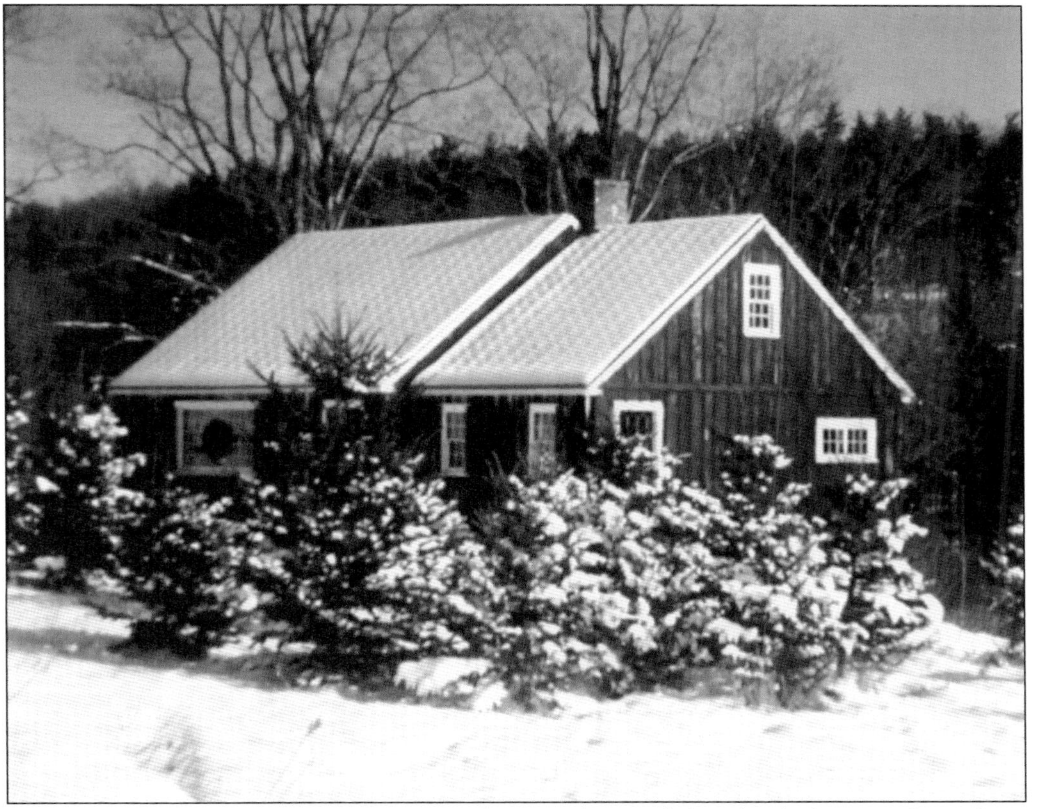

MUSTARD ANYONE? The Salmagundi Shop became the retail shop for the homemade products sold by Laura and Franklin Gregory under their Greylore Mustard Inc. label. Products made included mustards, relish, jams, and maple syrup. This shop eventually became a private residence and the Sugar Shack, located next door and used for the syrup production, was demolished.

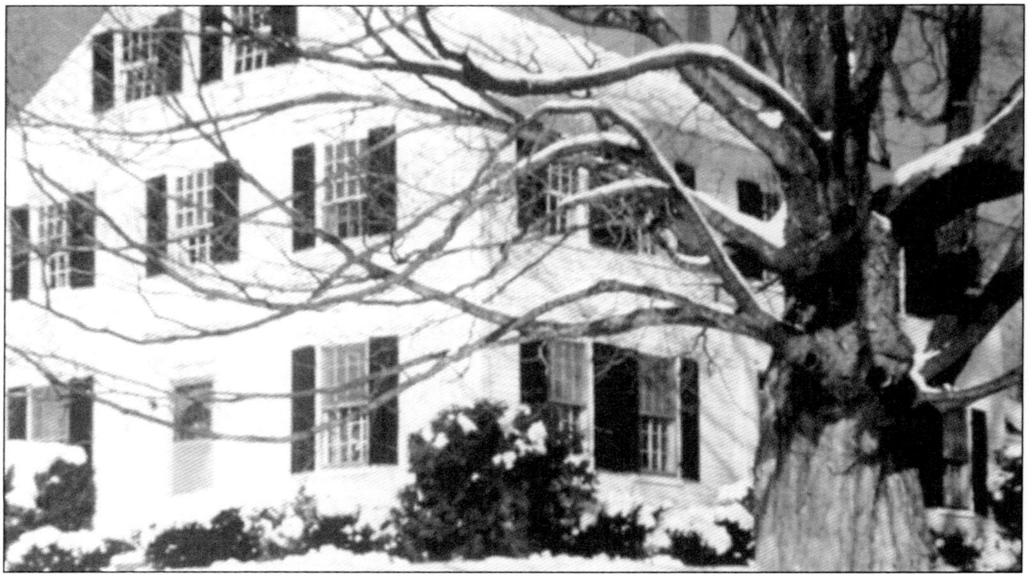

Specialty Farm. Samuel Rogers, one of the town's first residents, purchased this land in 1757. It was later owned by the Goodhue family. In this 1960 photograph, Laura and Franklin Gregory were the owners of the home. Incorporated as Greylore Mustard Inc., the property became known as a specialty farm. The barn burned in January 1974 and a barn raising was held in the spring. In 1979, after the property was sold, the land was subdivided into 21 house lots. The house and barn still remain.

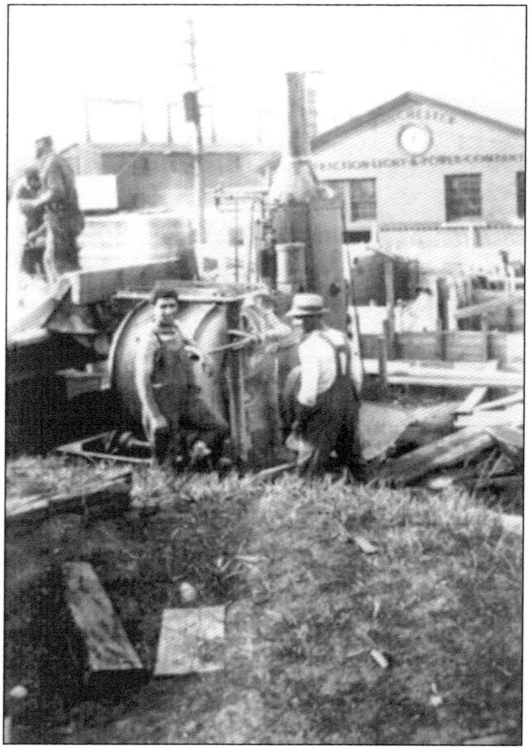

Garvins Falls. Jacob Carter had a mill on this site about 1788. The Manchester Traction Light and Power Company, whose workers are shown here, completed the first dam and hydroelectric facility here in 1907. The dam was 550 feet wide and 300 men were employed on the job at one time. Native American artifacts found along the Merrimack River indicate extensive use of this area for fishing and camping.

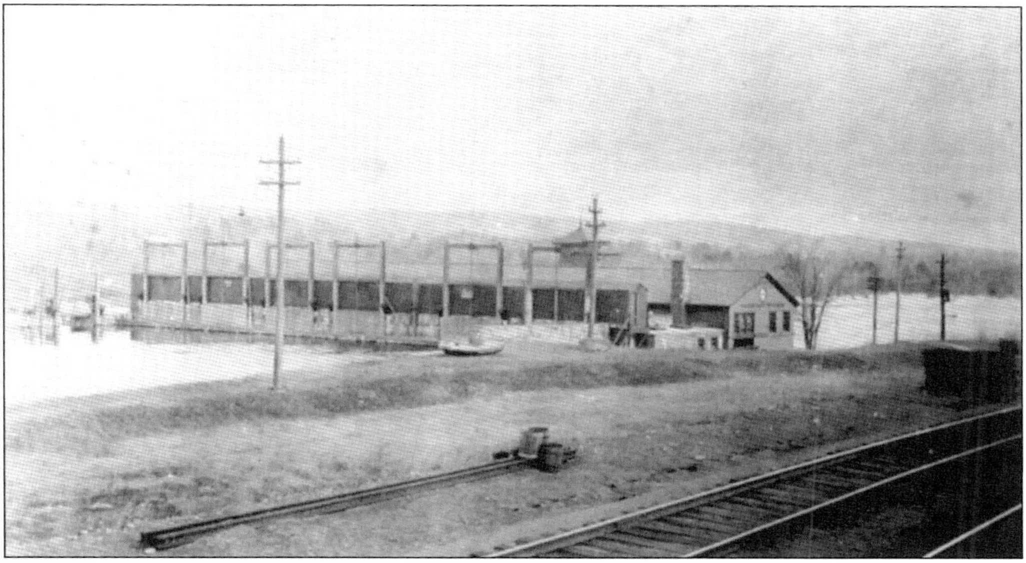

HYDRO. Fred Hogan, a selectman from 1914 to 1916, worked at the completed Garvins Falls plant. He lived at the power station and became the foreman. This plant (and later the Merrimack stations) paid a high proportion of Bow's taxes. The Garvins Falls facility has been modernized and developed, and produces electricity to this day.

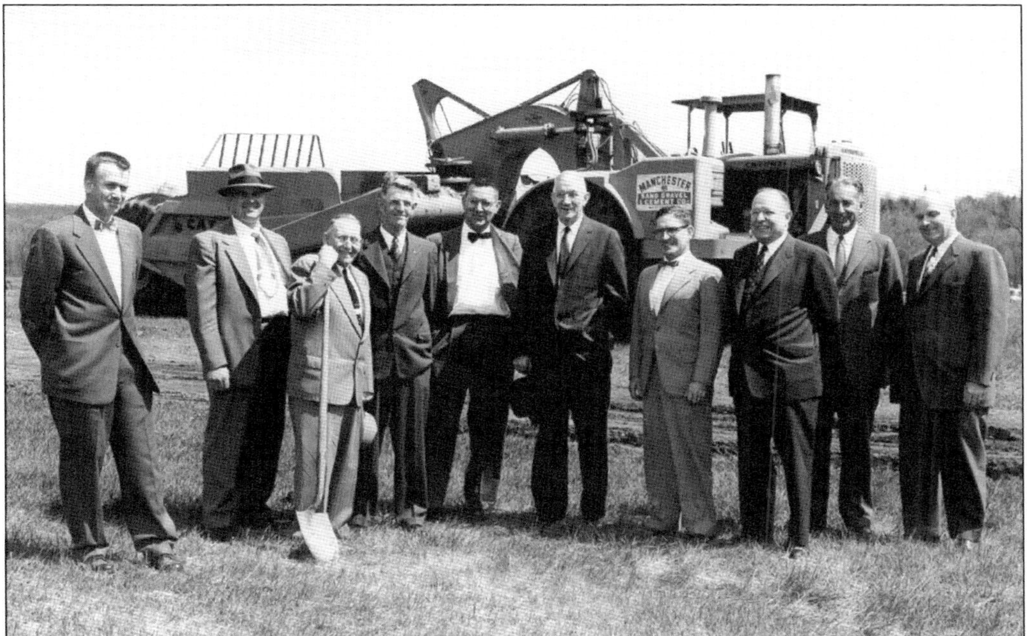

MORE POWER. Construction of the Public Service Complex on River Road began in 1958. Shown at the ground-breaking ceremony are, from left to right, Arthur Chadwick, Richard Hanson, Wilbur Vaughn, Harold Howe, and officials from the public service company. A new generating facility, Merrimack II, was constructed and opened in 1968. The favorable tax climate created by these two plants brought about tremendous residential and commercial growth.

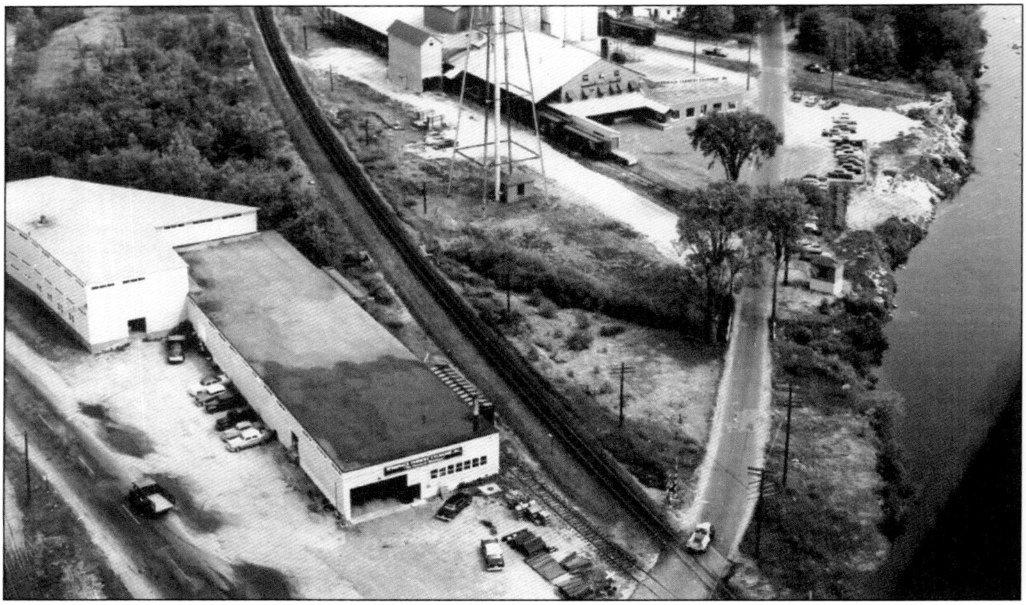

Merrimack Farmers Exchange. The Merrimack Farmer's Exchange was opened on December 6, 1941. According to *100 Acres More or Less*, it was designed to engage in "buying, selling, exchanging, leasing, mortgaging and generally dealing in farm products of all kinds." There was a 50,000-gallon water tower in the center to be used in the event of a mill fire. Residents also voted in 1942 to install a fire alarm box, wired to the Concord Fire Station, at the exchange building.

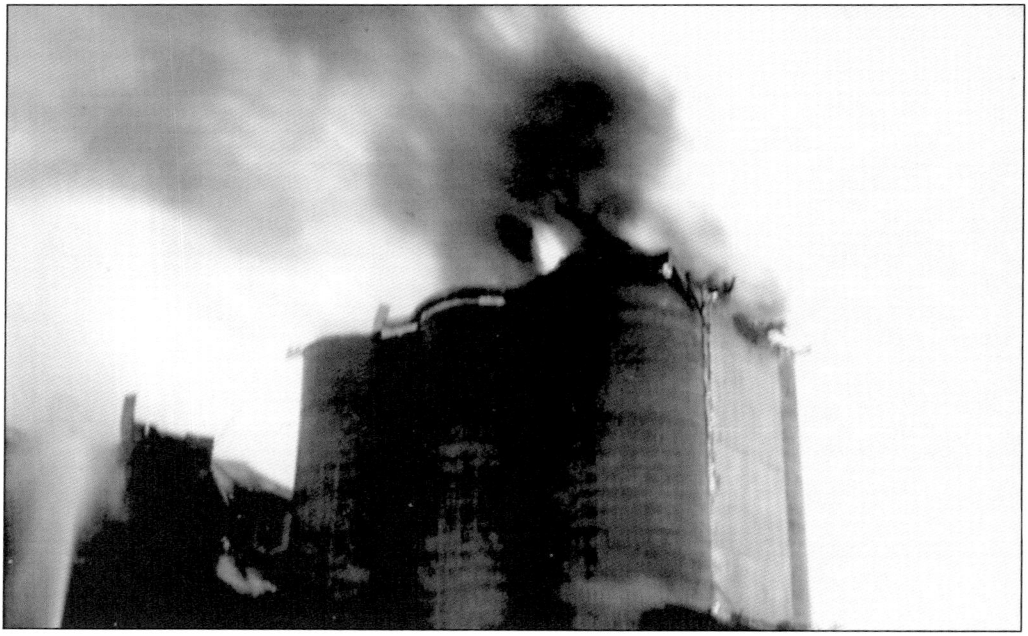

Mill Fire. In 1963, Merrimack Farmer's Exchange was destroyed in a spectacular early morning fire. Following the fire, the mill was rebuilt and expanded. It remained Merrimack Farmer's Exchange until the 1980s, when it was bought out by the Blue Seal Company. The warehouses on the west side of the railroad tracks are now owned by the Pitco Frialator Company.

Seven

GROWING PAINS

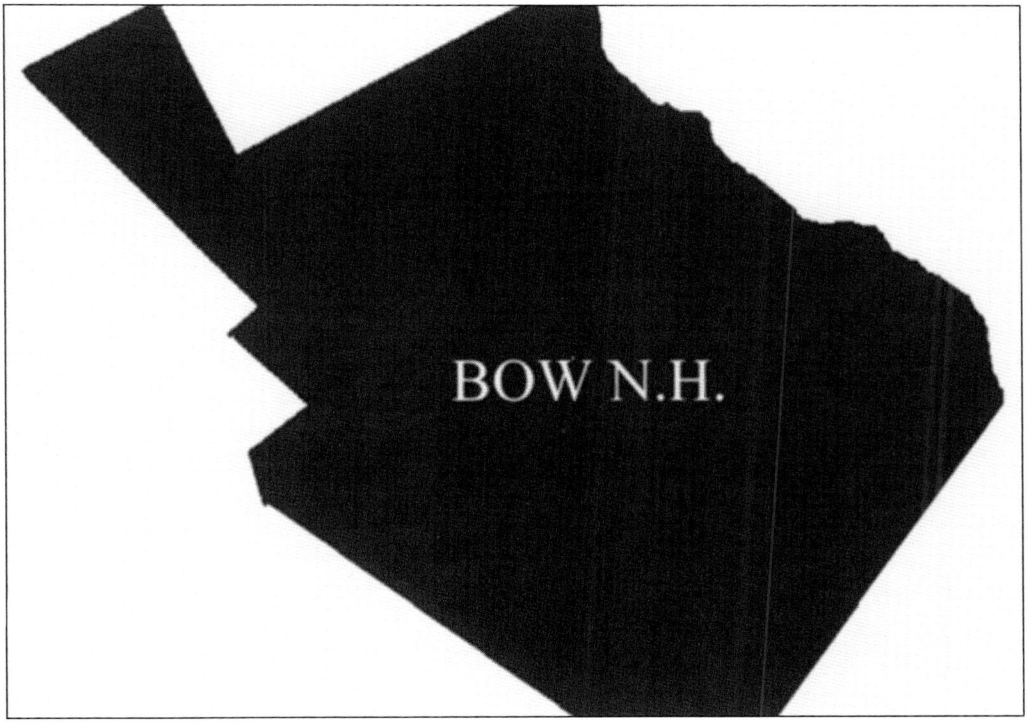

BETWEEN THE LINES. November 1748 was the date the Bow Proprietors chose a committee to perambulate the lines around the Bow Grant. By the end of 1749, the initial second division layouts were completed and accepted. The town boundaries were established and adjudicated several times over the coming years. As the population of Bow increased, so did the requirements for more services. Town meetings became quite interesting as budgets grew. Many fine people were elected to serve the town at the local, state, and federal levels. The demand for services such as fire, police, and highway has dictated the current government size. The board of selectmen has grown from three to five and a town manager has been hired to oversee the many town agencies.

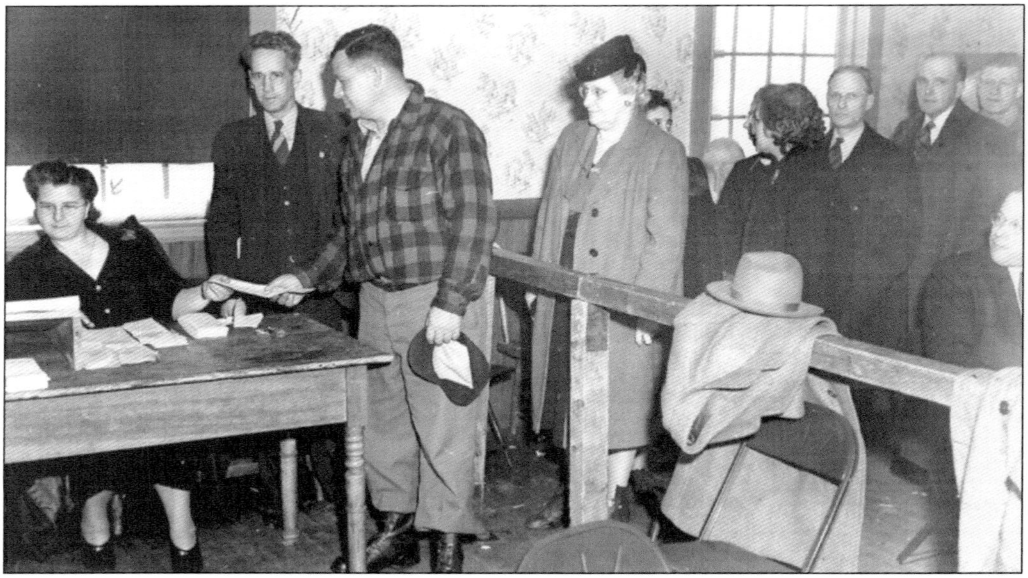

WE THE PEOPLE. Voting days and town meetings were important to the community. The first town meeting was held March 11, 1767, at William Robertson's house on Knox Road. This voting day picture held at the town house in 1948 shows Laura Sargent, ballot clerk; Phil Sargent, checklist supervisor; and voters Roy Wescomb, Edith Knauf, Bill Colby, Fran Colby, Alfred Jenks, and Ernest Morgan. Halstead Colby is seated at right. Beginning in 1957, voting was held at the Bow Community Building.

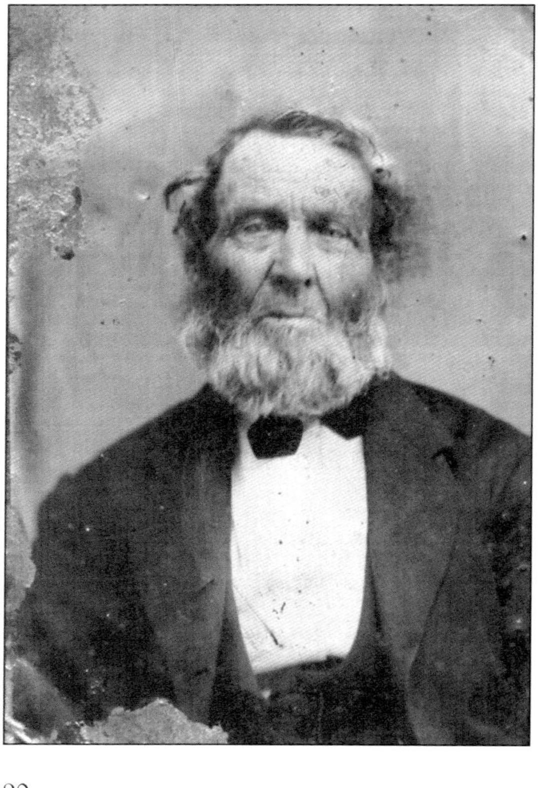

WILLABY COLBY. Willaby Colby was born in 1795 and lived at the intersection of Grandview and Logging Hill Roads, in the home now owned by Harvey Moody. He served on the committee that supervised building the Bow Bog Meeting House in 1835. In 1860, Colby opened a blacksmith shop at Bow Mills.

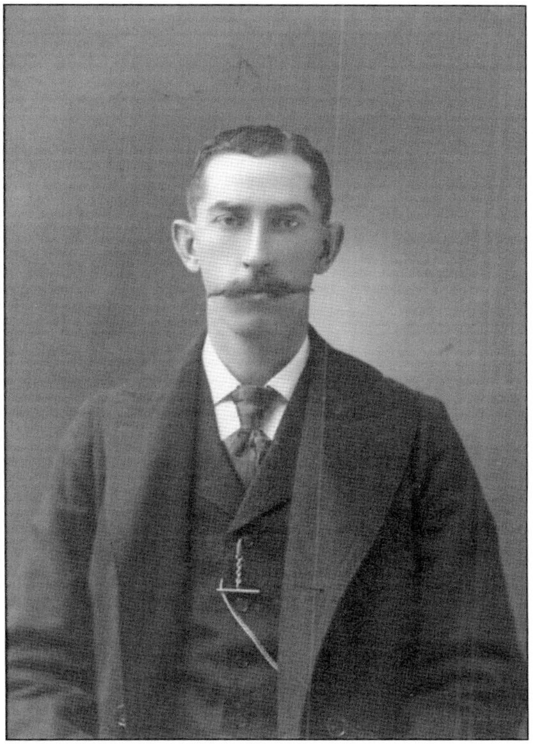

RUFUS BAILEY. Rufus Bailey was a selectman of Bow from 1859 to 1861. He was active in politics and served as head of the Democratic Town Committee. Bailey lived near the intersection of Route 3-A and Vaughn Road and worked as a farmer.

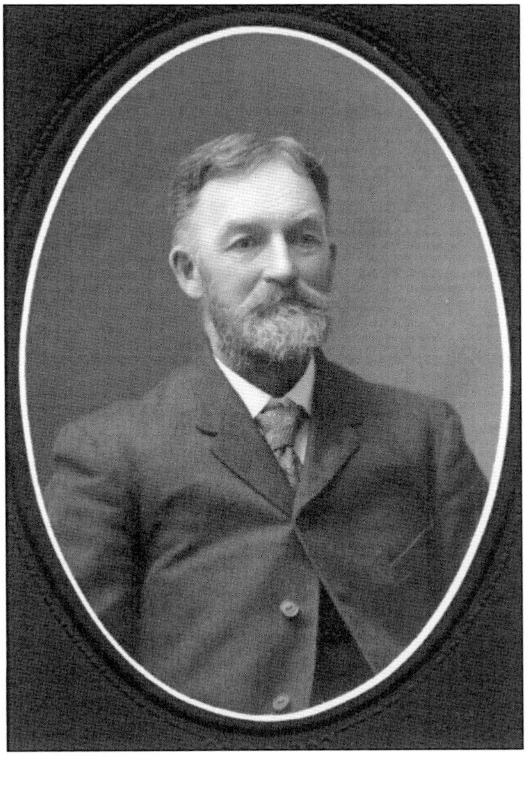

FRANK A. WHITE. Frank A. White lived on the Londonderry Turnpike (Route 3-A) on the farm now owned by David and Eva Lindquist. He was a graduate of the Agricultural School of Hanover, which was affiliated with Dartmouth College. White lived in Kansas for a few years, joined the Kansas Militia, and fought in the Indian Wars. He returned to Bow and enjoyed much success as a farmer and surveyor. White also served as a selectman.

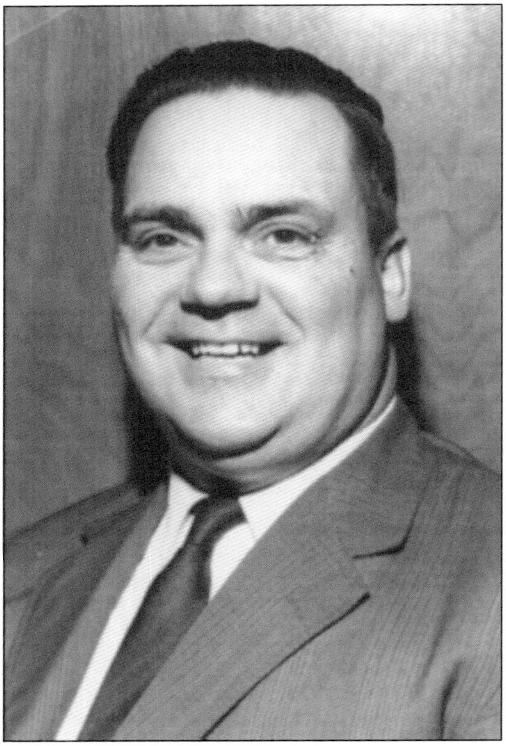

BEST KNOWN. Richard D. Hanson was elected as a selectman for the town from 1952 to 1973 and as a representative to the legislature. In the 1960s, Hanson was a key town developer, both residential and commercial. He was instrumental in luring the public service company to town, as well as locating Interstate 93 on the Bow-side of the Merrimack. He also built several housing developments.

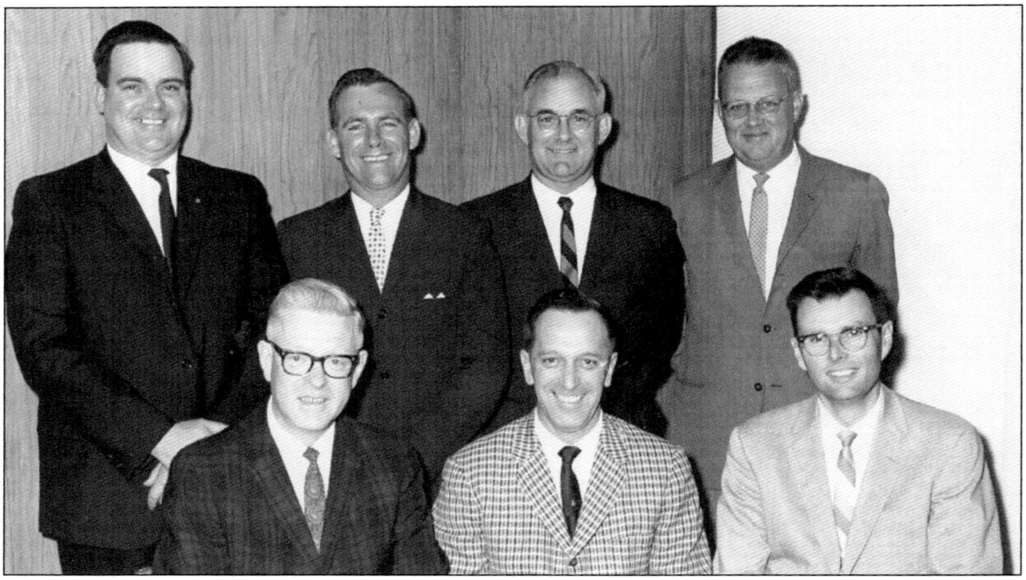

GROWTH OVERSEERS. The Bow Planning Board, pictured here in 1967, included, from left to right (first row) chairman Reginald Scott, Winfield Robin, and secretary Duncan Pearson; (second row) selectman Dick Hanson, Earl Wheeler, Ray Person, and Winton Fogg. It had been a busy year with public hearings held on five subdivisions; a survey was acquired covering industrial and commercial use. It was suggested that the town support the development of a comprehensive town plan.

NEW TO TOWN. Growing pains dictated that the size and make-up of the town's governing body be changed. After study and acceptance of the new idea, Bow changed to a town manager style. Al St. Cyr was hired as the first town manager in October 1989. Not an ordinary man, but one who diligently pursued better government for Bow; his imaginative ideas provided guidance for more than a decade.

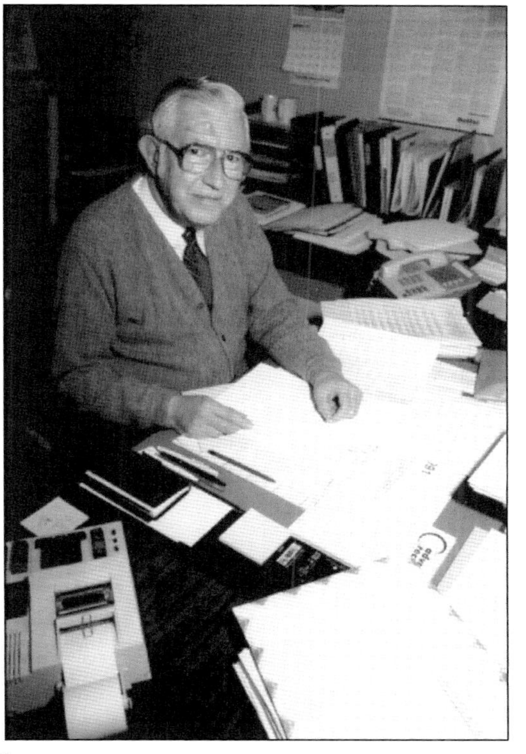

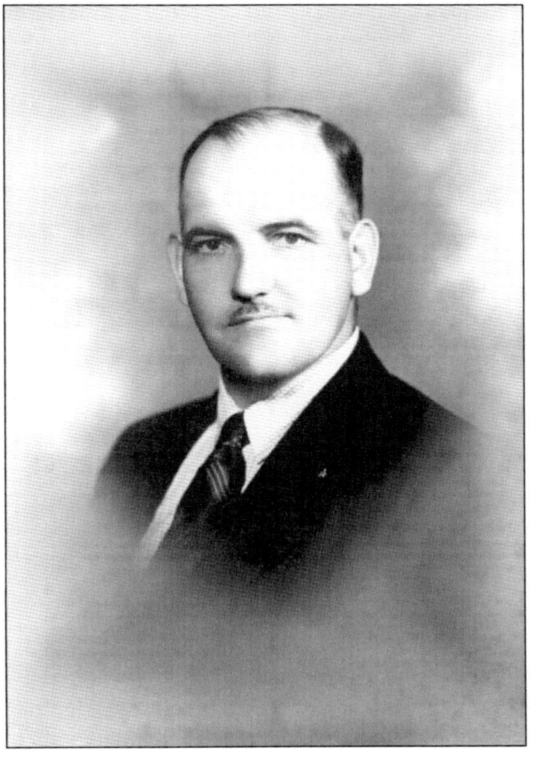

ERNEST MORGAN. Ernest Morgan, born in 1899, was a Bow native, going to school at the Bow Bog one-room schoolhouse. He was a locomotive fireman for the B&M until he was laid off in 1929, a casualty of the Great Depression. He and his wife, Lottie, built a small grocery store and gas station at Bow Mills. In 1940, Morgan was rehired by the railroad and worked as an engineer. He served the town as fire warden and as a representative to the New Hampshire legislature. Morgan was the fifth generation of his family to be buried in the Alexander Cemetery.

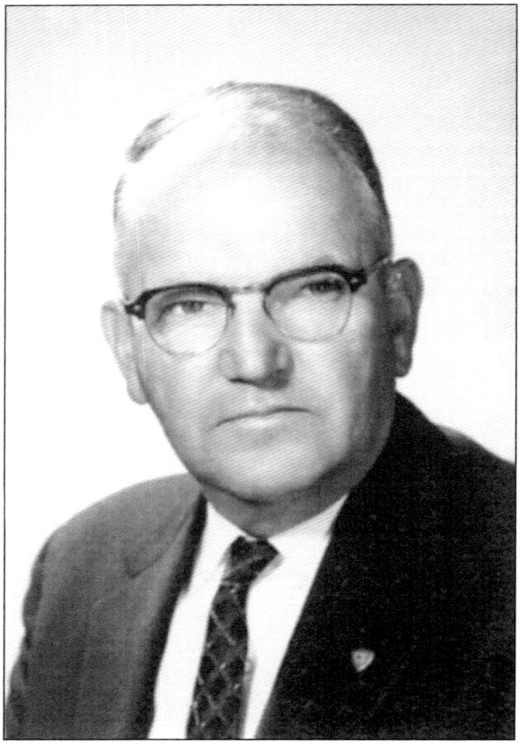

MANY HATS. Asa Morgan died May 2, 1994, after a life of service to the town of Bow, Merrimack County, and the state of New Hampshire. He was a selectman from 1933 to 1947, a New Hampshire state representative for four years, and a New Hampshire state senator for two years. Locally he was the overseer of the poor for 20 years and a school district moderator for 20 years. As a surveyor, he helped plan many housing areas in Bow.

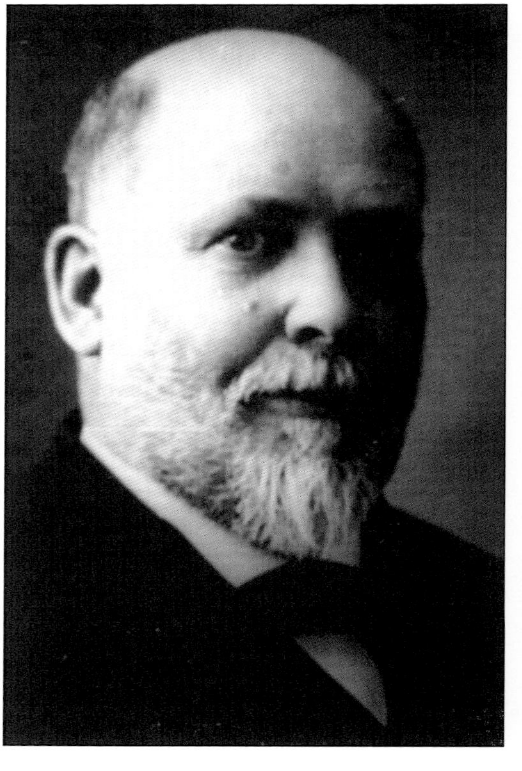

BOW TO WASHINGTON. During his lifetime of 71 years, Henry M. Baker was a mill operator with Mark Upton. He established the Garvins Falls Electric Company but sold his interest to the Manchester Traction Light and Power and became a prominent lawyer in Washington, D.C. He became a New Hampshire state senator, was admitted to the bar of the supreme court in 1882, and in 1886 was appointed judge advocate general for the New Hampshire National Guard. Baker was elected for two terms, 1892 and 1894. From 1903 through 1908 he was vice president then president of the New Hampshire Historical Society. Baker was an avid historian and had many articles published.

OUR BEST INTERESTS. Eric Anderson was first elected to the New Hampshire House of Representatives in November 1996. He has been re-elected six times and is still serving today. Anderson has been a member of the powerful House Finance Committee for the last eight years. He has also served on the Merrimack County Nursing Home Study Committee and has been vice-chairman of the Merrimack County Delegation. Anderson has also served the Town of Bow as a selectmen since 1986, and a library trustee since 2002.

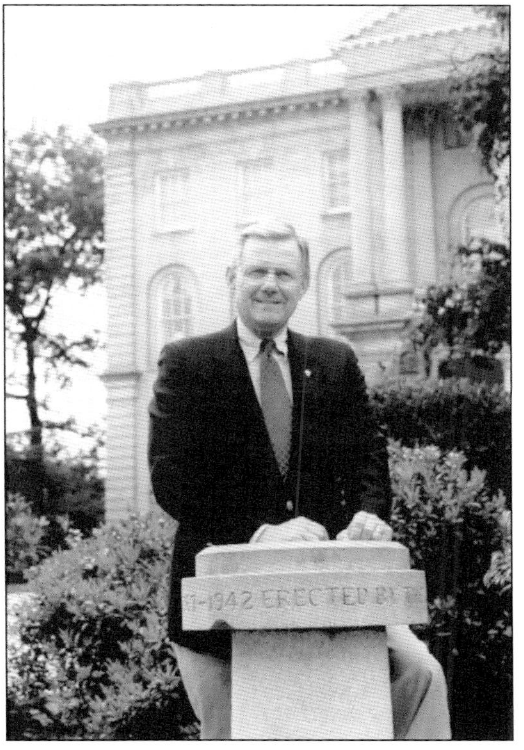

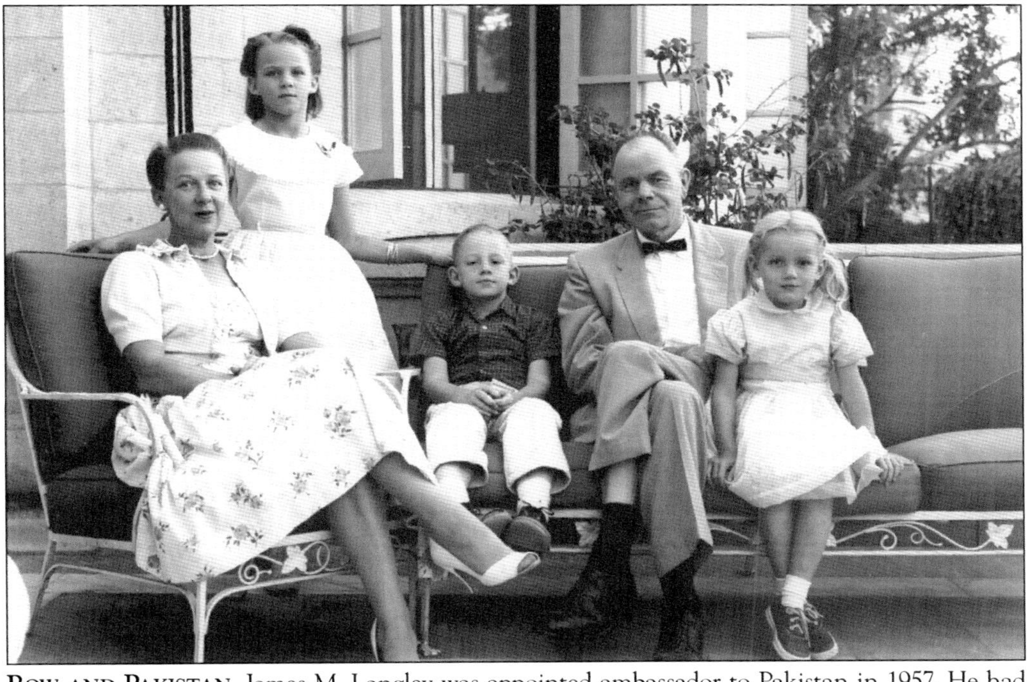

BOW AND PAKISTAN. James M. Langley was appointed ambassador to Pakistan in 1957. He had been owner and publisher of the *Concord Monitor* for three decades. In this photograph, Langley is shown at the embassy in Karachi with his wife, Lois, and children, Jane (standing), Jere, and Jill.

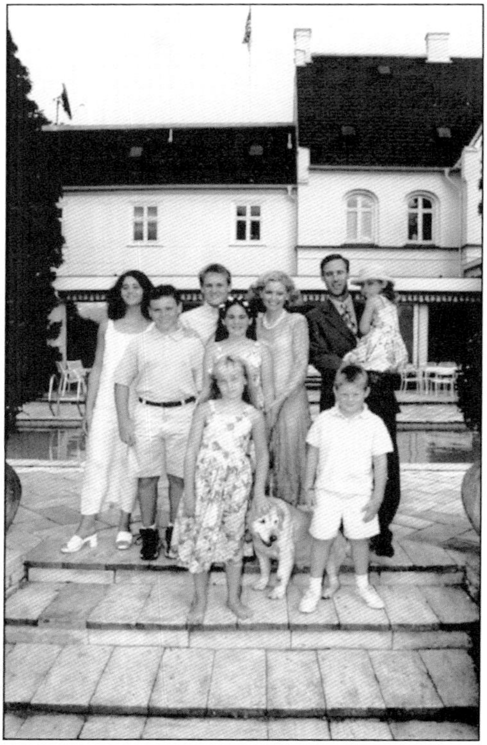

Bow, Washington, and Denmark. Richard Swett served in Congress as the New Hampshire 2nd District Representative from 1991 to 1995. After that he was selected to serve as ambassador to Denmark, arriving there in 1998. This picture was taken in front of the ambassador's residence in Copenhagen. Pictured from left to right are (first row) Kismet and Atticus; (second row) Keaton and Chanteclaire; (third row) Chelsea, Sebastian, Katrina, Richard, and Sunday.

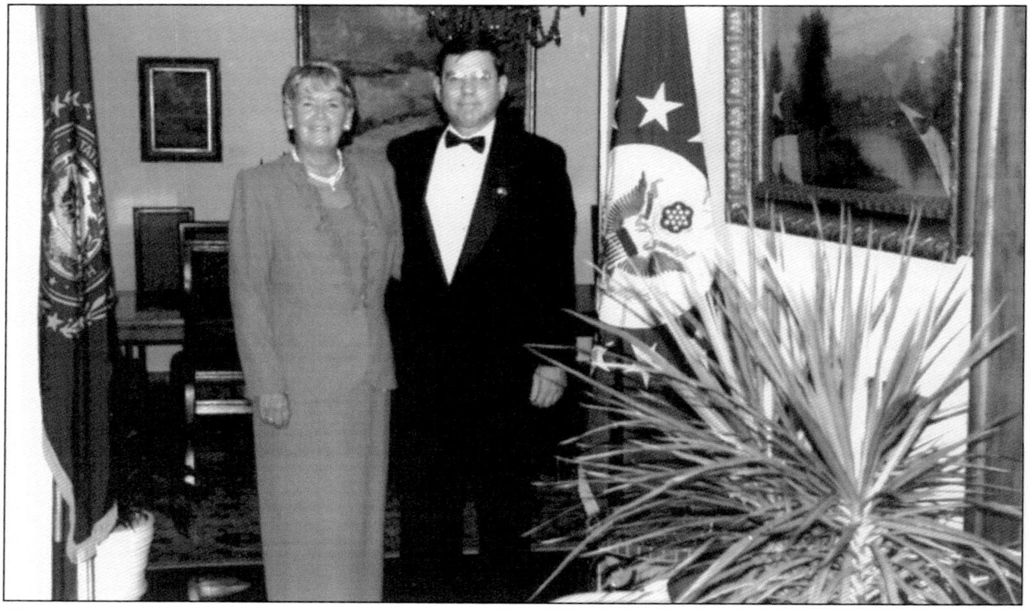

Report from Trinidad. Edward E. Shumaker III, better know as "Terry," was ambassador to the Republic of Trinidad and Tobago, appointed by Pres. William Clinton in 1997. He is a graduate of Dartmouth College and Boston University School of Law. Following his tour of duty, Shumaker returned to practicing law. He is shown here, in Trinidad and Tobago, with his wife, Molly.

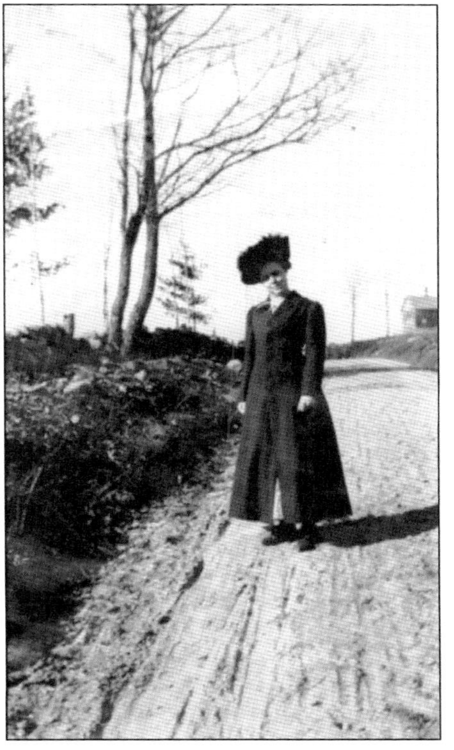

PAY HERE. Annie Colby Foote, daughter of Dr. Frank Colby, was town clerk from 1923 until her death in 1962. She was also the town librarian for 23 years, tax collector for 15 years, and school treasurer for 42 years. She also served as a president of the New Hampshire Cities and Town Clerks Association. This picture was taken at the fire station of Logging Hill Road, about 1910.

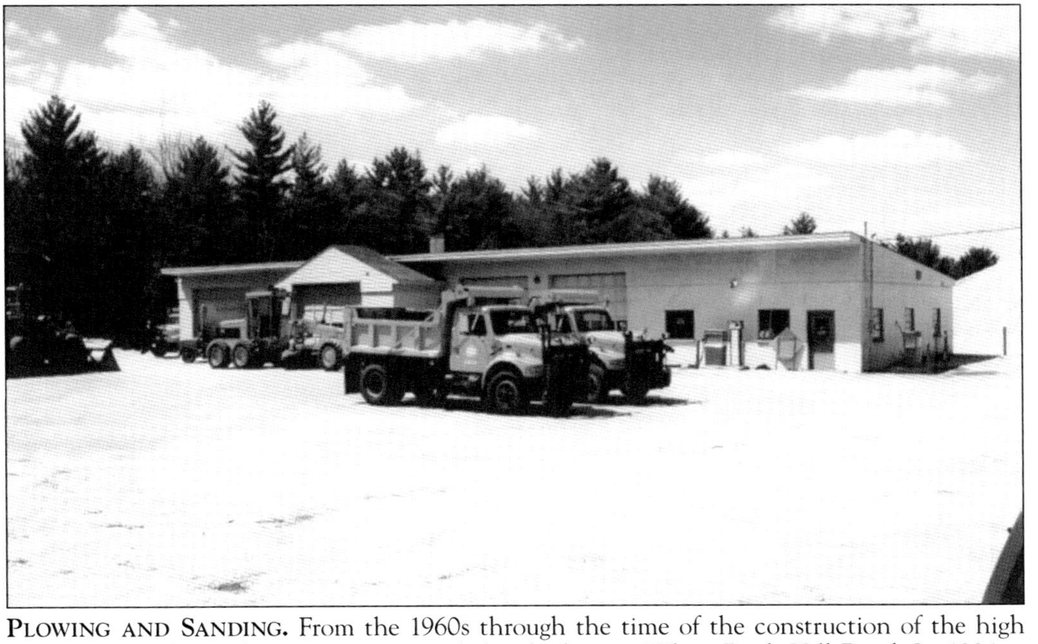

PLOWING AND SANDING. From the 1960s through the time of the construction of the high school, the highway department occupied this facility on White Rock Hill Road. In 1994, a vote was made to build a high school in town. The site selected for the high school necessitated moving the highway garage. The highway department was moved to a building on Robinson Road. The high school basketball court is now on the site of this garage.

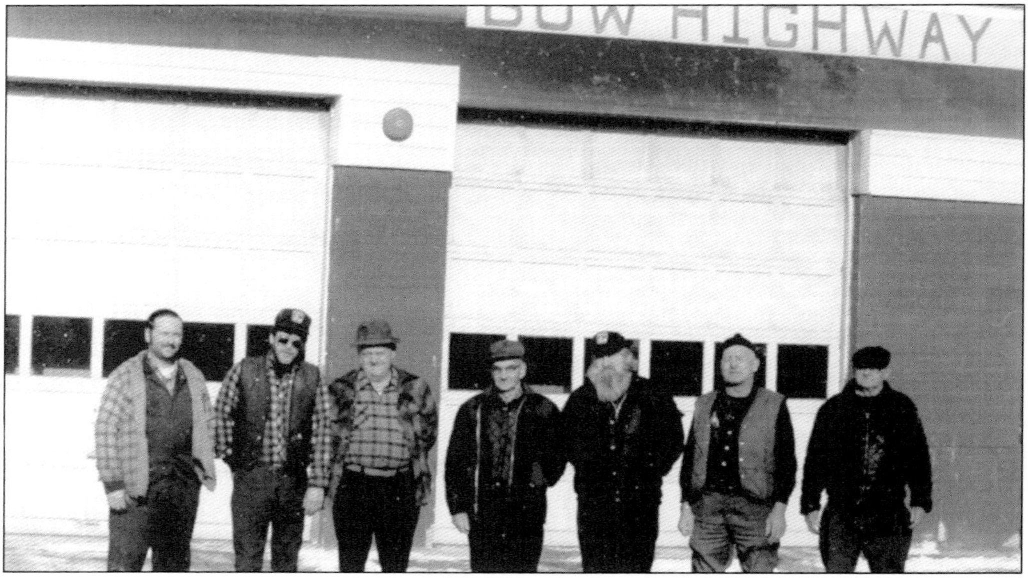

ON THE ROAD AGAIN. People travel everyday on the roads and highways; getting there safely is everyone's objective. An early picture shows the road agent, Paul Lindquist, with some of his crew. It is their job to see that the town's infrastructure is maintained, replaced, improved, and whatever else is necessary. Pictured in the photograph, from left to right, are Leonard Virgin, Donald Dunlap, road agent Paul Lindquist, Walter Alexander, Mark Goodwin, James Ordway, and Oscar Merrill.

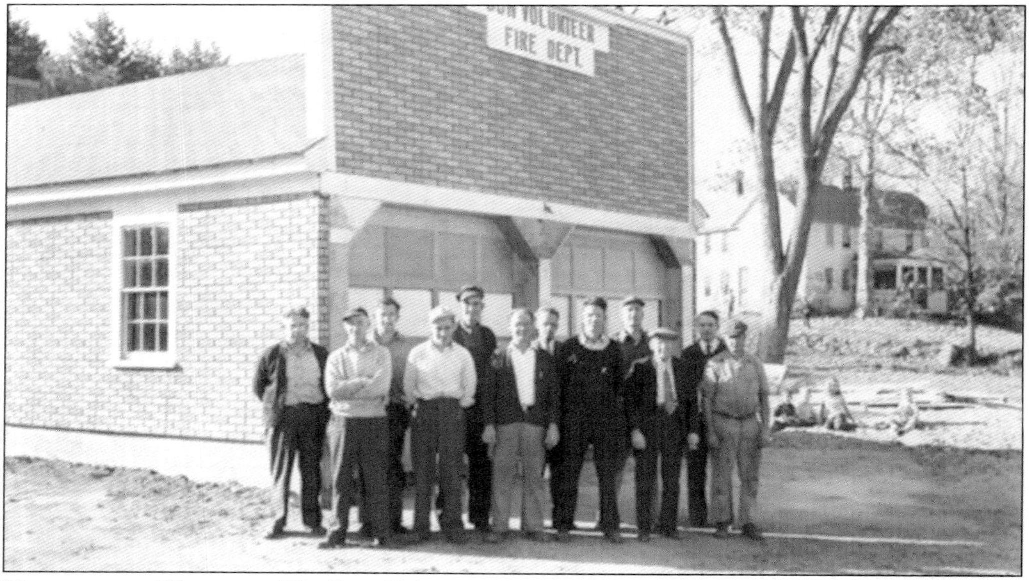

VOLUNTEERS WELCOME. The Bow Volunteer Fire Department was organized in 1945 following the March 13, 1945, town meeting. Charter members, as shown in 1946, from left to right, are Arthur Sargent, John Young, Earl Coulter, Elgie Goodwin, Maurice W. Whittier, Howard Day, Chief Harold W. Howe, Philip Sargent, Edward Cole, Norman Kilmister, Wilber Vaughn, and Harry Adams. They are standing in front of a two-stall garage at the foot of Logging Hill, which was originally the Morgan filling station and store.

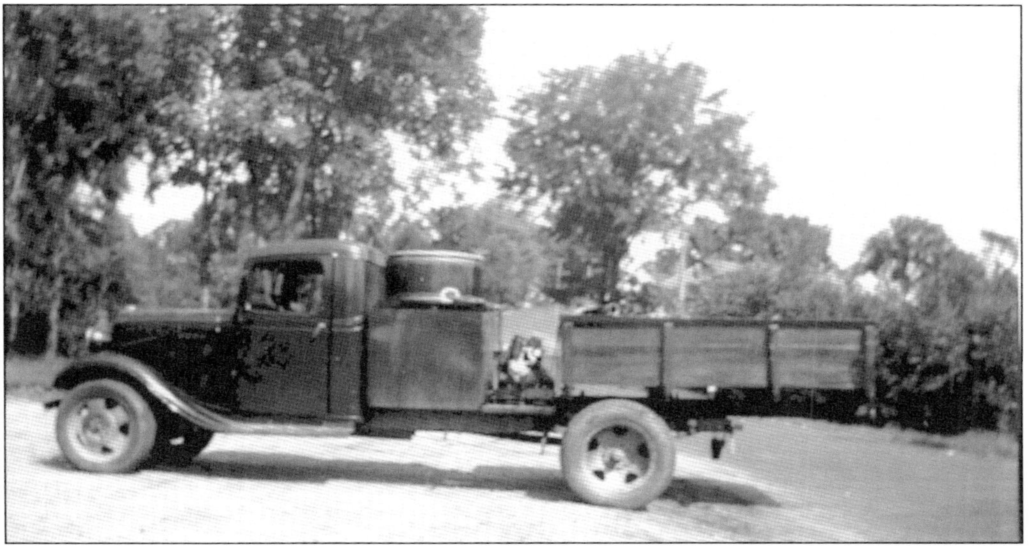

PARTS AND PIECES. According to a 1939 *Concord Monitor* article, Bow got a "well-equipped fire truck." Through voluntary subscriptions and $1,000 in tax money, enterprising citizens went to junk yards and second hand places to come up the makings of a complete fire truck. Fire warden Ernest Morgan was extremely pleased for the department to have its own equipment. Previously, Bow had to rely on the Concord Fire Department to answer calls.

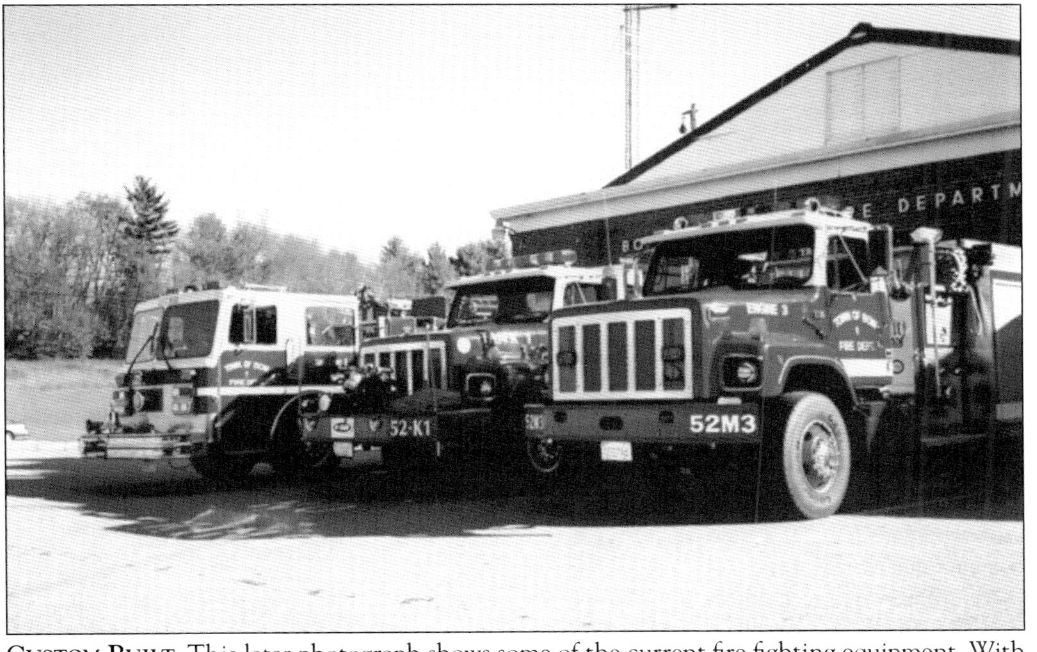

CUSTOM BUILT. This later photograph shows some of the current fire fighting equipment. With increased fire and medical calls, the department equipment and personnel have necessarily multiplied. Under Chief Dana Abbot and assistant chief Richard Pistey, volunteer coverage has been changing over to the hiring of permanent full time personnel.

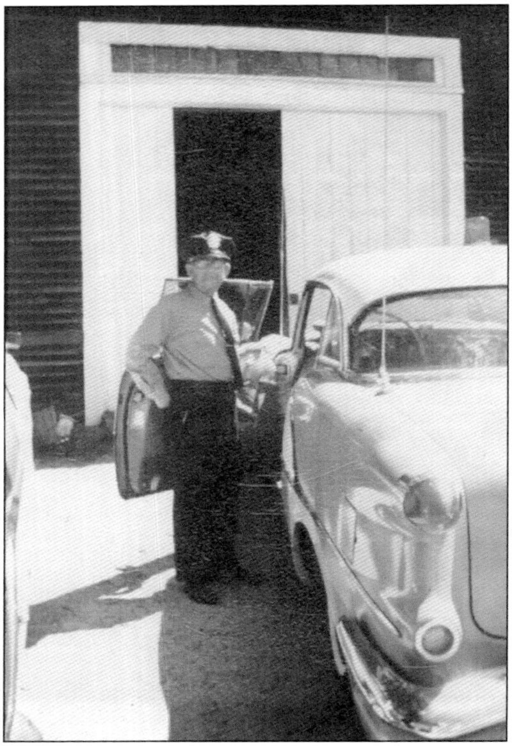

The Blue Light Special. Bill Colby, special police officer, stands by his cruiser ready to answer the call. Early Bow constables like Thomas Rollings in 1727, and John Carr in 1767, provided their own transportation. Horses, wagons, and surries all gave way to the automobile. Constables became special officers and patrolmen. Names such as Colby, Morgan, Geer, Ordway, Bailey, Cheney, and many more have served the police department well.

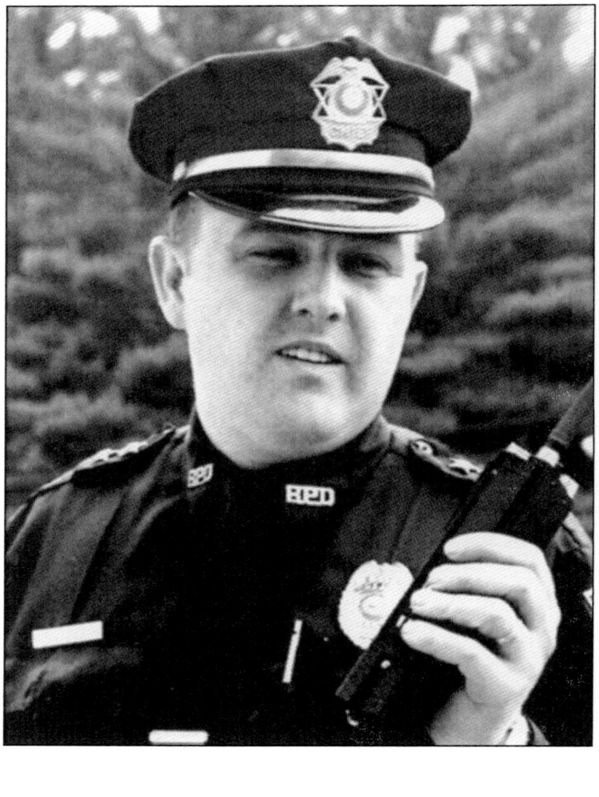

Full Time. Gary D. Nylen, a Bow resident and former Concord police officer, was chosen as Bow's first full-time patrolman in 1969 and was appointed chief the following year. Nylen, a graduate of the New Hampshire Police Academy, Command Training Institute, and the FBI National Academy, holds a bachelor's degree in management and economics from Franklin Pierce College. The department consisted of Nylen and 12 dedicated special officers during the early 1970s.

Eight

Remembering

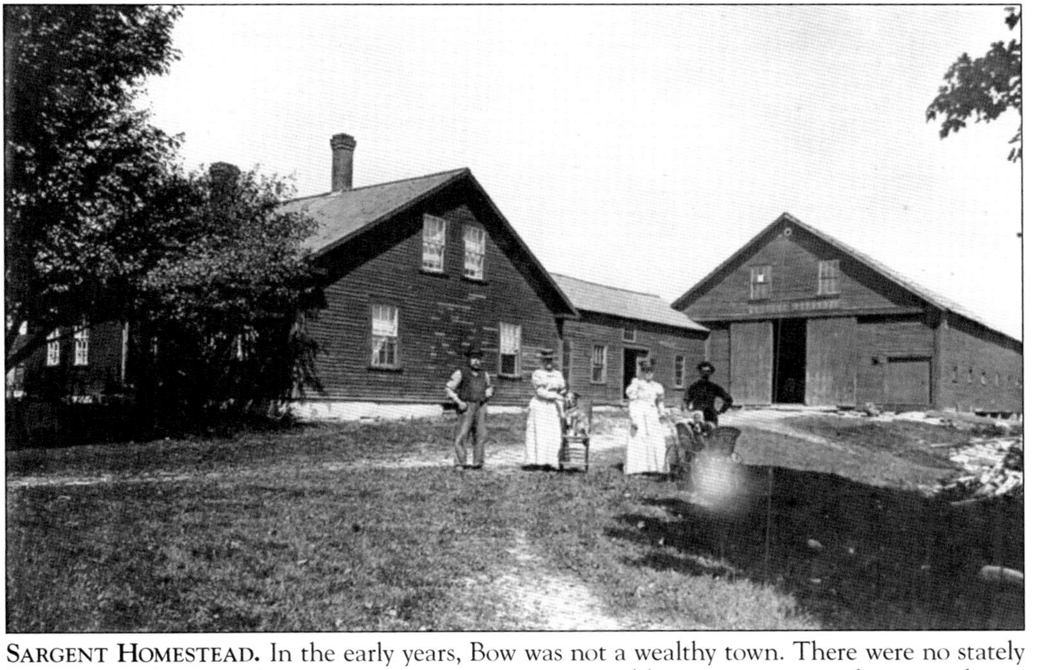

Sargent Homestead. In the early years, Bow was not a wealthy town. There were no stately homes around a central town square, no mansions owned by prosperous merchants, and very few fancy carriages. The people got by with few luxuries. Despite the long workdays, there were some times of leisure. Games, parades, and even posing for family photographs were times to be enjoyed. Here are three generations of one such Bow family standing in front of the Sargent homestead in 1897. From left to right are Cyrus and Maria Wheeler, grandparents; Samuel and Florence (Wheeler) Sargent, parents; and F. Marguerite Sargent in the carriage. Samuel was noted for his work as a stonemason, volunteering his skills for a barn raising in Dunbarton in 1879. Both Samuel and Cyrus served the town as selectmen.

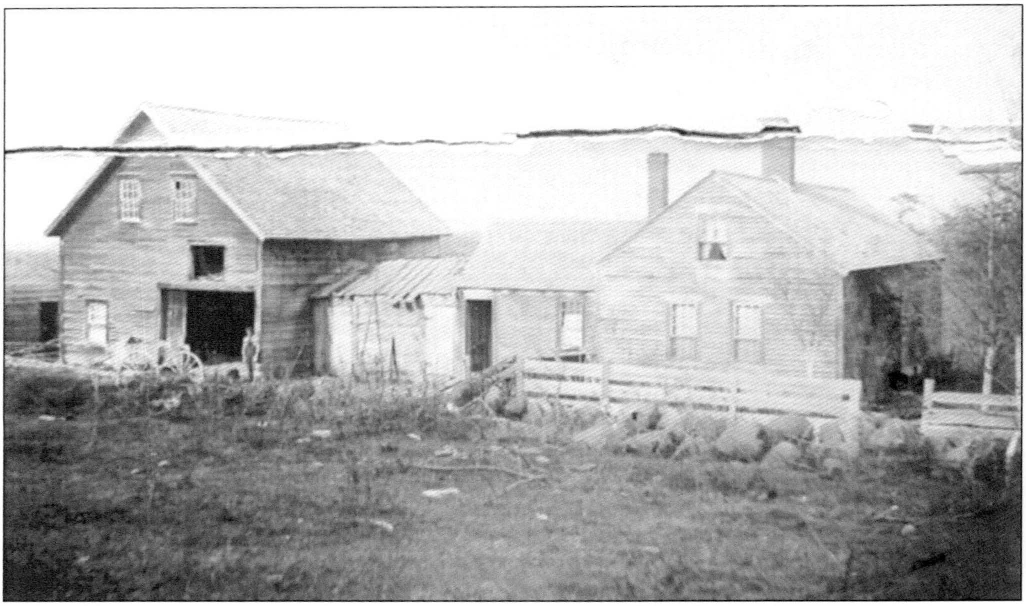

MAYS HOMESTEAD. The homestead at 51 Grandview Road, now owned by Mary Foote, is thought to be the oldest house in town. When the Footes moved to the farm in 1947, there was no running water, electricity, or heat. During renovations, the Footes found a beam with the date 1747. Unfortunately many of the old features such as the Dutch oven, floorboards, and original fireplace were beyond repair and had to be replaced.

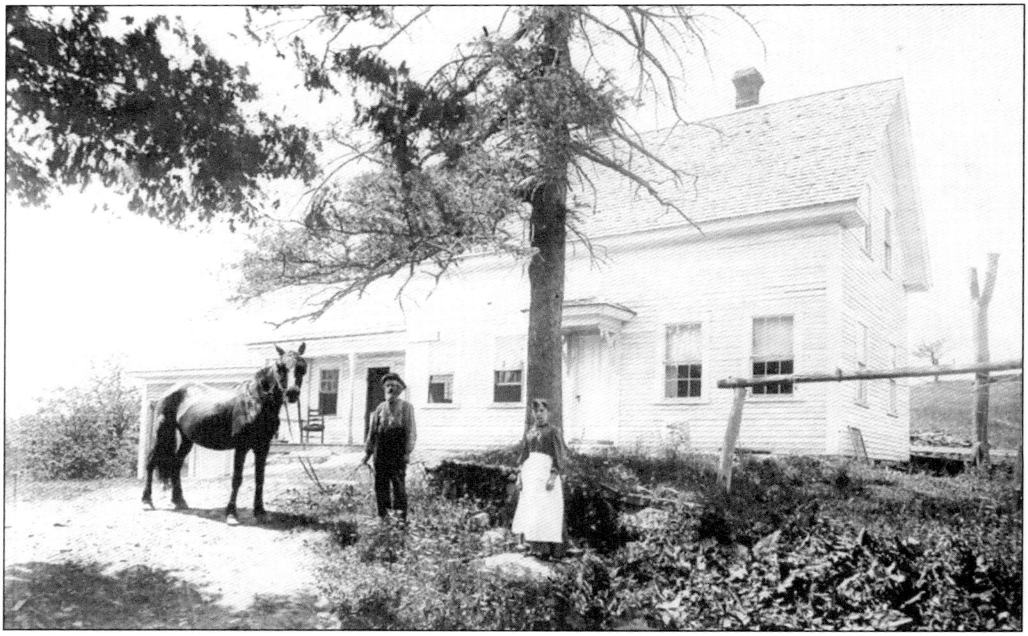

HAMMOND HOMESTEAD. This 1883 photograph shows Charles Hammond and his 20-year-old daughter Junia with the family horse. Hammond was a postmaster and operated the post office out of the house seen in the photograph. He and his wife Fannie are both buried behind the homestead in the Hammond Cemetery. Nancy Knapp now lives in the home.

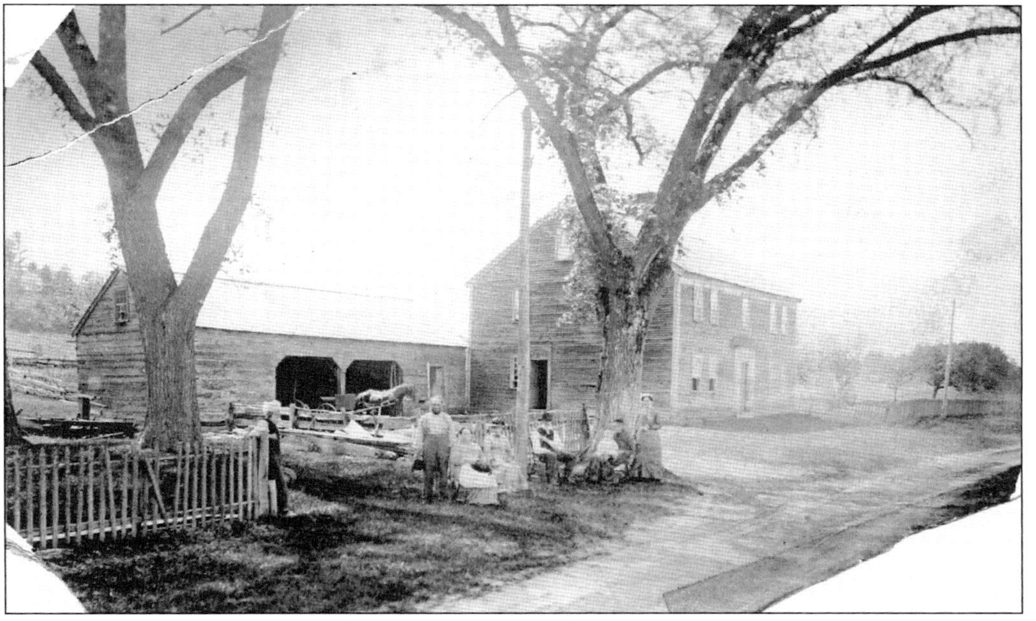

NOYES FARM. Hiram Noyes and family are seen enjoying the day at their home on River Road. A horse and carriage stand ready for the next trip or visit. Most homes of this vintage were plain board and shingle homes with none of the special exterior trimmings found today. Chances are the lumber for this house came from the several Noyes family sawmills.

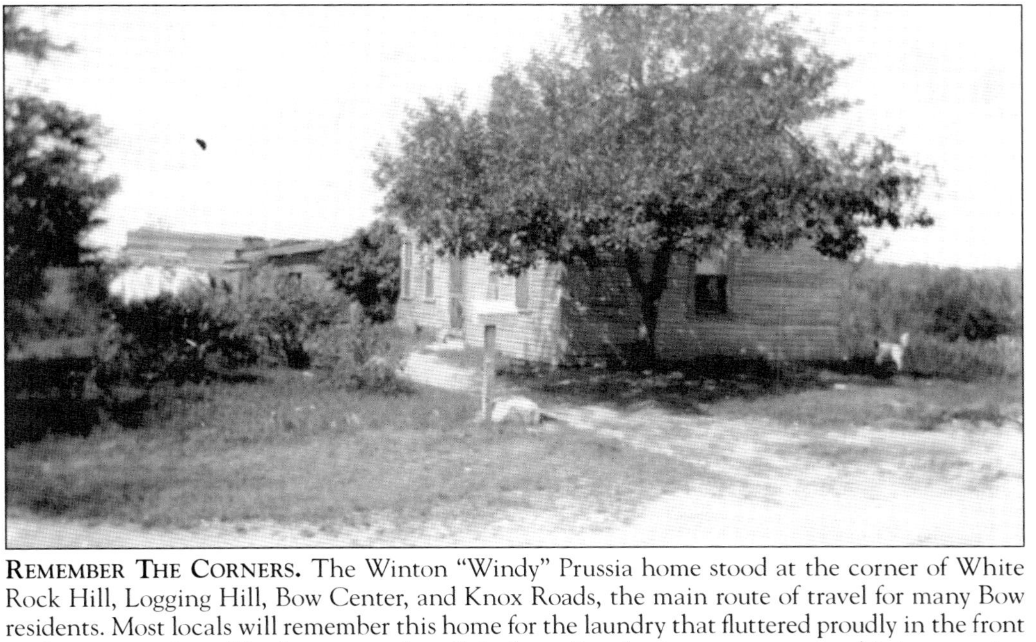

REMEMBER THE CORNERS. The Winton "Windy" Prussia home stood at the corner of White Rock Hill, Logging Hill, Bow Center, and Knox Roads, the main route of travel for many Bow residents. Most locals will remember this home for the laundry that fluttered proudly in the front yard on sunny days. The house was demolished to allow for improvements to this intersection following the construction of the high school. The well serves as irrigation for Rotary Park, which was built on the site.

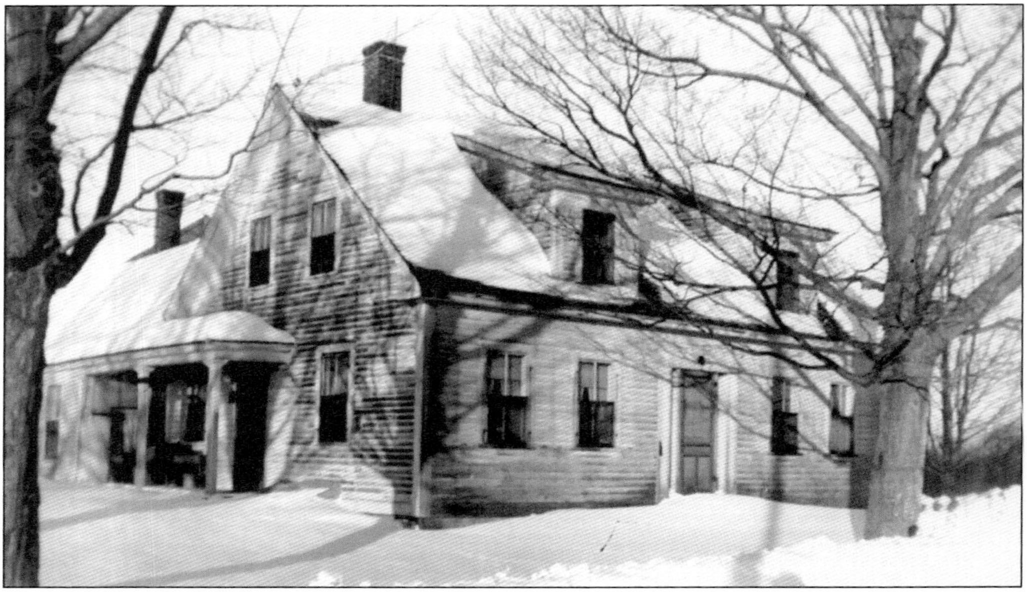

Meeting House Corner. Perley Clough's farm was at the corner of White Rock Hill Road and Page Road. It was one of the few remaining active farms following the Civil War. The Clough barn was the old Bow Meeting House, which had been moved by 20 yoke of oxen across White Rock Hill Road. Clough was the highway agent in 1894 and served from 1926 to 1928 as a representative to the legislature. The house remains today, but the barn was razed in 1955.

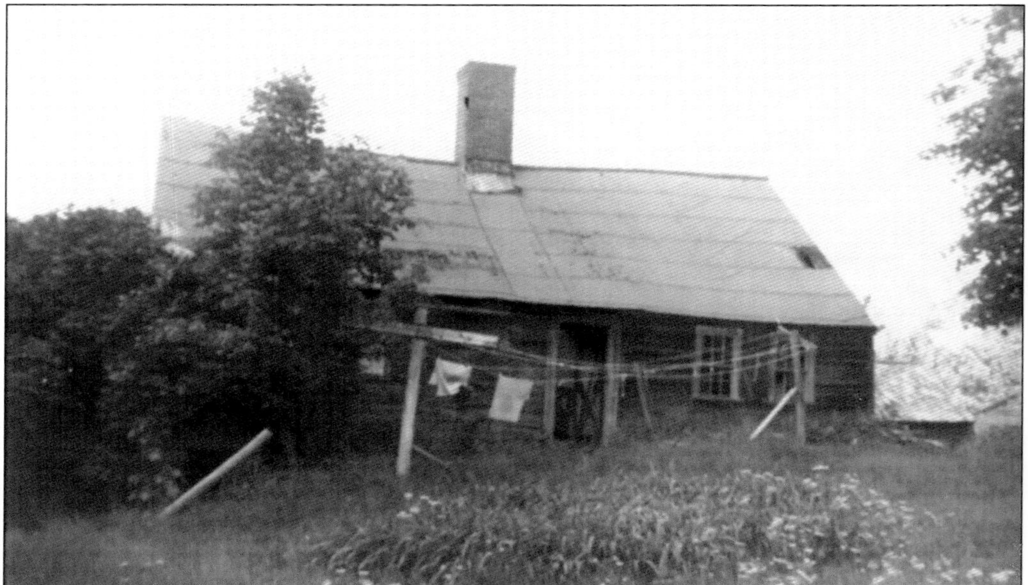

Town line dwelling. This home was built in 1765 and is one of the oldest houses in town. In 1777, the property was bought by John Nichols, whose family operated the Nichols-Colby Sawmill on Putney Meadow Pond. In the ell of the house is a room built like a jail cell that, as the story is told, was used to confine the Nichols' daughter who occasionally had violent fits. The home has now collapsed and only a portion of it remains.

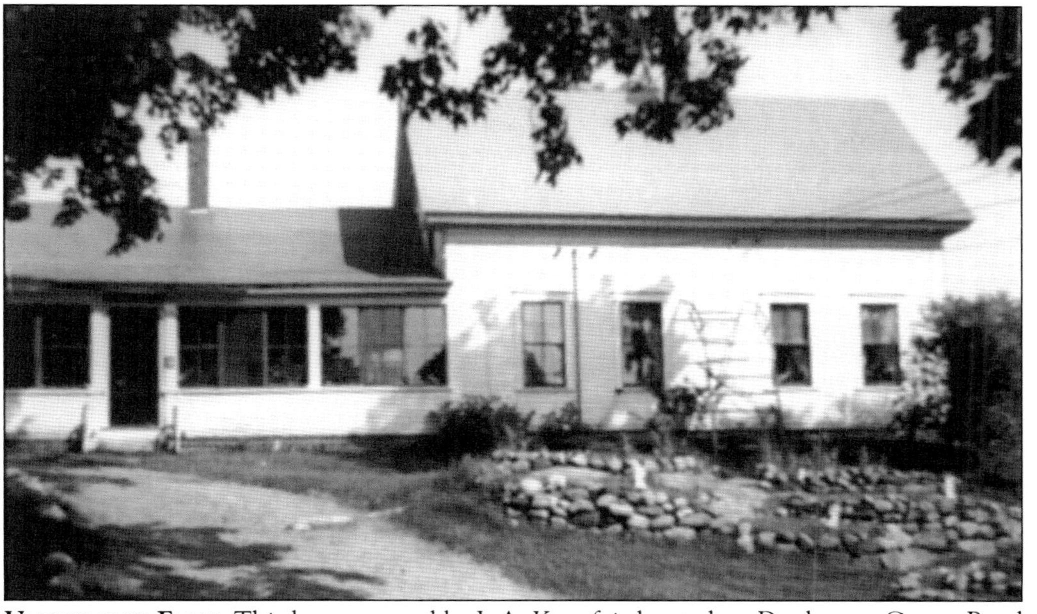

VALLEYNOOK FARM. This home, owned by J. A. Knauf, is located on Dunbarton Center Road and is now owned by Susan and Michael Wheeler. On the left, behind the porch is the kitchen and enclosed two-story shed—all that remains of the oldest part of the house dating back to the late 1700s. The main portion of the house was built in 1840. The home was deeded with 100 acres and typifies Bow's early farms consisting of "100 acres, more or less."

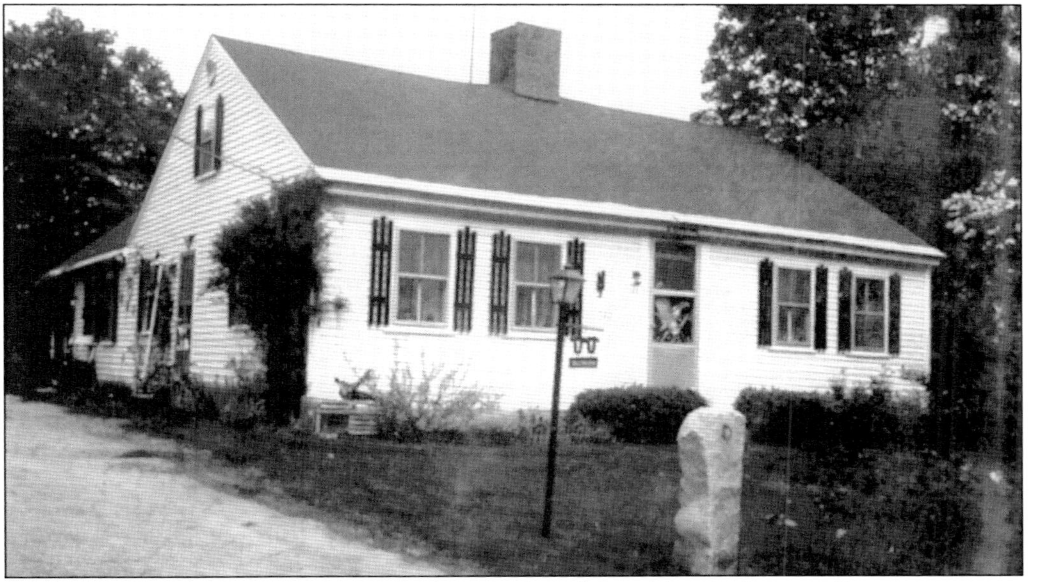

ORIGINAL HISTORY. This home on White Rock Hill Road has had many illustrious owners. It was the home of Francis Carr, who purchased this land during the second division of Bow; Capt. Benjamin Bean, who was recruited for the Bow Militia in 1776; and John W. Goodhue, who was a selectman from 1858 to 1859 and town clerk from 1856 to 1858. Until recently it was the home of Katherine Saltmarsh. The new owners of the home have made extensive renovations and additions.

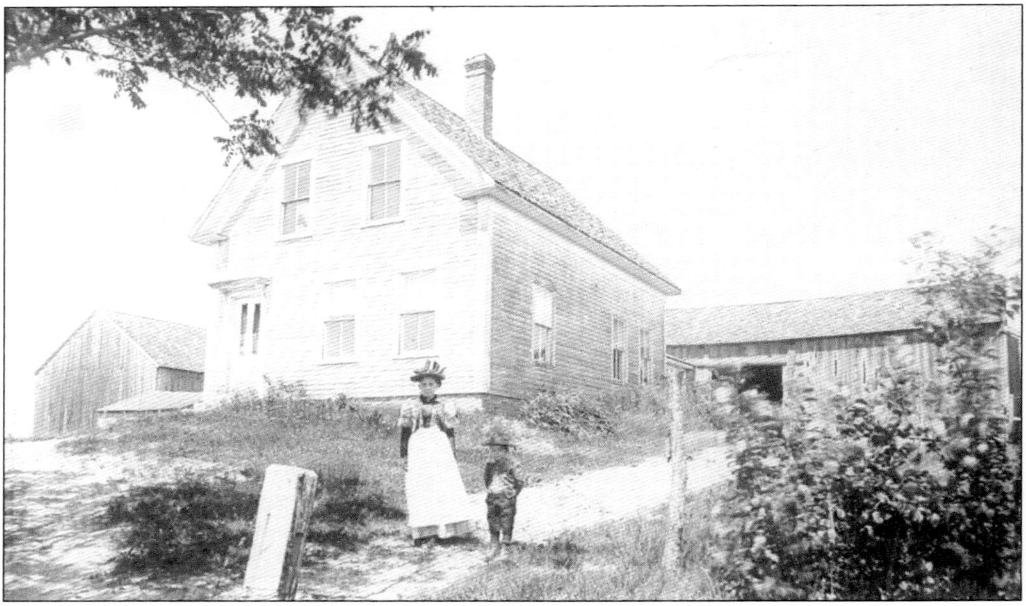

VISITORS. This house at 105 Brown Hill Road has had a long list of owners through the years and is currently the home of the Haubrichs. In the second decade of the 20th century, this was the home of Fred Shedd, who later became a selectman and a representative to the legislature. The two people seen in this early 1900s photograph are believed to be Junia Hammond and Roscoe Johnson, visitors to the home.

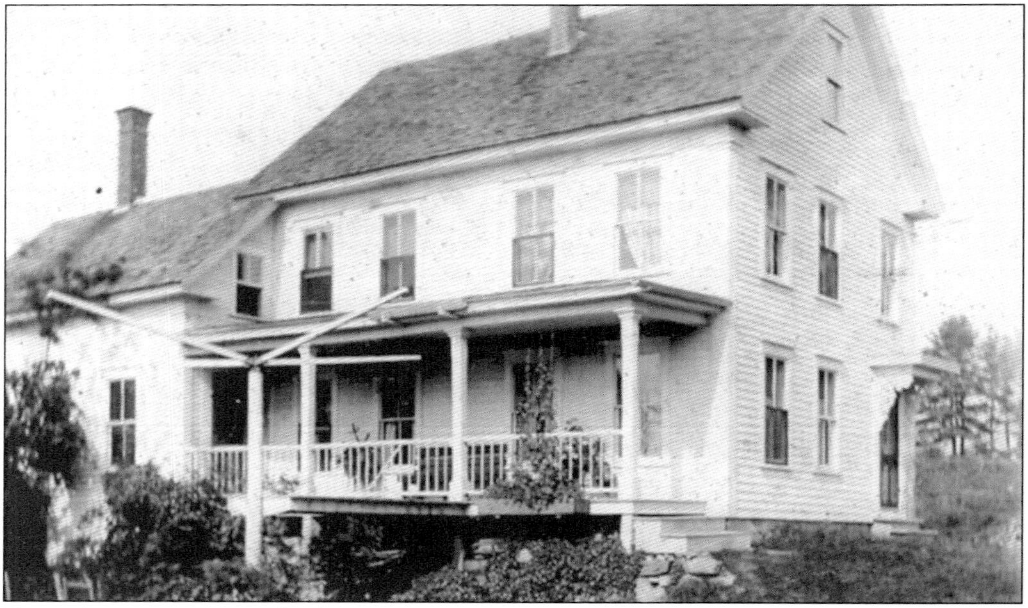

EARLY EXERCISE BUFF. This house on South Bow Road was the home of Edwin Colby, a noted schoolteacher, selectman, and legislator. He used to regularly walk from his home to the trolley stop in Hooksett, a distance of about five miles, and to school. Residents remember Colby refusing offers of a ride stating, "If I wanted a ride, I've got a horse in my barn and I would have taken it."

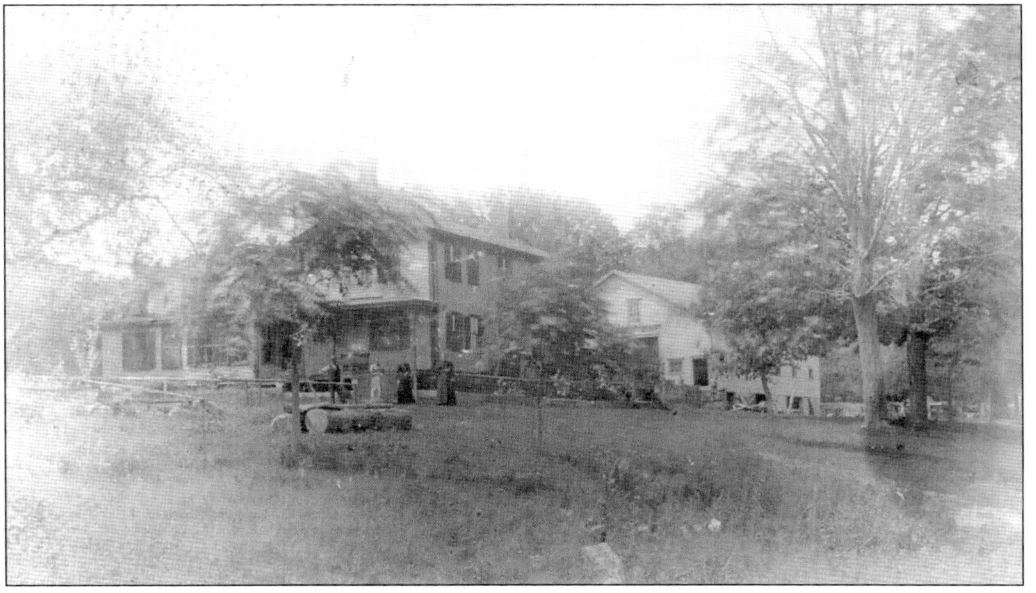

STURDY FOUNDATION. This farm was owned by Andrew Gault and was located on the west side of the Londonderry Turnpike (Route 3-A) at the intersection with Dow Road. Edwin Alexander bought the farm in the early 1900s. Bert and Eva May Alexander lived here until the late 1940s when the house and barn burned to the ground. A new house was built on the old granite cellar hole and, until recently, was owned by Elizabeth Alexander Bailey.

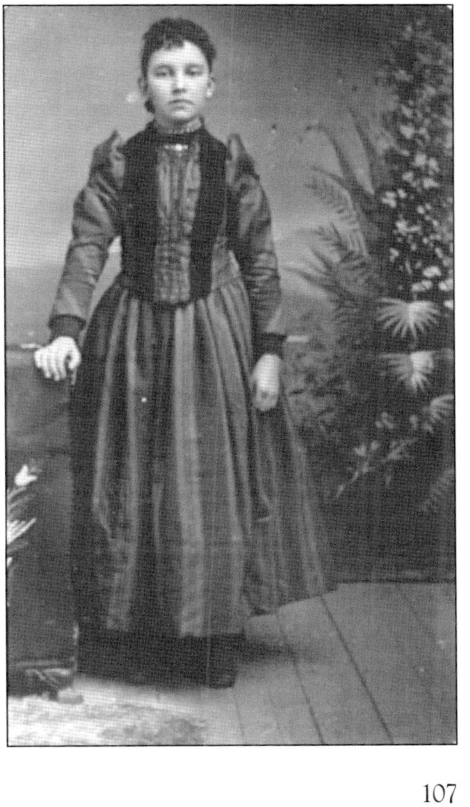

ALL DRESSED UP. Eva May Alexander, all dressed up for the photograph, is one glamorous teenager. Born in 1879, she lived in the family homestead on the Londonderry Turnpike (Route 3-A) across from Dow Road. She received the Boston Post Cane in 1968 at the age of 96. She lived to be 100 years old.

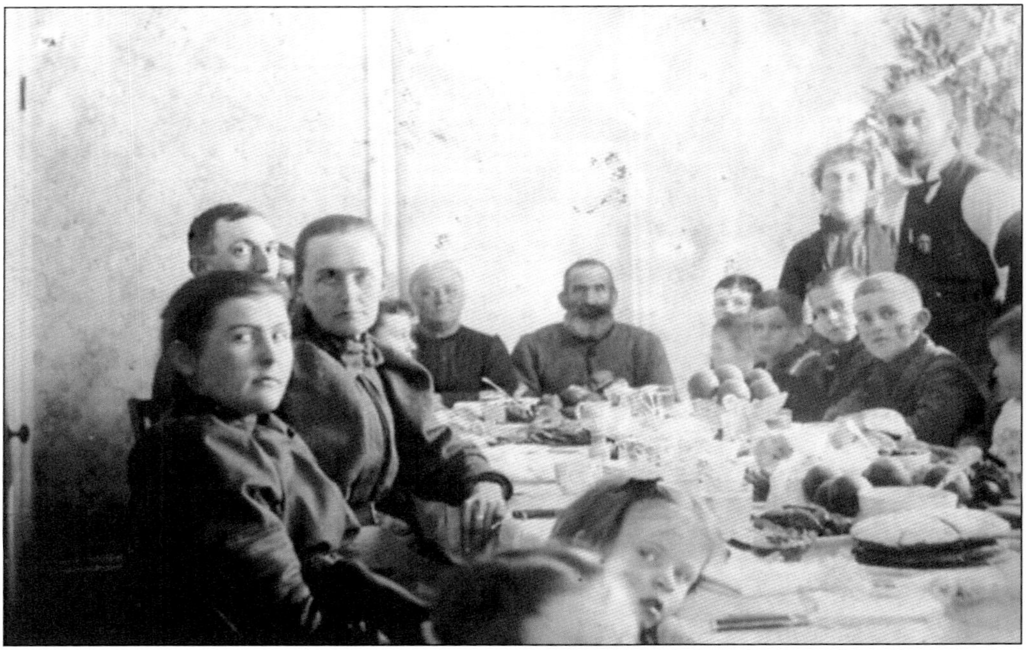

FAMILY LIFE. The Morgan family gathers here to enjoy good food, friendship, and family. Seated at the table in this late 1800s photograph are Ethel (Morgan) Saltmarsh, Laura (Morgan) Noyes, Otis Noyes, Martha (Elliott) Morgan, Asa Morgan, Elsie May (Clifford) Morgan, and Sam Morgan.

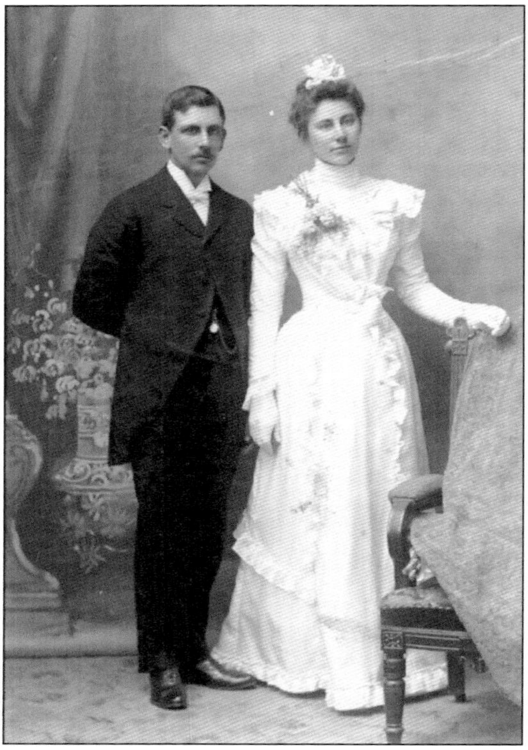

WEDDING DAY. Almond Sterling Colby is shown on his wedding day, March 5, 1899, with his bride Susan Tilton Hoyt. Colby was a lifelong Bow resident who lived on top of Wood Hill. He was a farmer but is remembered for being an avid rabbit hunter who was out at every opportunity with his beagles and his friend Harry Clough.

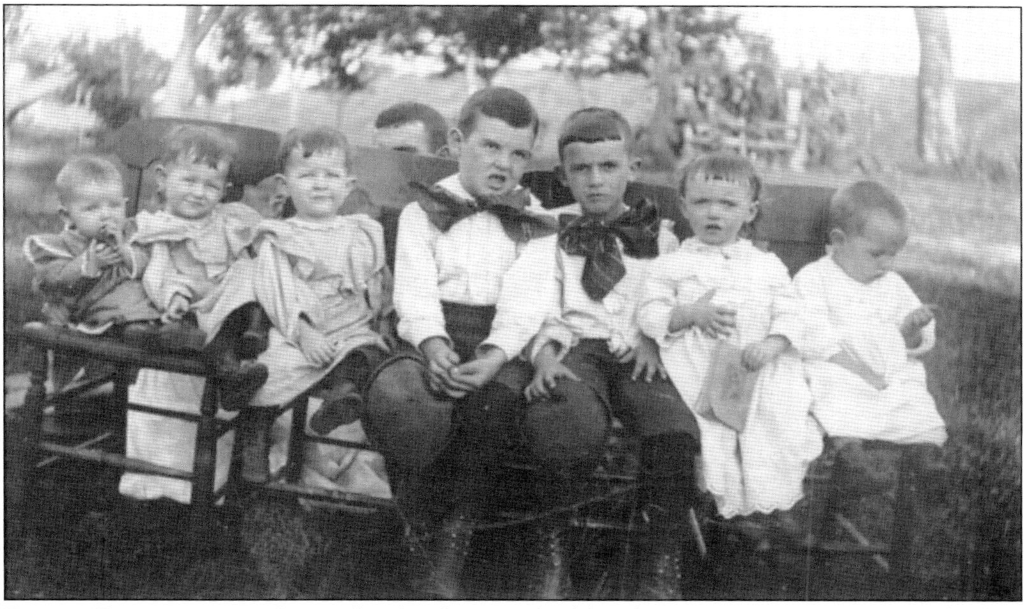

FAMILY PHOTOGRAPH. Group family photographs like this were very common in the late 1890s, the early days of photography. Morgan and Noyes children sit patiently for the picture to be snapped. From left to right are Rena, Nora, and Ella Morgan; Ivo Noyes; Ralph and Vivien Morgan; and Carl Noyes. Hollis Morgan, father of some of the children, hides behind the chairs.

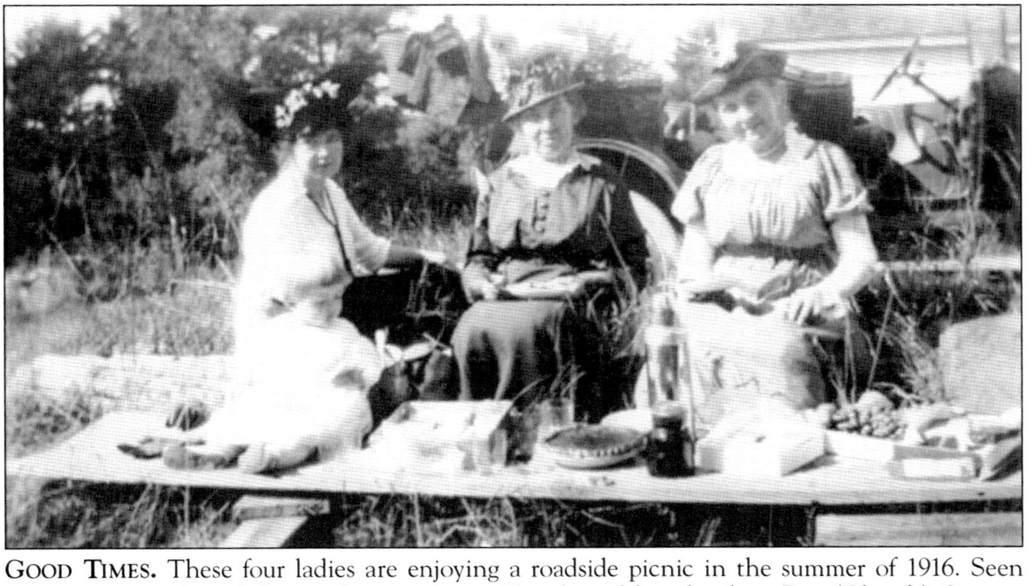

GOOD TIMES. These four ladies are enjoying a roadside picnic in the summer of 1916. Seen in this picture, from left to right, are Anne Clough and her daughter Rae (Clough) Carson, Mrs. Frank Clough, and Eva Allbee. Such roadside repasts were common in the days of dirt roads and low speed limits.

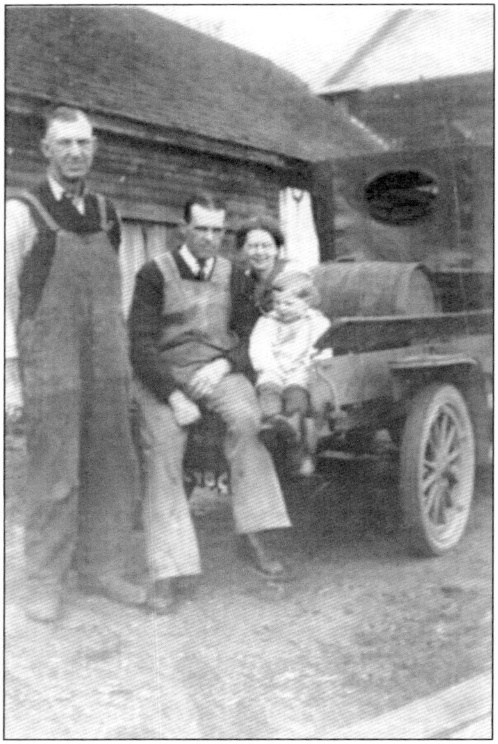

Three Generations. Three generations are seen in this photograph with grandfather Otis Noyes on the left. Son Ivo and his wife, Minnie Fowler Noyes, are standing in the center and their son Adin is seated in the truck. The Noyeses were farmers who lived on River Road. Prior to her marriage, Minnie taught at the River Road School.

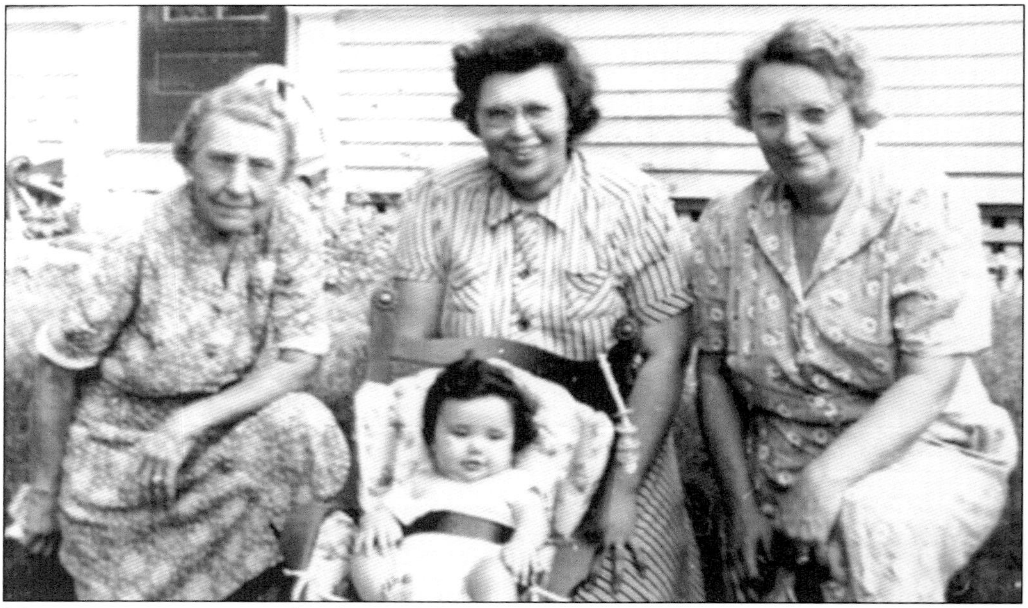

Valleynook Farm. Posed in front of the porch of the Valleynook Farm are four generations of ladies all living under the same roof. Pictured, from left to right, are Emma Wilcox, Gladys (Knauf) Goodsell, Edith (Wilcox) Knauf, and in the rocking chair, Carol Jean Goodsell. Today there is a return to the presence of several generations of a family living together for health and financial reasons.

ELIZABETH ALEXANDER. Elizabeth Bell Alexander Bailey looks across at her home on Londonderry Turnpike (Route 3-A). Bailey was a member of the Grange for 75 years and became famous for her apple pies. When she was called on the phone early in the morning and asked, "What are you doing today?" she would say, "I'm putting on my work clothes to see if they feel like working," said niece Linda Nylen. And work she did, doing her chores and mowing her lawn until her death. She was the last Alexander of her generation in Bow.

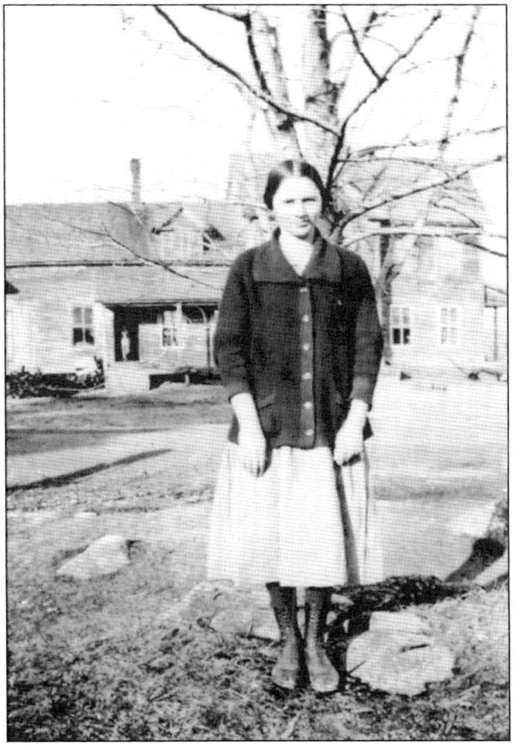

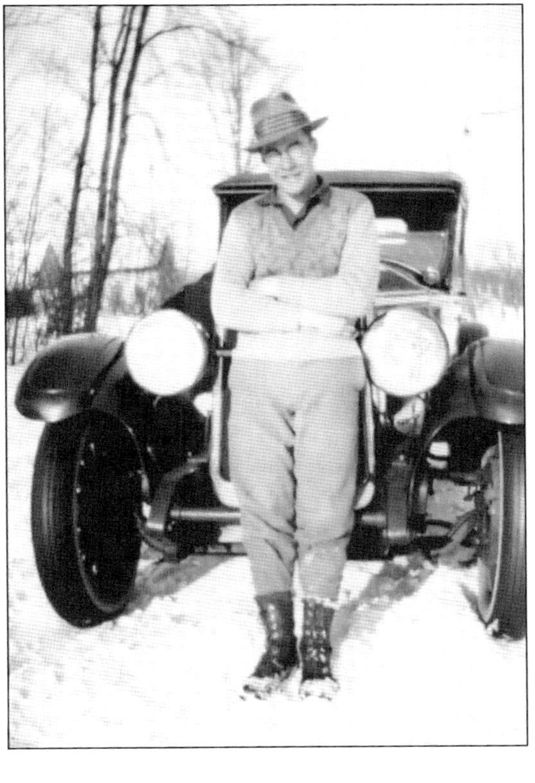

HALSTEAD COLBY. Halstead "Hap" Colby is seen here in front of his trusty car dressed for winter travel. Note the big tires that were winter ready. Colby was a professor of agriculture at the University of New Hampshire. He was an avid sportsman who enjoyed working field dogs and was well-known among dog handlers and breeders. Colby was a dedicated town volunteer, serving on many boards and committees, as well as selectman from 1973 to 1977.

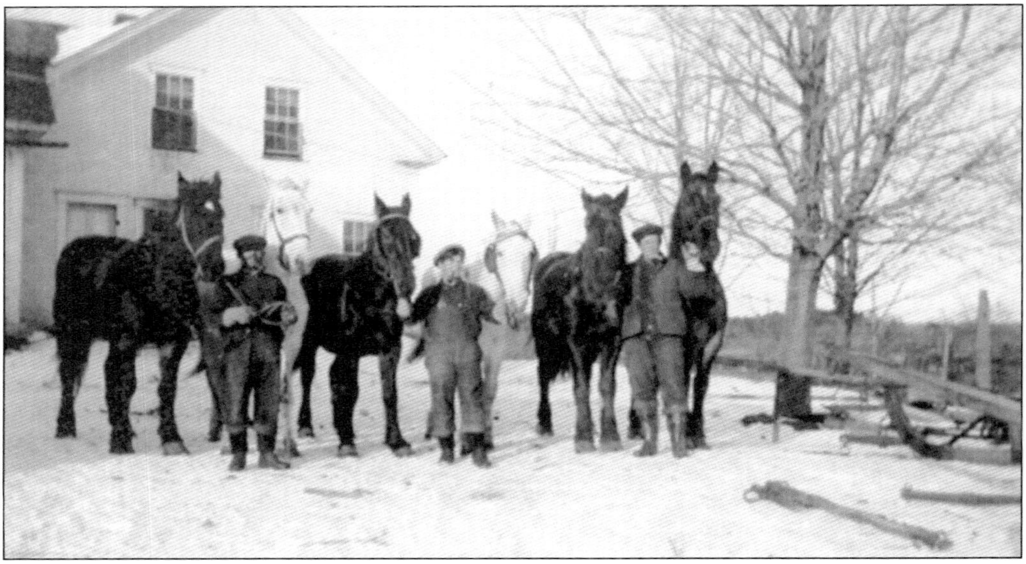

HORSEPOWER. Work or draft horses, such as those shown here at the Ordway Farm in south Bow, were used for multiple purposes. The Ordway family has lived in south Bow for many generations. They were primarily lumberman but also worked as farmers and participated in town government.

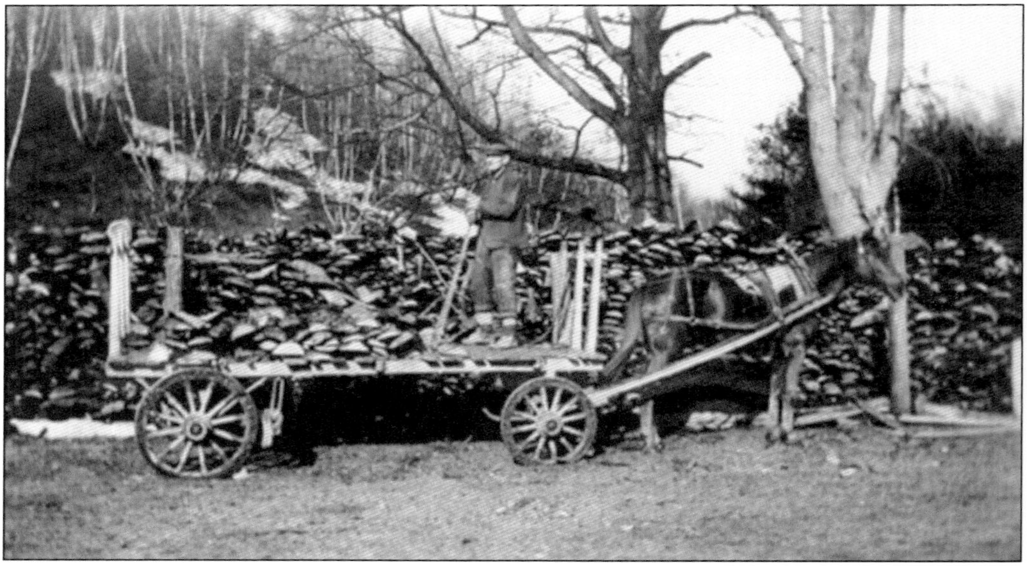

A LONG WAY TO GO. James Osgood Ordway is shown getting ready to load slabs onto his horse-drawn wagon in this photograph taken in south Bow. Ordway was a lifetime lumberman as well as a farmer. He worked for Warren Davis, the largest lumber dealer in Bow, who owned more than 50 woodlots, including what is now Nottingcook Forest.

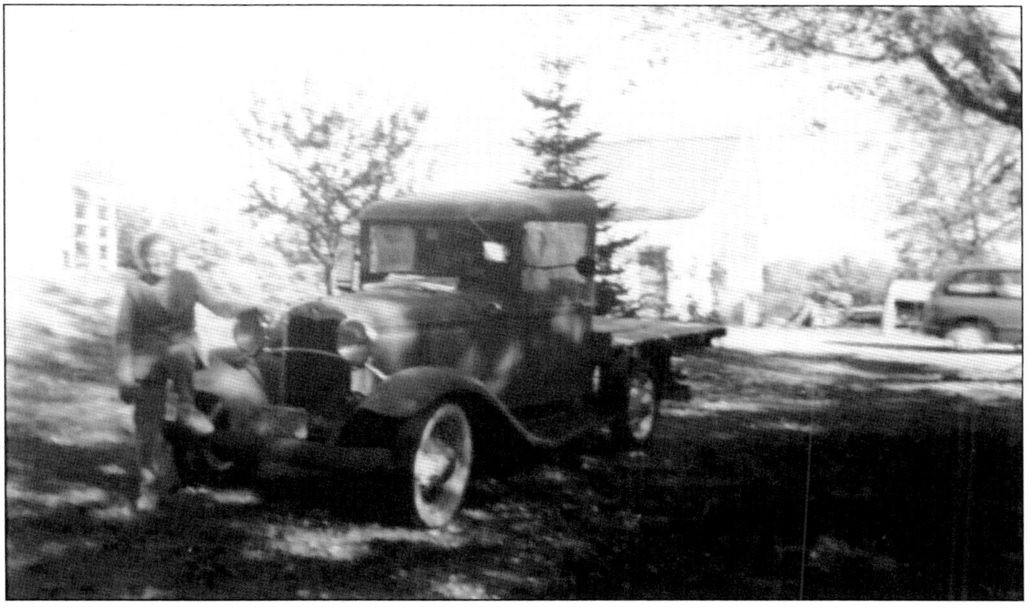

HOME AGAIN ON THE FARM. This 1936 Model B Ford truck was originally purchased by Warren Alexander for work on the farm. It started out as a sedan delivery truck and was converted to a hay truck. It was sold to Eric Anderson in 1949. Anderson kept the truck in his barn until 1984, when he sold it back to Alexander. Verna Alexander is shown standing next to the restored truck at the farm on Robinson Road. One of her grandsons Rick owns and runs the truck today.

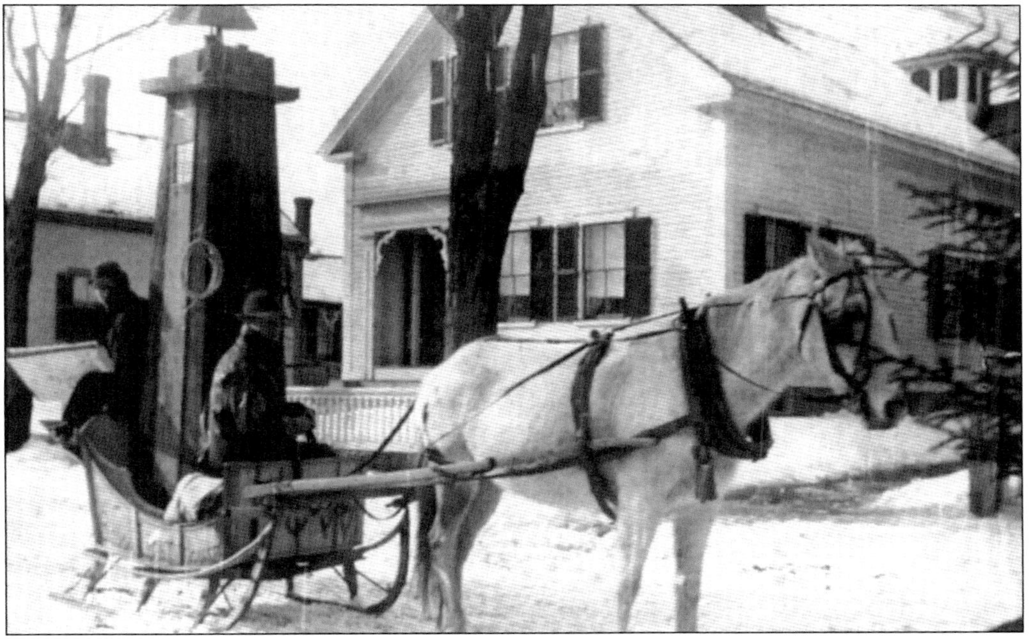

BOW LIGHTHOUSE. The history and humor behind the "Bow Lighthouse" have been lost to the ages, but what a story it must have been. What is known is that Bert Clough is driving the sleigh and he is in a parade lineup heading towards downtown Concord. The date is most likely around 1900.

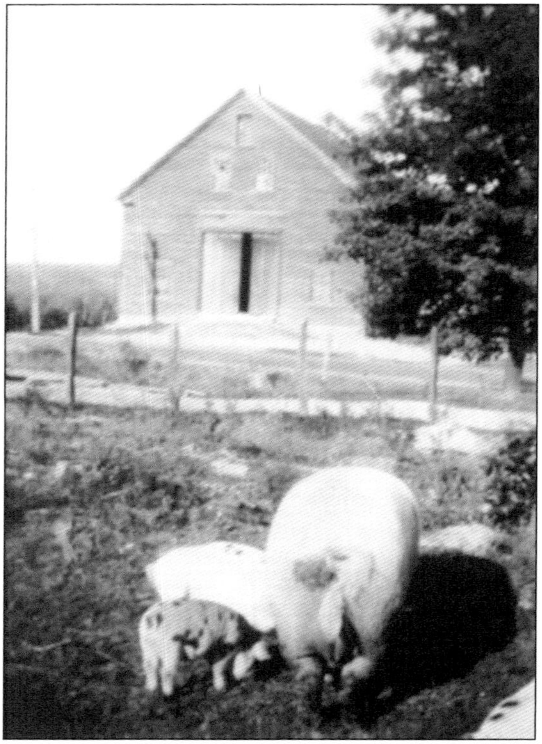

Bow Navy Yard. These hogs are happily grazing in their pasture at the Alexander Farm on Route 3-A. In the early days, loose hogs were a problem in town and pounds were built to house the strays. In the late 1800s, documents refer to the town pound as the "Bow Navy Yard." Again, the joke behind this reference has been lost. Could it be connected in some way to the lighthouse?

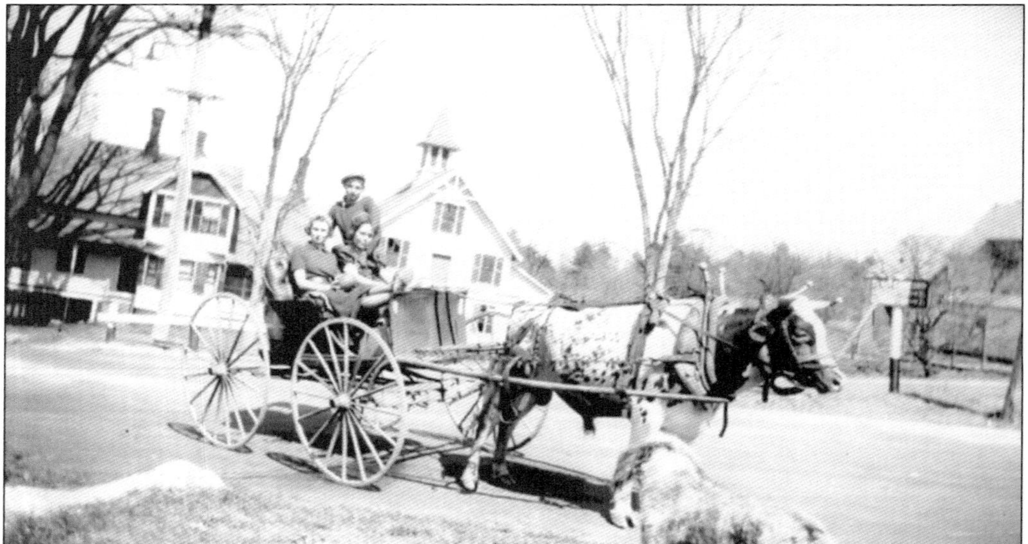

Before The Family Car. Farm kids were very industrious when it came to getting around. Bob Morgan took this photograph in the 1940s of a group driving their family ox back home to Dunbarton. In the background, Upton's Store and a road marker at the intersection of Grandview Road, Logging Hill Road, and South Street can be seen.

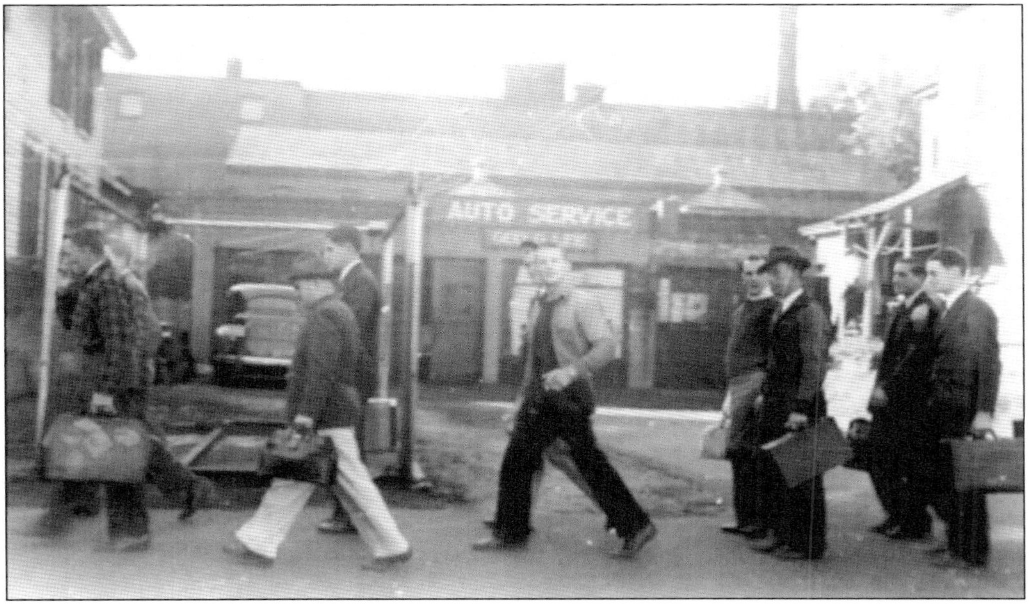

DUTY CALLS. Several young men from Bow responded to the December 7, 1941, attack on Pearl Harbor and were ready to fight in World War II. Seen here is young James Ordway on September 29, 1942, in the center with a cigarette and no suitcase. Ordway joined the army and served in the tank division. He returned to town and worked for the highway department, becoming the road agent.

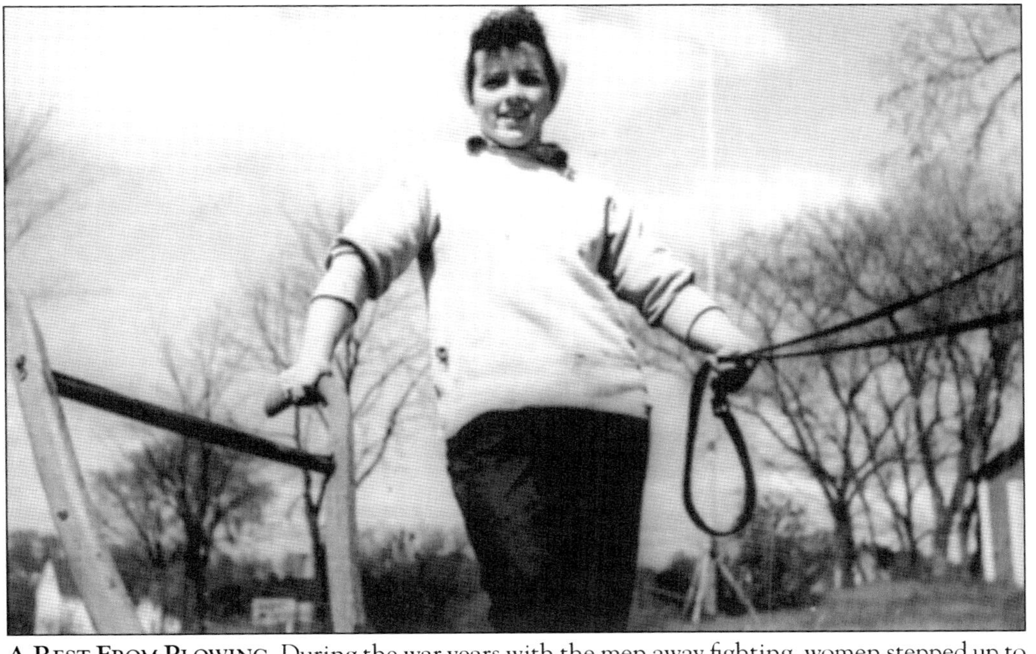

A REST FROM PLOWING. During the war years with the men away fighting, women stepped up to do most of the farm work. Jane Allbee Lindquist takes a break from spring plowing in 1944. She had given up an opportunity to serve with the National Weather Service in Washington, D.C., to stay home and help on the farm.

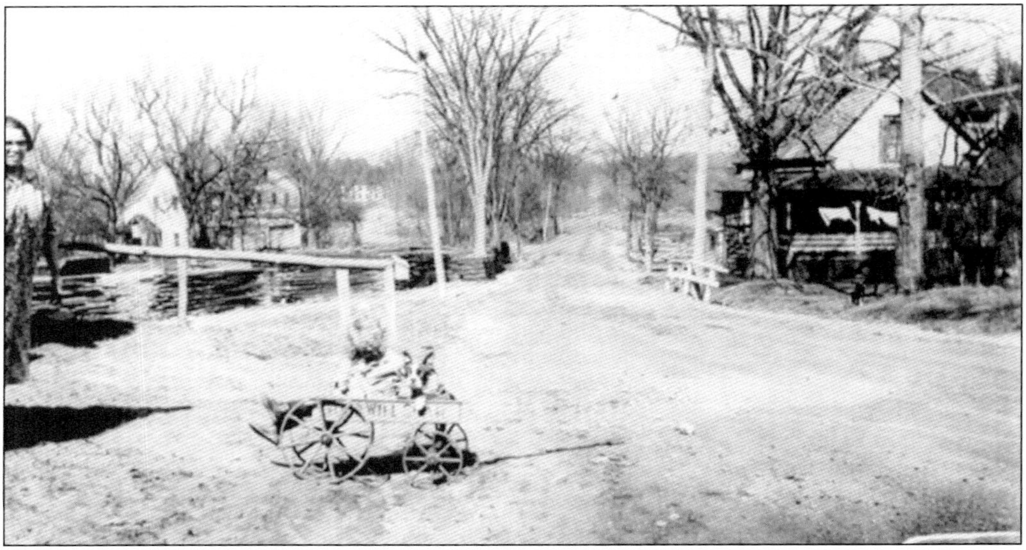

GOODWILL SOAP WAGON. In 1926, people made do with what they had. Hilda Morgan Sargent watches over Robert Ordway and pal in a wagon made from a Goodwill Soap crate. The photographer probably did not realize that they were capturing a piece of history in this shot looking down Valley Road. The home of Alice Hanson is on the right, Upton Shingle Mill is on the left, and the Women's Christian Temperance Union hall is off in the distance on the left.

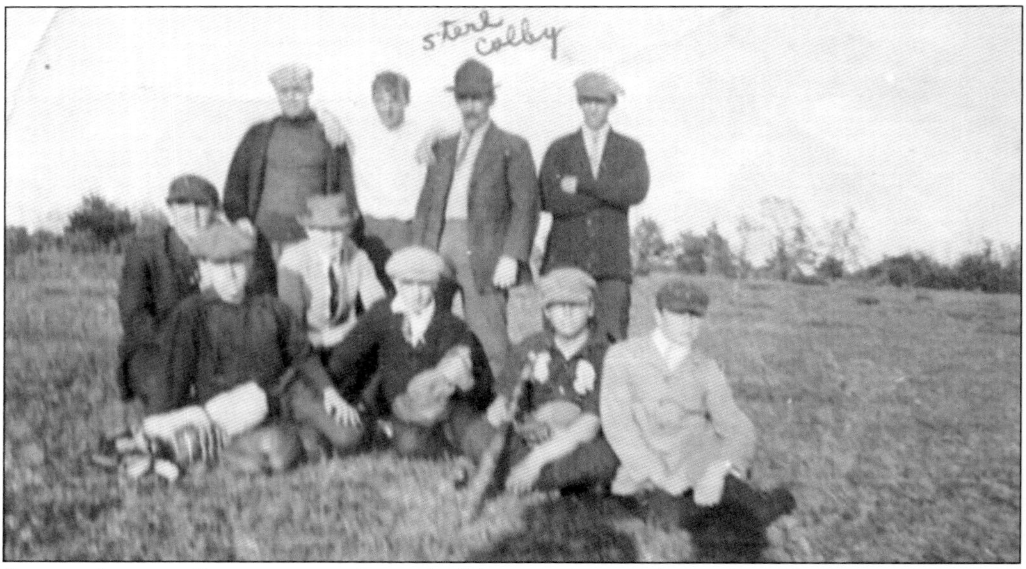

SUNSET LEAGUE BALLPLAYERS. Several of the young men of Bow formed a baseball team and competed in the Concord Sunset League late in the second decade of the 20th century. Those who can be identified in the photograph are Ernest Morgan, seated second from right; Hiel Allbee, seated on the far right; and Sterling Colby, in the second row third from the left.

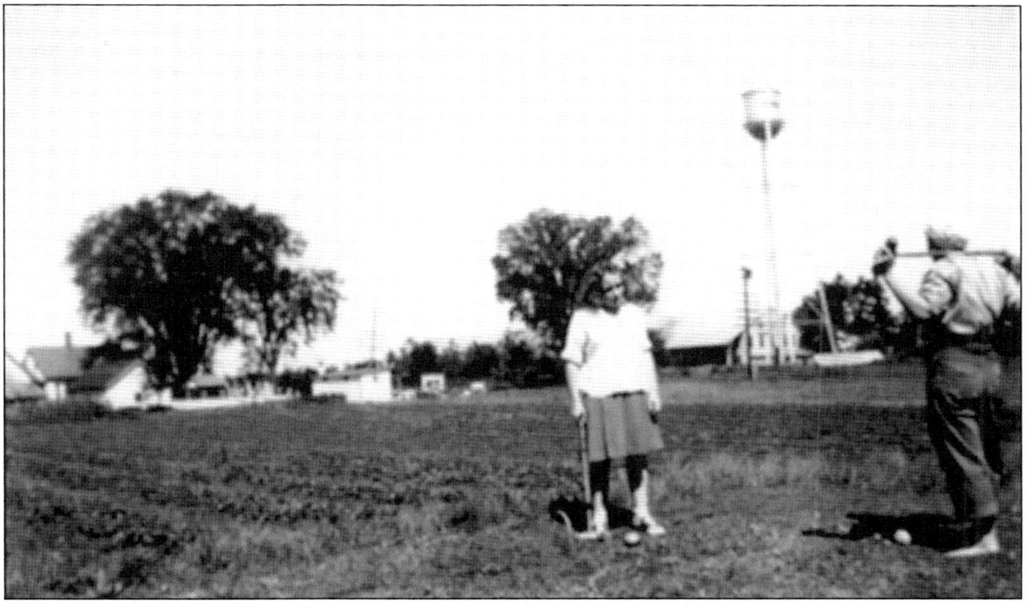

NOT JUST WORK. Carol Allbee Gouin contemplates her next shot in a game of croquet. It was not all work on her parents' Valley Road Farm, but those look like blossoms on the strawberry plants behind her, so picking cannot be far away. In the background, the Merrimack Farmer's Exchange warehouse and water tower can be seen on the right and Cote's farm and souvenir stand on the left.

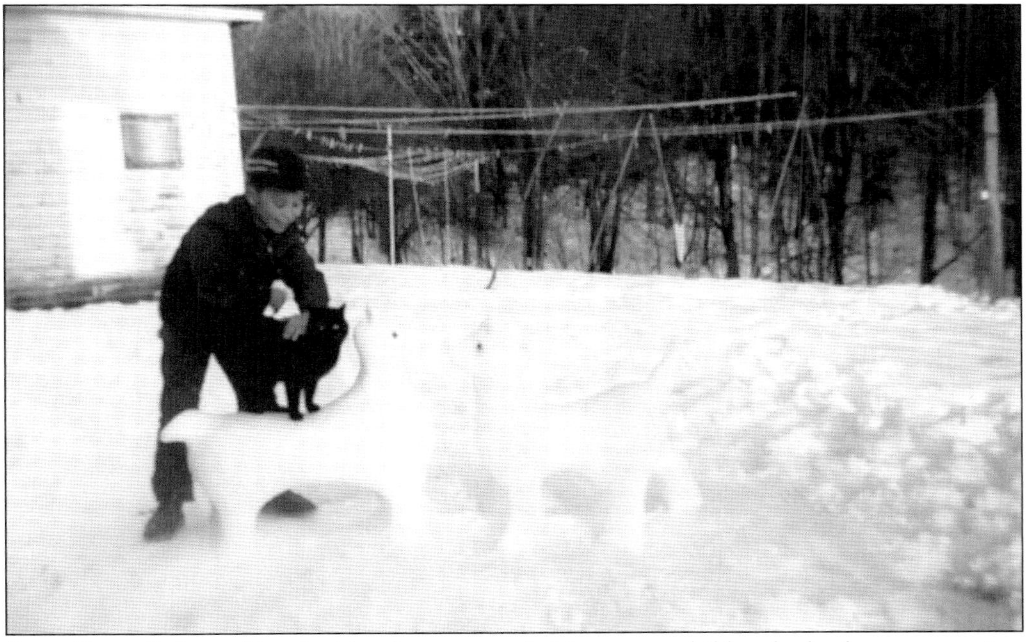

SNOW DAYS. Before cable television, Internet, and video games, children had to be more creative. Pictured here is young Robert Goodsell with the family cat on top of the newly sculpted snow deer. Other types of snow-animals over the years adorned the back, side, and front yards of this home on Dunbarton Center Road.

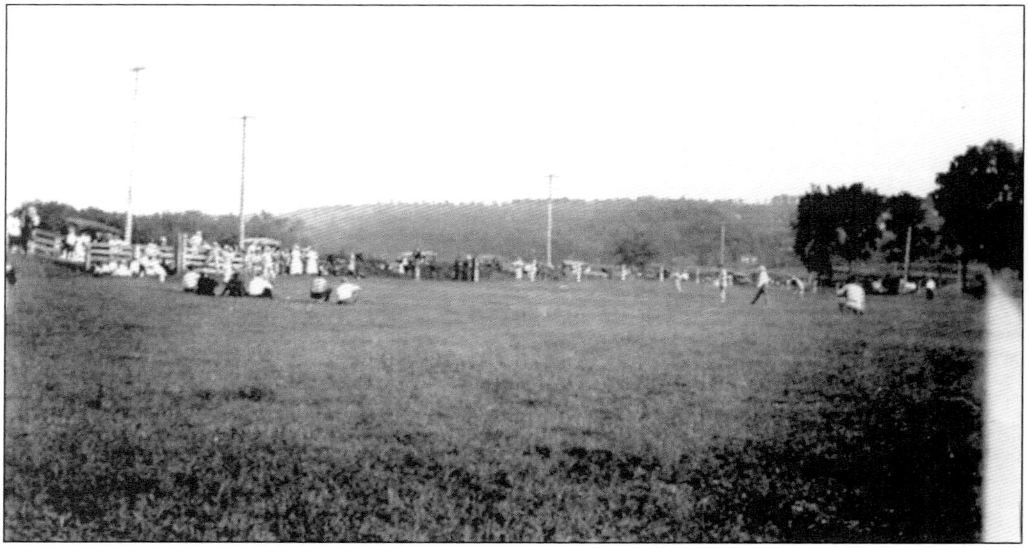

Old Home Day Ball Game. Teams compete in a friendly baseball game during Bow's Old Home Days in 1920. The field is on Hall Street, near the current site of Blue Seal Feeds. The earliest record of a Bow Old Home Week is 1906, when $50 was set aside for the event. Money continued to be set aside each year.

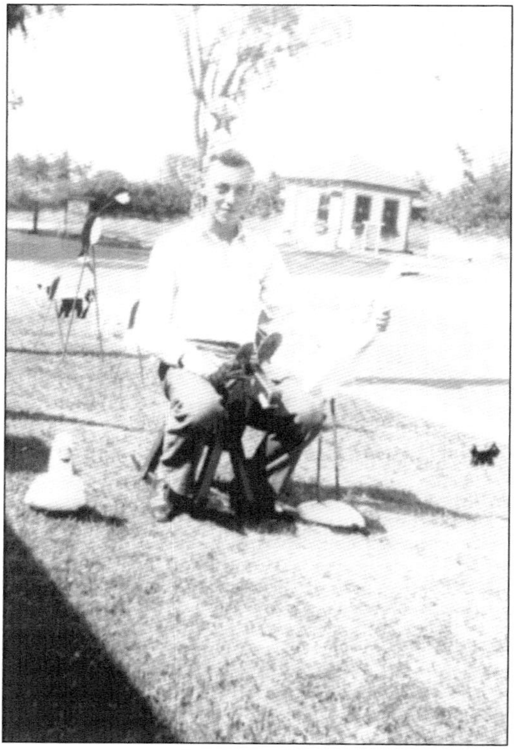

Souvenirs At The Cote Stand. Fred Bradley sits astride a homemade wooden rocking horse at Cote's souvenir stand. Tom Cote made the horse, the whirligigs, wooden bird, and dog lawn ornaments seen in the photograph. Bradley was a frequent visitor to the Cotes and lived just a ways down Hall Street.

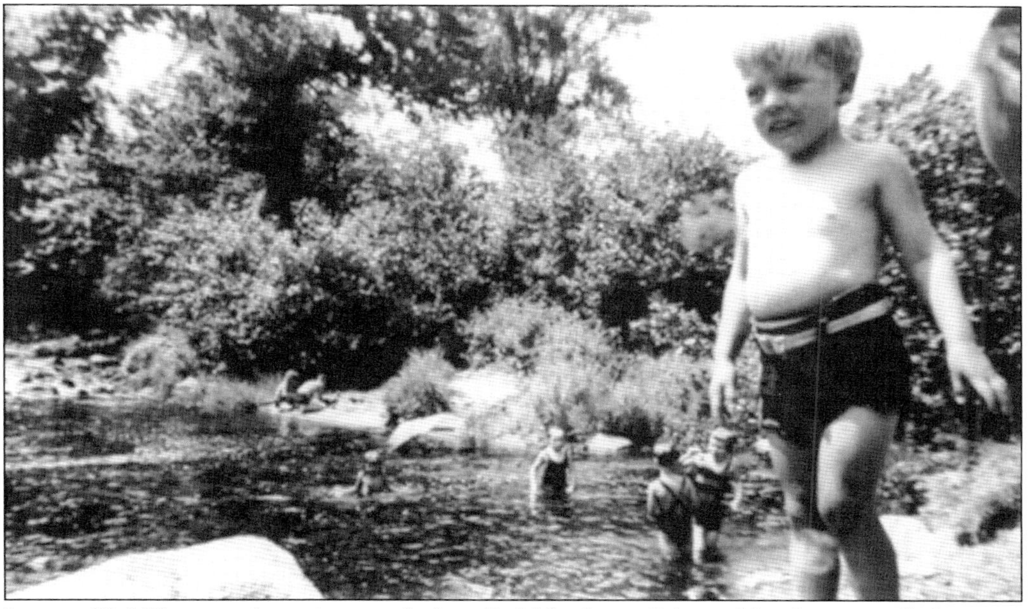

LIVE IT UP! This popular swimming hole called "the Lower," formed by the gristmill dam, was located at Bow Mills opposite what is now the Mobil Station. John Lyford, who later became principal of the Bow Elementary School, is pictured here enjoying the cool water of the Turkey River. Children and adults could be seen here on many hot summer days taking a quick dip or possibly having a picnic at the waters edge.

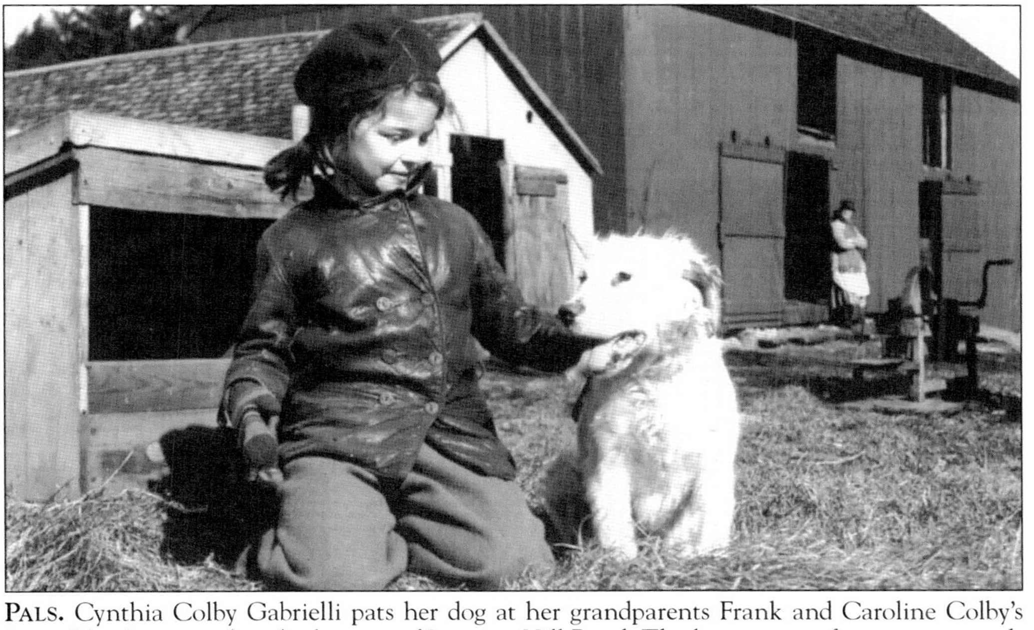

PALS. Cynthia Colby Gabrielli pats her dog at her grandparents Frank and Caroline Colby's farm. The farm stood at the bottom of Logging Hill Road. The house was a former stagecoach stop and was moved to the site. Frank was a doctor who later operated his father's apple orchard. The home still exists and is owned by a Frank Colby of this generation.

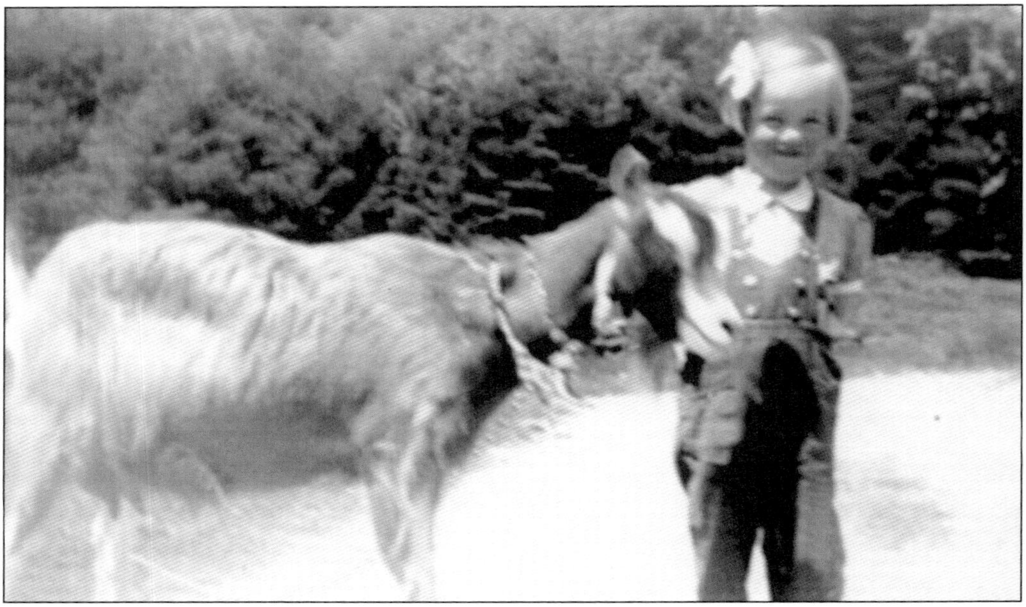

BUDS. Marjorie (Carleton) Nesbitt, age five, poses with her pet goat at the Carleton homestead on Wood Hill Road near the Dunbarton town line. Her family raised a menagerie of animals, including cows, a horse, a goat, and chickens. Her mother, Vivian Carleton, was a longtime lunch lady at the Bow Mills and Memorial Schools. She was a wonderful cook who made dinner rolls that would absolutely melt in one's mouth.

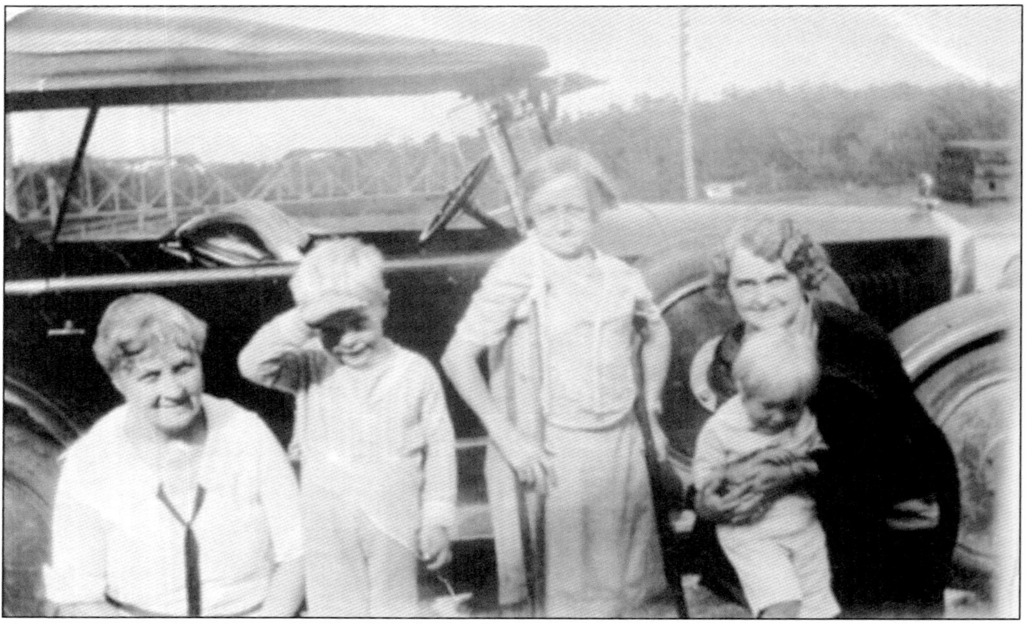

GRACE COTE AND FRIENDS. Tom and Grace Cote were one of the more well-to-do families in town. Grace owned an automobile, a luxury to many at the time. She would often give rides to schoolchildren who used to walk from Bow Junction to Concord High School. Shown here, from left to right, are Eva Allbee, Hollis Furbush, Allen Furbush, and Grace Cote.

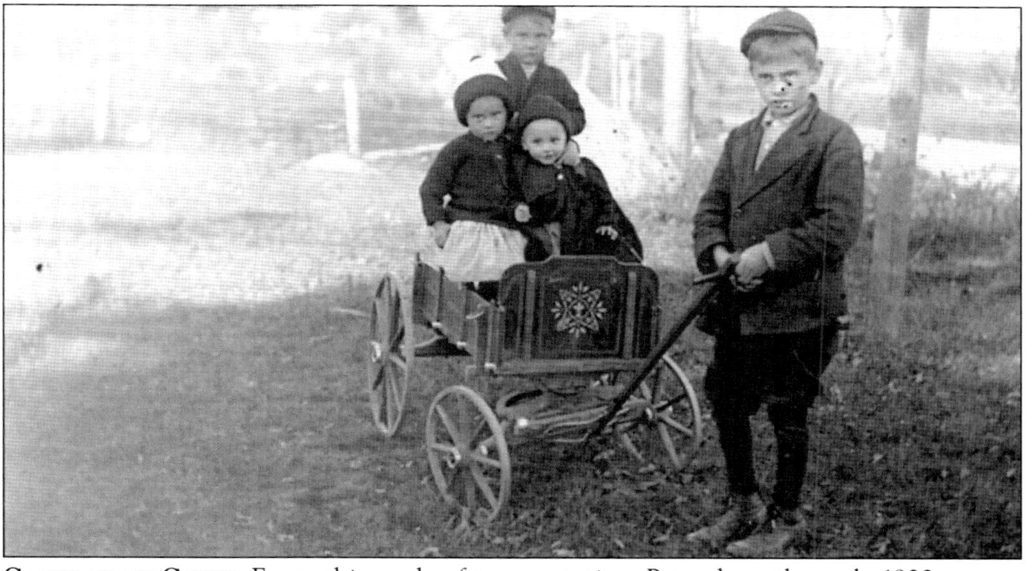

CADILLAC OF CARTS. Fancy this mode of transportation. Peter drags the early 1900s wagon while Walter stands in back, and Bernice and Elizabeth Alexander sit in front and enjoy a cart ride. Children raised on the family farm treasured such outdoor activities. Elizabeth and Walter Alexander were lifelong Bow neighbors, the former residing on the corner of Route 3-A and Dow Road, and the latter living in a home on Dow Road.

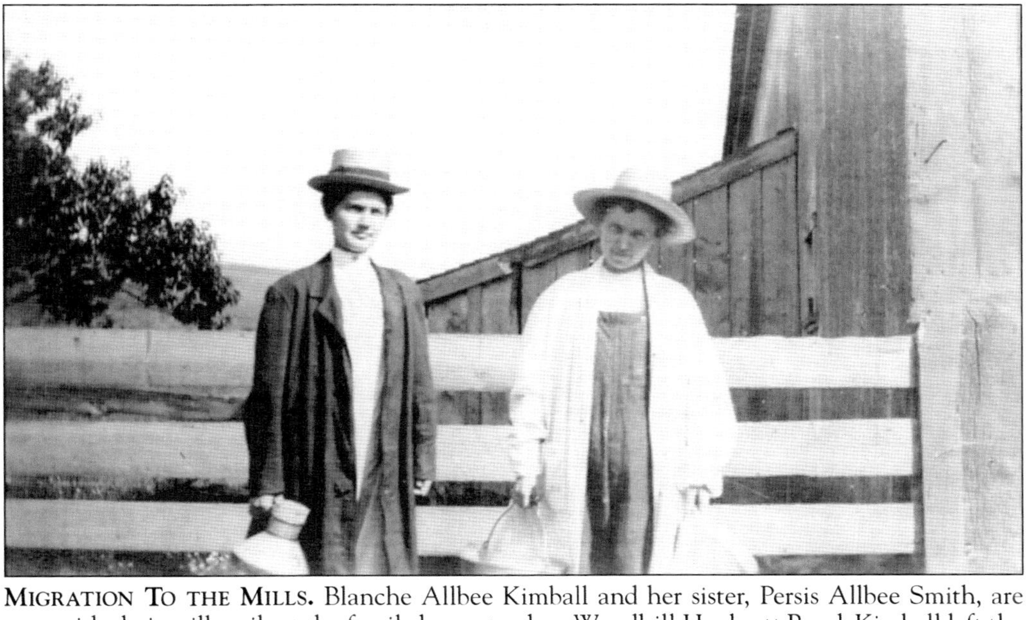

MIGRATION TO THE MILLS. Blanche Allbee Kimball and her sister, Persis Allbee Smith, are seen with their milk pails at the family homestead on Woodhill-Hooksett Road. Kimball left the farm when she was in her 20s to work at one of the mills in Manchester. She eventually married the owner of the mill to "better her family."

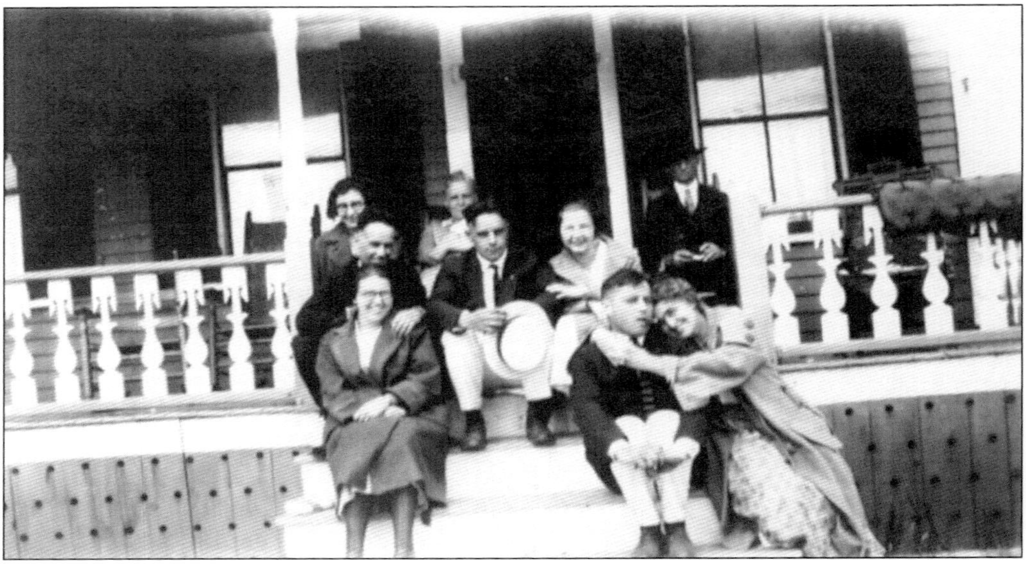

BEACH OUTING. A group of friends relax after an outing to Hampton Beach in the early 1920s. Pictured, from left to right, are (first row) Hilda Sargent, Hiel Allbee, and Grace Cote; (second row) Phil, Arthur, and Laura Sargent; (third row) Ruth Heath, Florence, and Sam Sargent.

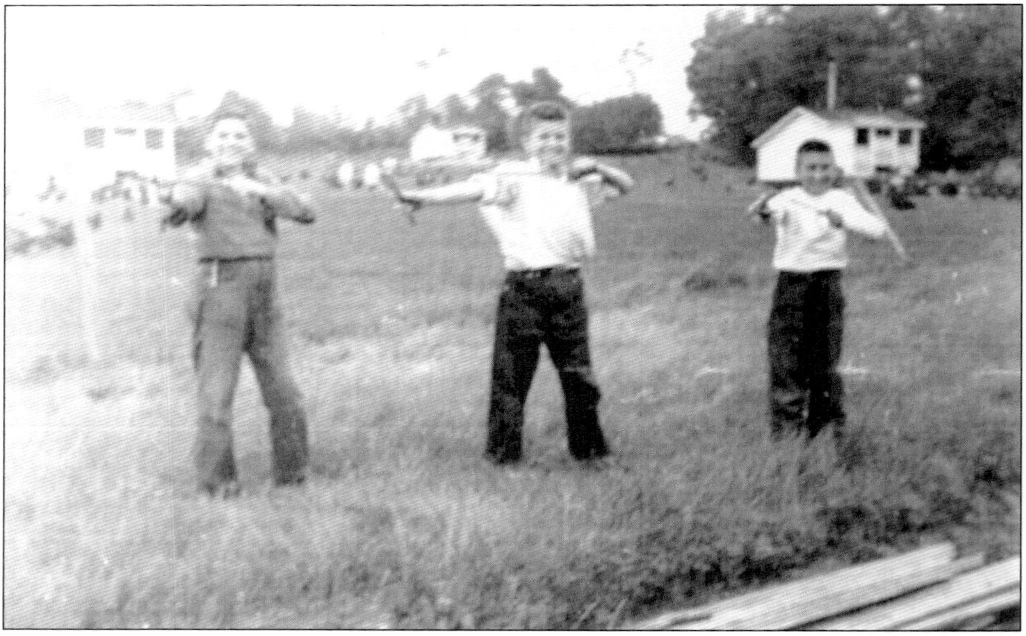

THREE WISE GUYS. These three brothers look like they are up to no good as they practice their aim with slingshots. The "three wise guys" in this 1934 photograph, from left to right, are Edward, Arthur, and Robert Cheney. Their parents were Helen and Henry Cheney, farmers who lived on Woodhill Road. In the background some of the chickens and coops can be seen.

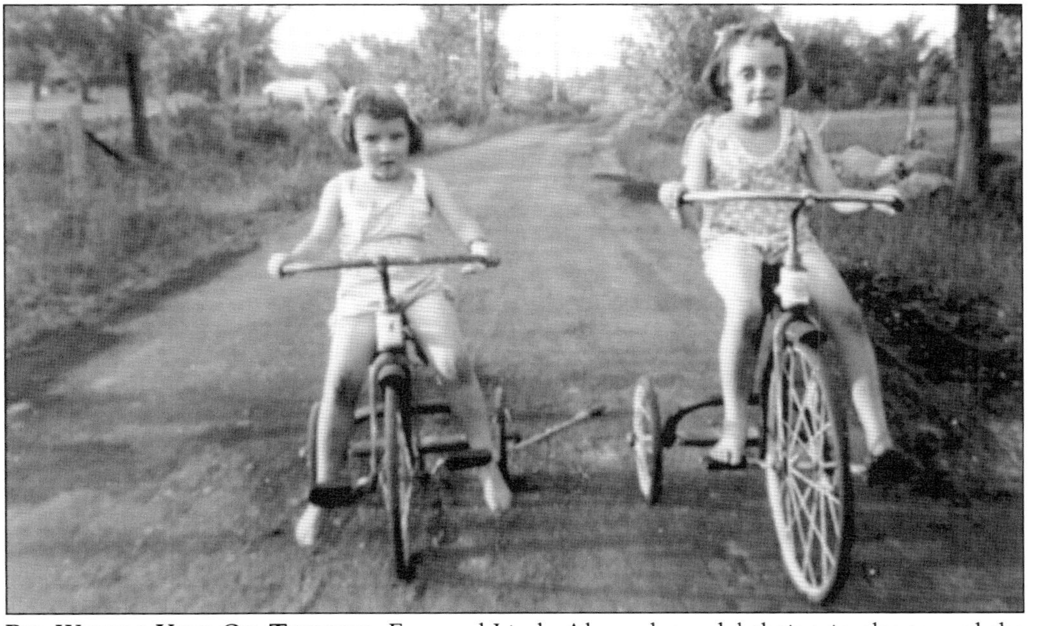

BIG WHEELS KEEP ON TURNING. Faye and Linda Alexander pedal their tricycles toward the intersection of Robinson and Knox Roads. In 1949, there were not many cars traveling on this road, partly because beyond this point, the pavement ended. Verna Alexander remembers only seeing "two or three cars a week" going by the farm.

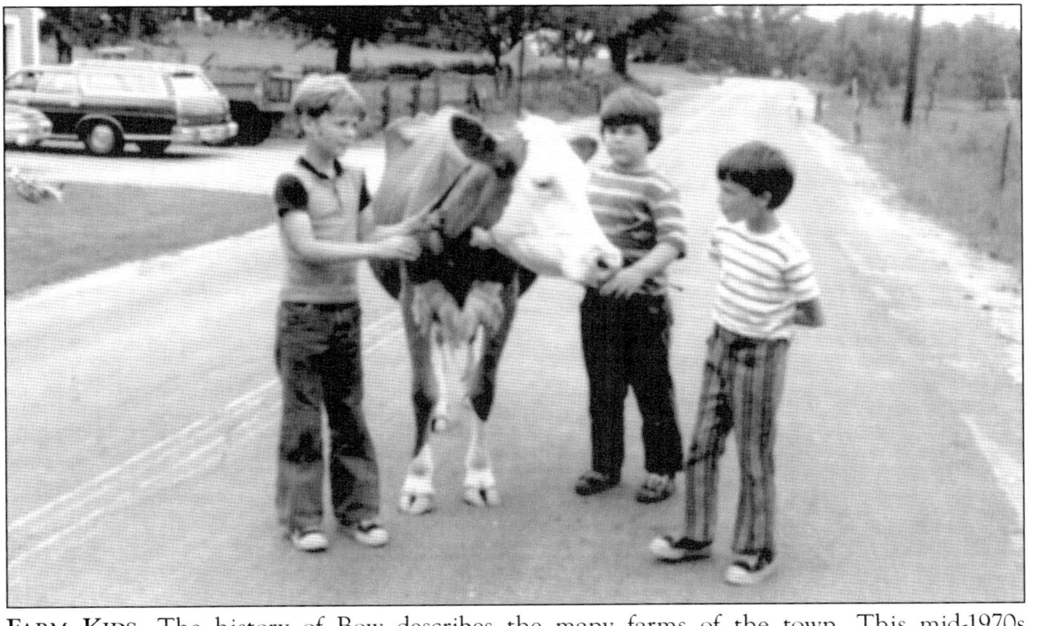

FARM KIDS. The history of Bow describes the many farms of the town. This mid-1970s photograph was taken in front of the barn at the Alexander farm, one of the two remaining dairy farms in town. Steven Cox (left), Patrick Nylen (right), who is the grandson of farm owner Mike Alexander, and Richard Guimond (center), discuss how to get Judy, the cow, back into the pasture. Even today, drivers are warned to beware of stray cows on this stretch of road.

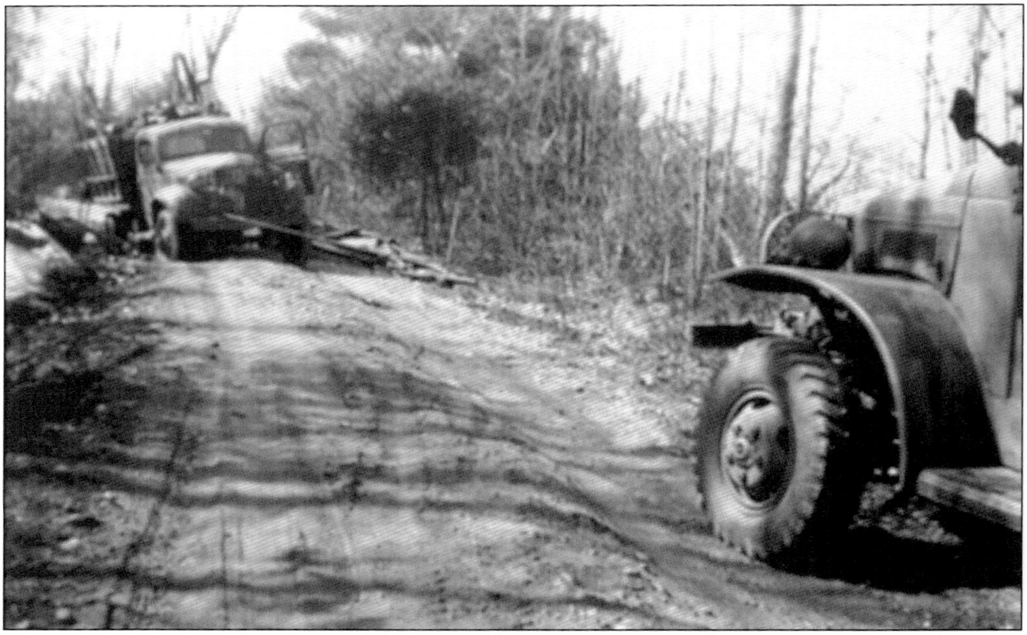

STUCK! Bow's roads were, for the most part, dirt and gravel through the 1940s. In the spring this made for many vehicles getting stuck in the mud. Mike Alexander can remember pulling many cars out of the mud on Knox Road with his tractor. Here a truck loaded down with wood on Johnson Road is about to be freed from the mire.

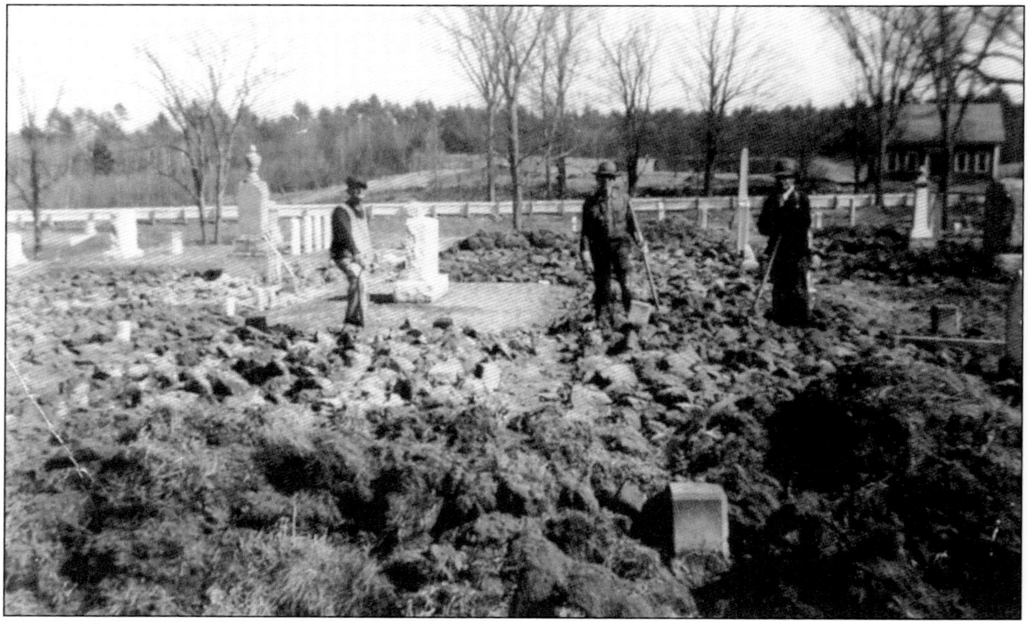

EVANS CEMETERY. John Foote (left), the town sexton, works to replace sod and expand the area of Evans Cemetery. Enos Foote works in the center, and the third man is unidentified. The cemetery was in use since the mid-1800s and as the town grew, so did the need for more grave sites.

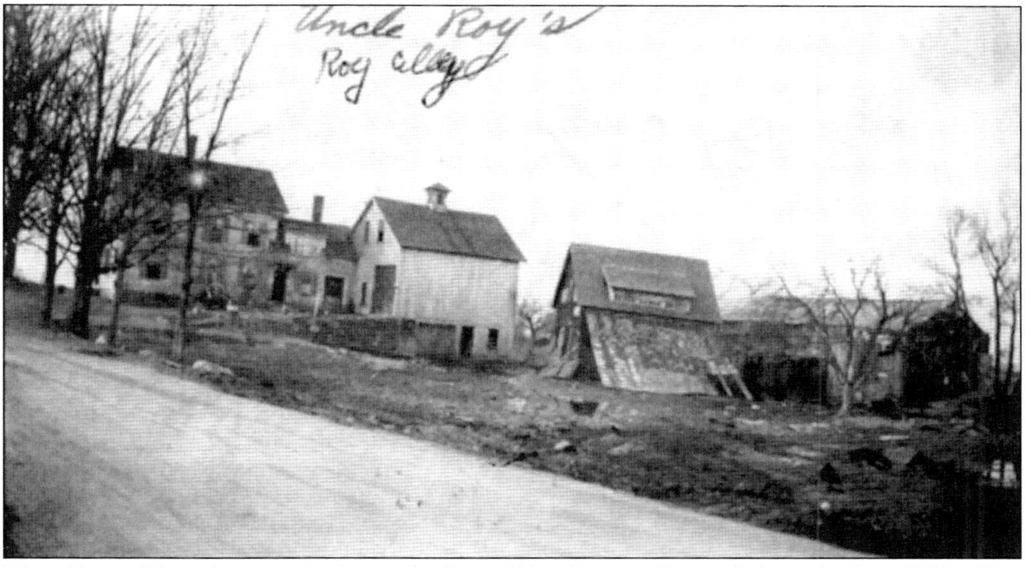

HOW SILLY. This photograph shows the Roy Cilley farm on Route 3-A in the late 1800s. The building on the far right was used to store blocks of ice cut from Ma Willey's Pond located behind their home. This homestead is now where the Exxon Station is located on the Concord line.

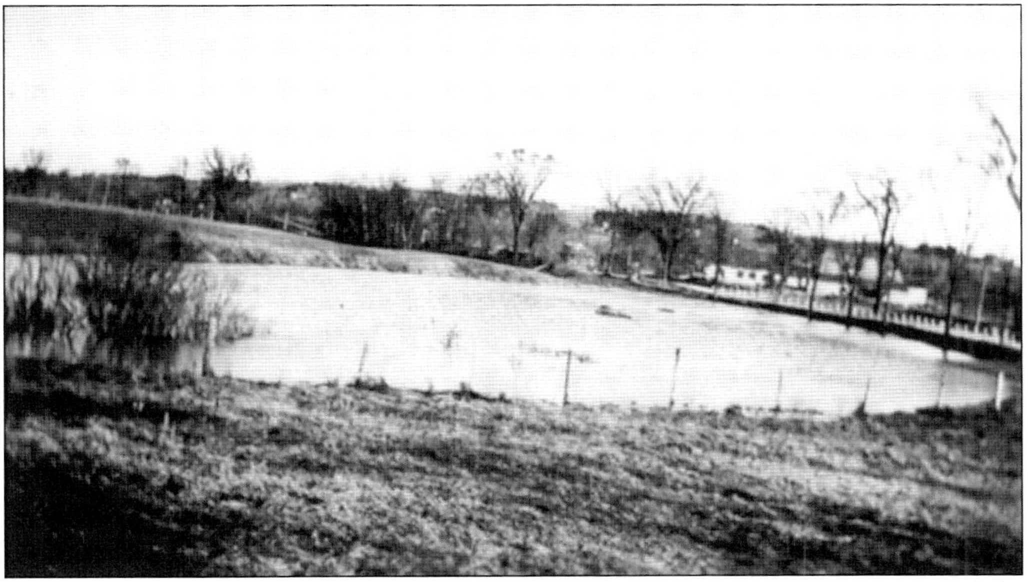

TURTLE POND. In the winter, Ma Willey's Pond was a popular skating spot and also supplied the Cilley family ice business. This photograph was taken from what is now the site of Grappone Honda, looking toward the Route 3-A and Hall Street intersection. In the distance, at the center, houses on top of Grandview Road can be seen.

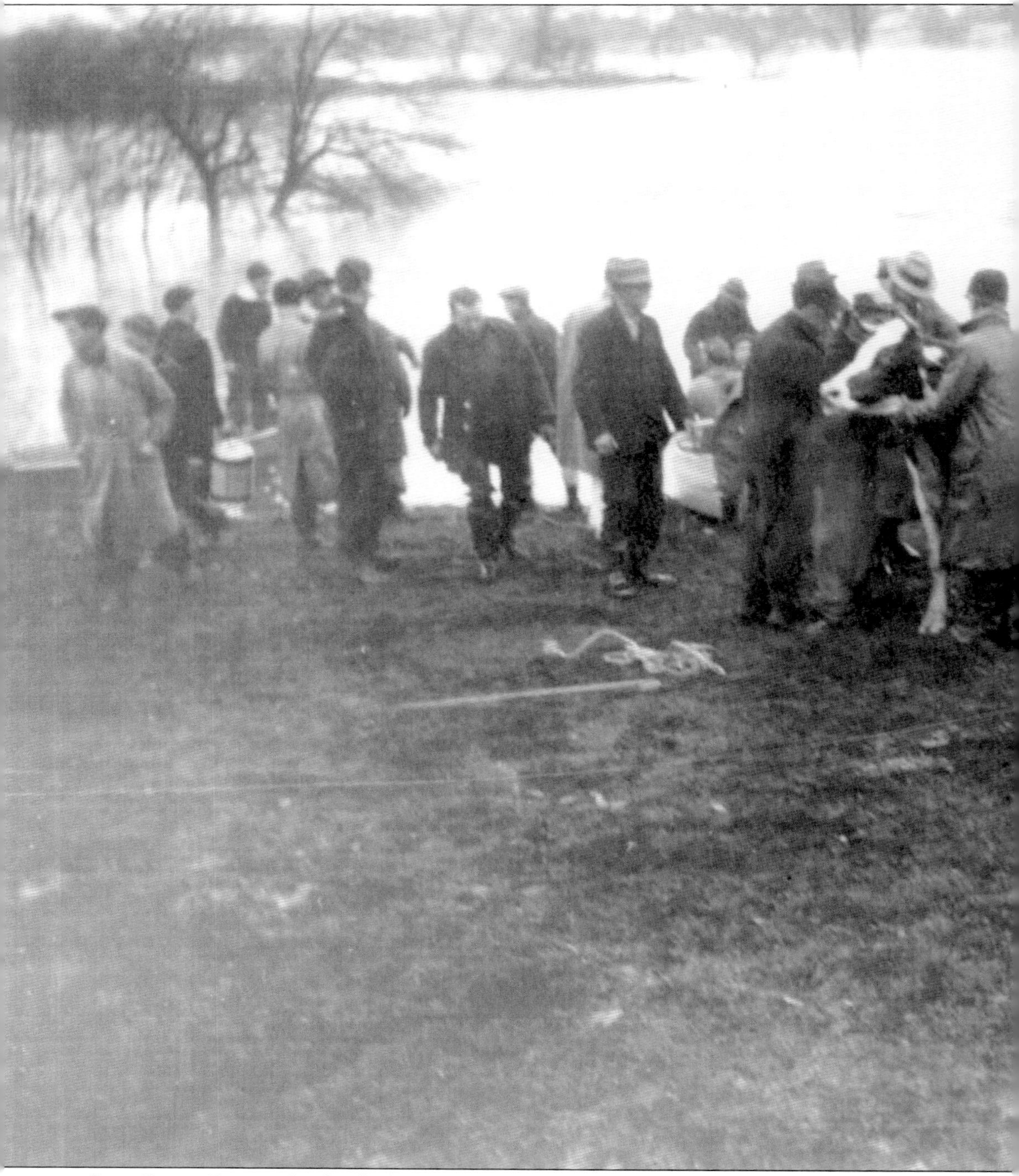

COW GONE. During the flood of 1936, several of the Allbee farm's cows were caught up in the quickly rising and fast flowing water of the Merrimack River. One of the cows was swept down the river, caught in the swift current and was lost over the Garvins Falls Dam. This lucky animal in the photograph was rescued by a group of men in a boat, who rowed out and shepherded the animal to this point of high ground where the Turkey River and Merrimack River converge.

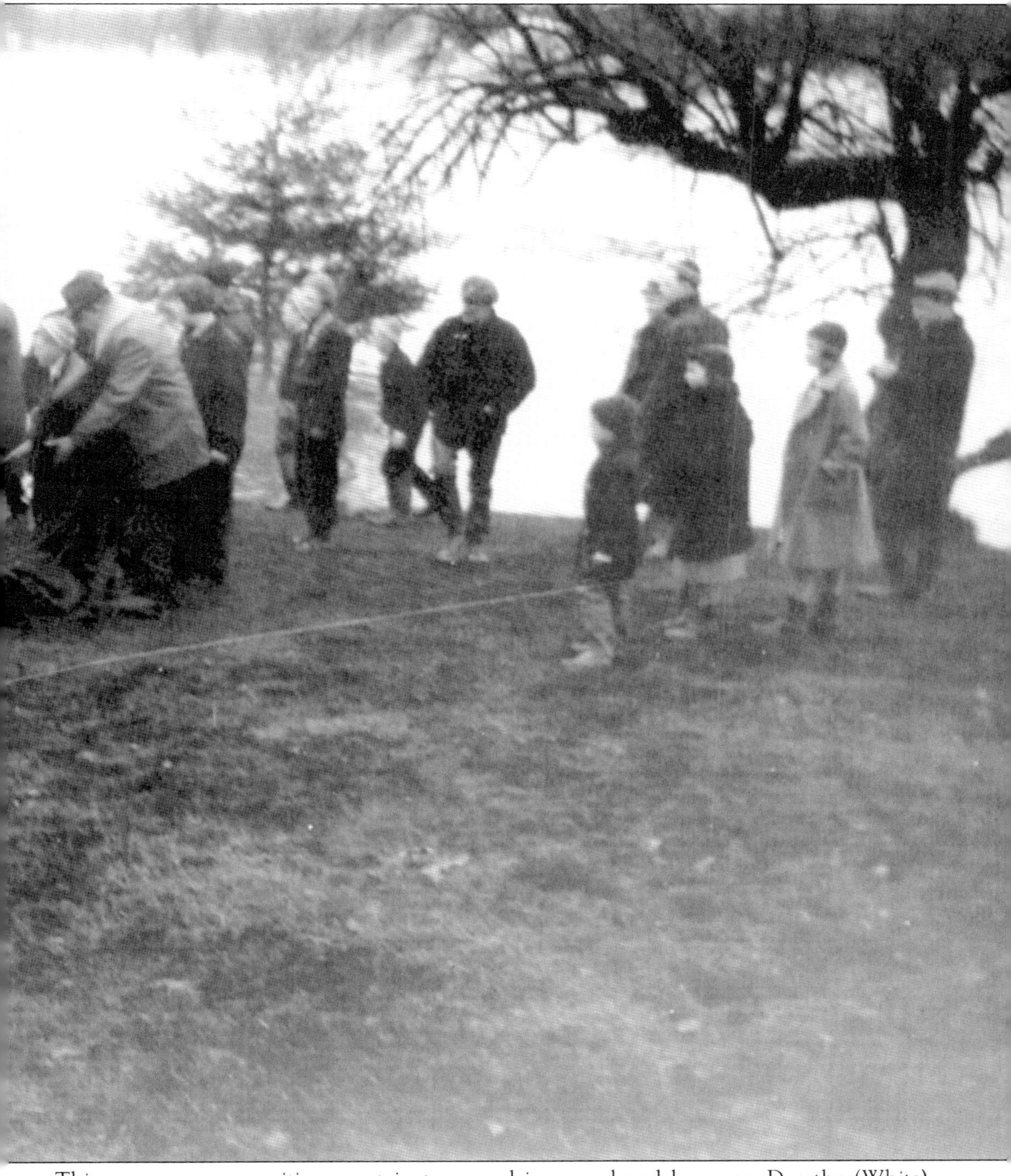

This rescue was an exciting event in town and is remembered by many. Dorothy (White) Shaw witnessed the drama from her home near the current Hampton Inn. Cyrus Wheeler Jr. had ridden over to the top of Woodhill with his father by horseback and watched from there. Carol (Allbee) Gouin was in the crowd of spectators seen in the photograph.